Breaking Boundaries
WITH
Global Literature

Celebrating Diversity in K–12 Classrooms

Nancy L. Hadaway   Marian J. McKenna

EDITORS

INTERNATIONAL
Reading Association
800 BARKSDALE ROAD, PO BOX 8139
NEWARK, DE 19714-8139, USA
www.reading.org

The International Reading Association attempts, through its publications, to provide a forum for a wide spectrum of opinions on reading. This policy permits divergent viewpoints without implying the endorsement of the Association.

Executive Editor, Books   Corinne M. Mooney
Developmental Editor   Charlene M. Nichols
Developmental Editor   Tori Mello Bachman
Developmental Editor   Stacey Lynn Sharp
Editorial Production Manager   Shannon T. Fortner
Design and Composition Manager   Anette Schuetz

Project Editors   Stacey Lynn Sharp and Christina Lambert

Cover   Design, Linda Steere; Art, © Images.com, Inc.

The publisher would appreciate notification where errors occur so that they may be corrected in subsequent printings and/or editions.

Library of Congress Cataloging-in-Publication Data

Breaking boundaries with global literature : celebrating diversity in K-12 classrooms / edited by Nancy L. Hadaway, Marian J. McKenna.

     p. cm.

   Includes bibliographical references and index.

   ISBN 978-0-87207-616-7

   1. Children's literature--Study and teaching (Elementary) 2. Children's literature--Study and teaching (Higher) 3. Children's literature--History and criticism. 4. Multicultural education--United States. I. Hadaway, Nancy L. II. McKenna, Marian J., 1954-

   PN1008.8.B74 2007

   372.64--dc22

                                007019301

Nancy dedicates this book to her husband
and fellow world traveler, Art Sikes.

Marian dedicates this book to her husband, Ralph Lee Allen,
for his support and numerous kindnesses,
and in memory of Jane E. Balvin.

TABLE OF CONTENTS

PART I

Diverse Perspectives in Literature

PART II

Themes of Diversity in Global Literature

PART III
Strategies for Using Literature to Promote Global Awareness

LIST OF AUTHOR REFLECTIONS

ABOUT THE EDITORS

Nancy L. Hadaway is a professor in the College of Education at the University of Texas at Arlington, USA, where she teaches graduate and undergraduate courses in literacy studies. Her research and publications have focused on literacy issues such as content literacy, the use of children's and young adult literature in English-as-a-second-language classrooms, and writing instruction with English-language learners. Hadaway has published in *The Reading Teacher, Journal of Adolescent & Adult Literacy, Book Links, The English Journal, Childhood Education, Ethnic Forum*, and *Equity and Excellence in Education* and has written chapters in books on literacy and multicultural education issues. Her books, *What Every Teacher Should Know About English Language Learners, Literature-Based Instruction With English Language Learners, K–12*, and *Supporting the Literacy Development of English Learners: Increasing Success in All Classrooms*, are helpful guides to working with the growing population of English-language learners in U.S. schools. She has served on various state and national committees of professional literacy organizations; presented at numerous state, regional, national, and international conferences; and received grants from the Adolescent Literature Assembly of the National Council of Teachers of English and the Association of Colleges and Universities. She has served on both the Orbis Pictus Committee and the Notable Books for a Global Society Committee. Prior to her university teaching experience, Hadaway was a public school teacher in Texas, Kentucky, and Colorado, USA, and taught adult education in Colorado and Germany.

Marian J. McKenna is a former public school teacher and a professor of literacy studies at the University of Montana at Missoula, USA. She teaches graduate and undergraduate literacy courses in the School of Education, focusing largely on secondary content literacy, the politics of literacy, and children's and young adult literature courses. Every one of McKenna's classes has a service-learning component in which students and professor are very active in the local and regional communities. McKenna has published in numerous professional journals and has written chapters in books, focusing especially on academic service-learning research and methodology. Her work in service learning and young adult literature, particularly global literature, has led to an international involvement that includes Great Britain and central Asia. McKenna is very active in regional, state, and national committees of professional literacy and service-learning organizations, serving as President of the Northern Rocky Mountain Educational Research Association and Chair of the Notable Books for a Global Society Committee.

CONTRIBUTORS

Carolyn Angus
Director, George G. Stone Center for Children's Books
Claremont Graduate University
Claremont, California, USA

April Whatley Bedford
Associate Professor, Department of Curriculum and Instruction
University of New Orleans
New Orleans, Louisiana, USA

Evelyn B. Freeman
Dean and Professor of Teaching and Learning
The Ohio State University at Mansfield
Mansfield, Ohio, USA

Cyndi Giorgis
Associate Professor, Department of Curriculum and Instruction
University of Nevada, Las Vegas
Las Vegas, Nevada, USA

Nancy L. Hadaway
Professor, Literacy Studies
University of Texas at Arlington
College of Education
Arlington, Texas, USA

Linda Leonard Lamme
Professor, School of Teaching and Learning
University of Florida
Gainesville, Florida, USA

Barbara A. Lehman
Professor of Teaching and Learning
The Ohio State University at Mansfield
Mansfield, Ohio, USA

Janelle B. Mathis
Associate Professor of Literacy, Department of Teacher
    Education and Administration
University of North Texas
Denton, Texas, USA

Jeanne M. McGlinn
Professor of Education
University of North Carolina–Asheville
Asheville, North Carolina, USA

Marian J. McKenna
Professor of Literacy Studies
The University of Montana at Missoula
Missoula, Montana, USA

Mary Napoli
Assistant Professor
School of Behavioral Sciences and Education
Penn State Harrisburg
Middletown, Pennsylvania, USA

Patricia L. Scharer
Professor of Teaching and Learning
The Ohio State University at Marion
Marion, Ohio, USA

Terrell A. Young
Professor of Literacy Education
Washington State University
Richland, Washington, USA

Notable Books for a Global Society: The Beginning

Our life experiences play an important role in molding us as individuals, and so, too, do these experiences influence our understanding of the texts we read and the world around us. Being raised in a certain neighborhood, city, state, and country shapes not only who we are but also how we interpret what we read and how we perceive the world.

In the fourth grade, I remember reading in my social studies textbook, "The Midwest is the breadbasket of America." Because I had grown up in O'ahu, Hawai'i, USA—a rock in the middle of the Pacific Ocean just a bit over 240 square miles in size—this sentence befuddled me. The environment I lived in consisted primarily of the ocean and sea life; pineapple and sugar cane fields; chickens, rabbits, and turkeys raised for food; banana, avocado, mango, and papaya trees; and volcanoes, tidal waves, hurricanes, and floods. Therefore, I did not understand that in the Midwestern United States wide expanses of wheat crops are a natural part of the vast and seemingly limitless landscape, and I was too embarrassed to ask what this sentence meant. In my mind's eye, I saw breadbaskets across the middle part of the United States map stapled on the bulletin board. When answering the test question "What is the Midwest?" I wrote dutifully that "The Midwest is the breadbasket of America," but I had no understanding of what this meant. It wasn't until I was in high school, when I traveled to the continental United States for the first time, that I saw wheat fields covering the panoramic land, swaying to and fro with the wind, their hues changing as the sun moved across the crops. Only then did I grasp why the Midwest is called the "breadbasket," or heartland, of America.

Just as our life experiences influence our understanding of what we read, we are each, in turn, influenced by the books we read in and outside of school. I grew up reading about Dick, Jane, Sally, and their dog, Spot, and felt odd in comparison, wondering, "Why isn't my family like theirs?" Until the ninth grade, the schools I attended did not have libraries, and the reading texts portrayed

Breaking Boundaries With Global Literature: Celebrating Diversity in K–12 Classrooms, edited by Nancy L. Hadaway and Marian J. McKenna. © 2007 by the International Reading Association.

families very much unlike mine. No one struggled with money, inter- and intra-personal relationships, or identity issues. I read about and saw pictures of white children who lived in nice, clean, suburban single-family homes. Their mothers were neatly dressed in beautiful clothing; their fathers went to work wearing suits, carrying briefcases.

In contrast, my life was so different. My home was crowded and small. I shared a bedroom with my parents and my younger brother until I was 9 and then shared a bedroom with three younger brothers until I was 17. Our home backed up directly to a portion of the H-1 freeway, and I was able to touch the chain-link fence from the front porch where the on- and off-ramp to the freeway was situated. My family lived with the sounds from the freeway. We slept with soot on the bed sheets and breathed carbon monoxide from car exhausts. My father went to work in steel-toed boots carrying a black lunch pail; my mother ironed other people's clothing and babysat five children. An uncle and his family lived together with mine until I was 21 years old.

My situation was so unlike Dick's, Jane's, and Sally's, and that of the other characters in the assigned school readings—in fact, almost all of the books I read until I graduated from high school concerned characters, living conditions, and situations with which I could not relate. I ached to read books about families and cultures like mine and have my experiences validated, but instead my reading was mostly limited to the Scott Foresman reading books and the boring, factual textbooks for social studies, science, and math.

On those rare occasions when I went to the only public library on O'ahu, I would sit in front of the two huge bookcases stacked with fables, tales, and legends of Hawai'i, China, and Japan. This was the one place I could thumb through books that captured my interest. Books like these were not used as regular reading material when I went to school. Sometimes my father took me to a bookstore, and if he had enough money he would let me purchase a book. Because I didn't know what to select, and there was a dearth of realistic, historical fiction, biographies, nonfiction, and poetry written for young people my age, I would choose a book with short tales about the Hawaiian culture—stories of King Kamehameha I and how he united the islands by pushing his enemies off the Pali cliff on O'ahu, Hawaiian gods and goddesses, or *Akuas* (Pele, the goddess of fire; Maui, the time shifter; Kane, the god of fire; other Hawaiian deities), and the *menehunes* (Hawaiian fairies who did good deeds for people). When I was 20, a friend recommended that I read the book *Hawaii* by James Michener. I stayed up all night reading this book; I couldn't put it down. Michener's *Hawaii* was the first self-selected novel written by a renowned author that I read from cover to cover. Fortunately, as an undergraduate at the University of Hawai'i, I was required to take courses in world literature and American literature, and my little island world became a bit more expanded.

After teaching for the Hawai'i State Department of Education at Ka'ahumanu Elementary, Waipahu Intermediate, and Pohakea Elementary Schools, during the summer of 1969 I moved to East Lansing, Michigan, USA, to attend graduate school and teach in the Lansing School District. In Michigan, everything was different from what I was used to. I was far away from the salty, buoyant ocean—its smell and sounds, the fragrance of tropical flowers, my parents, three brothers, and other members of my very large extended family. I went swimming in Lake Michigan, but it didn't taste, feel, or smell like the ocean. Yet at first glance I thought it would be like swimming in the ocean for, like the ocean, it appeared to go on forever. I saw trees turn brilliant colors and lose their leaves in the autumn, leaving them bare and naked in the winter. I experienced seasons and spring fever. The children I taught were mostly from European American descent, with some from African American descent. Some of my students' parents questioned my ability to speak English and my knowledge of American history and queried if I grew up in a grass shack. Though my moving to the mainland was a grand adventure and I marveled at every experience, I experienced cultural shock.

However, I managed to find great comfort in my graduate courses in children's literature. I loved reading *No Promises in the Wind* (Hunt, 1970) and was enchanted with Bill Martin Jr books and his lyrical language and by *Crow Boy* (Yashima, 1955). I fell in love with Judy Blume books because I could identify with many of her characters, even though their backgrounds were different from mine. Blume's characters experienced the same issues and problems I had growing up. I took heart in knowing that even the children from the dominant "white" culture had concerns and identity questions like I had at their ages. How I wished I had read books like this when I was young and was experiencing apprehensions about my family and background. It was at this juncture that I discovered the power that quality literature has to influence our perceptions of the world around us and lead to greater cultural understanding and knowledge of self.

Despite the universal themes reflected in some literature for children, adolescents, and young adults, such as the aforementioned books, in my own classroom and for my students I felt there was still a great need for books written by people of color about people of color in the United States as well as from different countries. My students—all from diverse backgrounds—needed to read about young people from cultural, social, economic, and environmental surroundings different from their own in order to better understand themselves and other cultures. I felt that my role as a classroom teacher was to help my students (as well as myself) learn and reflect about cultural diversity, understand the historical context of a culture, and appreciate the values of a culture that shape people's behavior and beliefs. Thus, I became an advocate of global literature and its integration into the classroom. I believed—and still believe—that teachers have a great role in helping their students understand human values common to all cultures and those distinctive of a particular culture. By reading books that reflect their own lives and lives of others different from themselves, our young people wouldn't feel as I did during my childhood—weird—and would instead appreciate their own unique experiences and culture and realize that, though we are different, there are elements of the human condition that are common to all.

Looking back, I know I should have read more in school, participated in reading discussions instead of letting my mind wander, and not have been as afraid about putting my ideas, feelings, and hopes on paper. Though the books set in the mainland United States made me wonder about that region, the seasons, and the people who lived there, I would have read wider and been a better writer if I had been exposed to books representing *many* different cultures, because I would have been able to identify with characters like me who had lives like mine as well as learn about cultures and life experiences so different from my own.

A few weeks before I attended the International Reading Association's (IRA) 1993 Annual Convention, I came across a newspaper article in which a journalist wrote about an interview I had with him regarding the literature that minority children are given to read. Morson (1993) reported about the instructional benefits of reading diverse literature with which students can relate but also stated that not everyone agrees that reading literature representing an array of cultures is beneficial. He writes, "But critics insist that the emphasis on multiculturalism substitutes 'political correctness' for common sense" (p. 28A). Morson cites Jeff Walin, the president of American Academy for Liberal Education, who reportedly thinks that schools should instead emphasize the nation's common culture:

> After all, all these kids in our schools are American, whether they came here five generations ago or, like my family, one. You take any of us and put us back—you take me back to Yugoslavia—we wouldn't be very happy. That's not my culture any more. That doesn't mean individuals should forget their ethnic roots. But they should forget the ethnic divisions that are tearing apart most of the world. (p. 28A)

When I read this article, I realized that some people did not think that bringing multicultural perspectives into the classroom was a good thing to do. Unfortunately, many of those who disagreed with using multicultural literature for young people apparently didn't understand that multicultural literature actually *helped* young people understand an important concept—this world is composed of many cultures, peoples, languages, religions, customs, and celebrations in addition to a variety of histories, foods, dress, transportation, topography, and ways of living. However, this particular newspaper article did help me to recognize that the word *multicultural* made some people feel uncomfortable. I recalled the issues the state of Colorado was facing with regard to standards being drafted by the National Council for Accrediting Teacher Education Programs, and the importance of those studying to become teachers being sensitive to the needs of minority students—African American, Hispanic American, Asian American, immigrants, and children adopted from other countries—and these future teachers' ability to reach and educate them. Thoughts about what could be done about this issue at a national level started churning in my head. I wanted young people to be able to embrace their own cultures as well as those different from their own.

Because there was no K–12 listing of multicultural or global books at this time, I decided to discuss this newspaper article with IRA's Children's Literature and Reading Special Interest Group. We decided that this would be a good project for this committee to pursue. Criteria for selection and a timeline were developed. Along the way, I toyed with the booklist's name. I did not think including the word *multicultural* would be a good choice. I felt that, for many people, the word *multicultural* triggered certain ideas, beliefs, and practices and would therefore be limiting. In addition, I wanted this list to be inclusive and advocate for cultures of different countries, ethnic groups, religious beliefs, lifestyles, and backgrounds and not to be limited to a particular level of schooling. I wanted this booklist to be comprehensive. I eventually decided on "Notable Books for a Global Society: A K–12 List." The decision to use the word *global* was made because this word represented what I had in mind—this word took into account all the different characteristics that make up a person, capturing the variety and complex nature of individuals, yet at the same time conveyed the commonalities of cultures throughout the world. In addition, I wanted this booklist to extend beyond the national boundaries of any country; I felt strongly about the notion that students in the United States and elsewhere need to learn about each other.

In addition to publicizing the list in *The Dragon Lode*, the journal of the IRA's Children's Literature and Reading Special Interest Group, we wanted to reach a wider audience. I asked the then-editors of *The Reading Teacher*, Nancy Padak and Tim Rasinski, if there might be space in an issue to publish this list. Auspiciously, the editors agreed, and the first list, "1996 Notable Books for a Global Society (Books published in 1995)," was published in the March 1997 issue of *The Reading Teacher*. Although *The Reading Teacher* no longer publishes this list, it continues to be published in *The Dragon Lode*. This yearly article discusses the 25 chosen books and features annotations, teaching ideas, and related books and websites. The K–12 booklist and information about the selection program are available at http://www.tcnj.edu/~childlit/.

The many people who contribute to and generate interest in IRA's Notable Books for a Global Society booklist should be applauded. Without these brilliant authors, courageous publishers, and hardworking, knowledgeable educators, there would be no list.

In 2005, Notable Books for a Global Society: A K–12 List celebrated its 10th year. As I look to the future, my hopes are that there will continue to be an active interest in global books that help young people and teachers appreciate and revel in the diversity in this world, as this is so important for humanity to flourish. Embracing diversity, not uniformity, enriches and makes our world a better place for all of us. Enjoy this treasure trove of information and the chapters that follow. The contents of this book are not only theoretically sound but also practical in nature.

Savor the information, bring this knowledge to your classrooms, and know that how you spend time with a child lasts a lifetime. In the end, test scores do not really matter. Learning involves matters of the heart first, then the mind. For facts to make sense, they have to be presented as more than just a collection of information—the information needs to have a story context to seem sensible. Stories are important because they are a part of how people make sense of themselves and the world around them. Stories are people, just as people are stories; that is, when we read or hear stories, we learn about and deepen our understanding about others and self. Stories provide a way to understand the past and present, project toward the future, and celebrate both the multiplicity and commonalities among all peoples so that humanity can evolve toward peace, acceptance, and harmony throughout the world.

—Yvonne Siu-Runyan
University of Northern Colorado

REFERENCE

Morson, B. (1993, April 4). Johnny can't read because Johnny can't relate: Teachers look for new ways to reach minority students. *Rocky Mountain News*, p. 28A.

LITERATURE CITED

Hunt, I. (1970). *No promises in the wind*. Chicago: Follet.
Michener, J.A. (1959). *Hawaii*. New York: Ballantine Books.
Yashima, T. (1955). *Crow boy*. New York: Viking.

Considering Diversity Through Literature

The goal of this book is to consider the importance of global literature and to examine the recent progress in children's and young adult literature to offer diverse perspectives and appeal to *all* readers. As a primary source for specific examples of quality global literature, this book draws from the first 10 years of the Notable Books for a Global Society: A K–12 List (1996–2005), although other excellent books are also noted in some of the following chapters (see chapter 1 for more in-depth discussion of the Notable Books for a Global Society booklist and an analysis of books selected). Our hope is that readers will find this book a valuable resource with chapters that both explore current themes in global literature and offer ideas for implementing global literature in classrooms.

Who Should Use This Book

Just as the booklist itself was created to have global appeal, this book, too, is targeted to a global audience. Designed for educators both within and outside the United States, each chapter targets themes and books that address society and culture within the United States as well as the global society. Although chapter 4's portrayal of immigration issues and chapter 5's depiction of language diversity in children's and young adult literature are discussed in the context of American society and schools, these are still universal themes that may spur readers to consider such issues from the perspective of their own geographic setting.

More specifically, as the full title of the booklist indicates, this book is targeted at K through 12 students and teachers as well as teacher educators working with both inservice and preservice teachers of grades K through 12. Although the K through 12 grade range naturally includes a wide spectrum of variance in students' age, grade, ability, and maturity, this book does not categorize the literature and corresponding activities by age appropriateness

Breaking Boundaries With Global Literature: Celebrating Diversity in K–12 Classrooms, edited by Nancy L. Hadaway and Marian J. McKenna. © 2007 by the International Reading Association.

or grade level. Using age ranges or grade levels to indicate a targeted level for use seems somewhat narrow given the variance just noted as well as the tremendous diversity of language, culture, background knowledge, and experiences in classrooms today. Add to those factors the rich variety of themes and topics explored in the books highlighted in the following chapters, and the designation of age and grade level might lead some educators to overlook books that would actually be valuable resources. Therefore, while individual chapters may give general guidelines for classroom application, this book does not use age or grade levels as labels, as doing such may incorrectly and unnecessarily limit the usage of literature that by nature is meant to appeal to *all* readers. This book allows teachers to instead rely on their own discretion and judgment for what books are appropriate for individual classrooms.

In the place of age- or grade-level indications, a book's genre may be a better indicator of usability for teachers. Some of the booklist titles address mature or controversial themes such as genocide, human trafficking, drug use, or sexual orientation. The authors of these books may choose to introduce these controversial topics in a picture book format in order to offer a means of developing awareness and understanding among younger learners in the elementary grades. However, despite the picture book format, such books also have the potential to be used through the high school grades, and certainly to educate future and current educators. On the other hand, we are aware that most chapter books and novels are not appropriate for younger students due to their reading level—and sometimes because of the more mature content and events depicted in these longer books.

As the genre breakdown chart in Table 1.2 in chapter 1 indicates, there were 57 fiction picture books in the first 10 years of the booklist and 34 nonfiction picture books. In addition, most of the folklore books on the list would fall into the picture book category. All of these books would be appropriate for students and teachers in any grade level, K through 12. Conversely, most realistic and historical fiction novels are intended for secondary students and teachers in grades 6 through 12, but teachers could certainly choose a novel for reading aloud to an intermediate-grade classroom. Thus, if examining the booklist only by genre in order to better gauge the appropriateness for different grade ranges, roughly 50% of the books could be considered as elementary level and 50% could be considered as secondary level. A helpful reference to assist teachers with their selections of the best books for their particular classroom or teaching situation is the online supplement's categorical breakdown of books on the list according to genre (see page xxiv for more discussion on the online supplement).

How to Use This Book

Organization

This book begins with an introduction and is divided into three sections. The introduction and the first two sections of the book build a knowledge base on global literature in general and explore specific themes within such literature in order to apply the techniques discussed in the final section. The Introduction, "Building Bridges to Understanding" by Nancy L. Hadaway, sets the stage for the chapters that follow by explaining the need to represent the diversity in children's and young adult literature and the need for increased attention to international literature. The introduction also notes the many terms that have been used to categorize children's and young adult literature written by diverse authors and from different perspectives and explains the use of the comprehensive term *global literature* in this book.

Part I: Diverse Perspectives in Literature includes two chapters. In chapter 1, "An Analysis of the Notable Books for a Global Society, 1996–2005," Nancy L. Hadaway reinforces the importance of global literature and highlights some of the issues surrounding the selection of quality global literature. In addition, the chapter serves as a road map to the booklist's first 10 years, analyzing dimensions such as authors, illustrators, publishers, genres, categories, and different cultural and social groups. This analysis will provide a databank for educators to compare and contrast and to connect books for study and discussion. In addition, readers can consider both the strengths and limitations that exist in the list over the first 10 years.

Chapter 2, "The Challenges and Opportunities of International Literature," reminds us that we live in a global community, and that the need for social justice throughout the world is apparent. Through global communication, children view the horrors of war, natural disasters, poverty, and sickness on a daily basis. They witness firsthand the lack of social justice in the world around them. In this chapter, authors Evelyn B. Freeman, Barbara A. Lehman, and Patricia L. Scharer focus on the international perspectives in children's literature or, more specifically, books originally published outside the United States, books by immigrants to the United States, or by authors from countries outside the United States, as well as literature that addresses settings beyond U.S. borders. The authors contend that international children's literature is a powerful, but often forgotten, resource for use across the school curriculum. The chapter explores the relationship between global perspectives and international children's literature and, more specifically, the place of international literature in the literary canon, teacher interest in and access to international literature, and the publication of global literature.

Part II: Themes of Diversity in Global Literature consists of four chapters that deal with key themes in global literature. Recommended titles from the booklist and a few additional resources that relate to each of the themes are woven into the discussion throughout each of these chapters. At the end of these chapters, the Literature Response Activities integrate spotlighted global literature and themes directly into the classroom.

The first chapter of Part II, chapter 3, "Finding Our Stories Through Her Stories: Strong Females in the Global Tapestry," explores the theme of gender, reflecting the chapter authors' belief in the need for stories about strong women. Stories of successful, active, and bold female characters provide opportunities for readers of both genders to escape the stereotypes that have prevailed of the submissive role of women in society and to extend females' identity and a realization of their role in the global society. Cyndi Giorgis, Janelle B. Mathis, and April Whatley Bedford discuss books from a variety of genres, historical eras, and diverse cultures that portray strong heroines who use their strengths to meet life's challenges and to make their world a better place.

In chapter 4, "Coming to America: The U.S. Immigrant Experience," Jeanne M. McGlinn analyzes the traumatic and, at times, exhilarating experience of immigration as explored in several books of realistic fiction for young adults. Many children's and young adult writers have explored the immigrant experience in the United States in a variety of genres with a goal of educating readers about the complex problems surrounding immigration and providing a human face to this intense debate. These authors create their stories from the tensions that exist for people who have chosen or been forced to leave their homes and countries, hoping for economic success and upward mobility in the United States. They detail the reasons people emigrate to foreign places and the difficulties of forging a new identity in a culture that often does not value their traditions or ethnicity.

Closely related to the theme of immigration is that of linguistic diversity. An examination of recent demographic statistics shows that English-language learners are the fastest growing population in U.S. schools, a direct result of the increasing number of immigrants whose first language is not English. In chapter 5, "Language Diversity in the United States and Issues of Linguistic Identity in a Global Society," Nancy L. Hadaway and Terrell A. Young examine language through the lens of children's and young adult books that portray the diversity of languages around the world, the joy (and the challenges) of knowing more than one language, and the difficult transitions to be made when you don't speak the language of school or the community.

In chapter 6, "Resilient Children in Times of War," Linda Leonard Lamme considers oppression caused by the special geopolitical events that occur in different cultures around the world. The ways children and young people endure and rise above oppression are often heroic and should be known and celebrated by other children around the world. This chapter brings to light the wide range of oppression and heroism that children around the world encounter as highlighted in selected children's and young adult books.

Part III: Strategies for Using Literature to Promote Global Awareness focuses on the integration of global literature into classrooms. In chapter 7, "Keys to Global Understanding: Notable Books for a Global Society Text Sets," Carolyn Angus shows readers how to pair books to develop text sets or literature clusters (collections of books that focus on a particular theme). Text sets cluster books that vary in genre, reading level, and subject and enable students to explore common themes in their discussions. Teaching suggestions that support intertextual connections are included.

In chapter 8, "Using Poetry to Explore Social Justice and Global Understanding," Mary Napoli illustrates how global poetry addresses international issues and social justice themes and promotes recognition, understanding, and acceptance of cultural diversity and individual differences. Sharing poems from the selected global literature, Napoli discusses how she guides students in her children's literature classes to celebrate their own heritage and fosters conversations about social justice. The poems serve as a site for engagement, critique, and global understanding, which in turn help teacher education candidates create participatory lessons and spaces within the context of their field experience placements with students.

In chapter 9, "Transformative Literature: A Teaching/Learning Model for Using Global Literature to Positively Influence Our World," Marian J. McKenna presents a three-level model designed to help readers discover the transformative process that results from reading global literature. McKenna considers the ways books may move readers beyond the world of their neighborhoods, their schools, and their immediate concerns, helping them realize that they live in a global village and challenging them to develop compassion, insight, and perhaps even constructive activism as a result of being exposed to such books.

As evidenced from the focus of the preceding chapters, literature serves as an avenue for compassion in a turbulent world. Now that we have "built the bridge" through our discussion of global literature, how do we move forward? The conclusion, "Crossing the Bridge" by Marian J. McKenna, offers a summary of the key ideas in the preceding chapters and considers the future for children's and young adult literature with diverse perspectives.

Author Reflections

Because no discussion or celebration of literature would be complete without the voices of children's and young adult authors, several authors whose works have been selected to the booklist offer personal insights on the importance of global literature. These short Author Reflections complement the chapters by revealing the authors' own connections and commitment to diversity and encouraging teachers to use global literature to build bridges to understanding. The authors featured are Joseph Bruchac, Chris Crowe, Jane Kurtz, Ben Mikaelsen, Pat Mora, Nikki Grimes, Suzanne Fisher Staples, Michael O. Tunnell, and Janet S. Wong.

References

A complete listing of the Notable Books for a Global Society by year of selection can be found at the end of the book. Within each chapter, the Notable Books for a Global Society are noted as NBGS with the year of publication and the booklist selection year noted (e.g., 2000/2001 NBGS). Citations for children's and young adult books discussed in a chapter, but not on a Notable Books for a Global Society booklist from 1996–2005, are found at the end of each chapter.

Online Supplement

To further extend the educational reach of this book, an online supplement providing the complete list of and full annotations for all 249 titles can be found on the International Reading Association's website at www.reading.org. The supplement organizes the books from the booklist's first 10 years into a variety of categories that teachers will find helpful for instructional purposes. Teachers can refer to the supplement to locate excellent books for their own class library, for independent reading suggestions, or for read-aloud options. Most importantly, the online supplement can be easily used to plan genre, author, or culture units.

Acknowledgments

The contributions of many people have made this book a reality. We first wish to thank the authors of the chapters found in this volume. This book is a tribute to their scholarly expertise and great concern for global literature and social justice.

We also want to recognize the support we received from the Publications Division of the International Reading Association. We are grateful to Corinne Mooney and Stacey Sharp for the time, skills, and guidance they devoted to this project.

In addition, we would like to express our gratitude to the many publishers whose generosity in submitting hundreds of newly published books each year fuels the work of the Notable Books for a Global Society Committee. Similarly, we would like to acknowledge the members of the Notable Books for a Global

Society Committee who work tirelessly each year to read and review the works submitted by publishers.

Most importantly, we would like to acknowledge the many outstanding authors whose books have been selected to the Notable Books for a Global Society booklist since its inception in 1996. Special thanks are extended to the nine Notable Books for a Global Society authors who shared their personal insights on the importance of global literature in the Author Reflection essays.

Without all of these partners, this book would not have been possible.

—*Nancy L. Hadaway*

Building Bridges to Understanding

Nancy L. Hadaway

"Literature educates not only the head, but the heart as well."
—Rudine Sims Bishop (1994, p. xiv)

L iterature reflects the experiences, values, and beliefs of a group of people. As such, it can provide insights on a culture, promote empathy, and support a developing sense of identity. Through literature we can extend our knowledge as well as our personal boundaries, developing new perspectives and expanding our understanding of who "we" are.

In my own life, from childhood onward, literature has been an extension, my window to other possibilities. Growing up in the 1950s and 1960s, I lived on the same street in a small town for 17 years. Whereas some may feel comfort in being surrounded by sameness in neighborhood and school, I felt strangely out of place. I wondered about the world beyond my narrow slice of life. I was intrigued by the idea of other places, ways of life unlike my own, and different languages. Through literature, I forged a connection with settings and characters that, while foreign in so many ways, seemed surprisingly familiar. For me, literature was a window onto lives and experiences different from my own.

Literature as window is only half the perspective needed, however. In addition to providing a window to look beyond ourselves, literature must also serve as a mirror reflecting the reader's own cultural values, attitudes, and behaviors. Herein lies the problem. "Until recently, children of color have had almost exclusively the book as window, while white, middle class children have almost exclusively been offered book as mirror" (Bishop, 1994, p. xiv).

Breaking Boundaries With Global Literature: Celebrating Diversity in K–12 Classrooms, edited by Nancy L. Hadaway and Marian J. McKenna. © 2007 by the International Reading Association.

The Need to Represent U.S. Diversity in "Multicultural Literature"

The critical need for literature that offers both a mirror *and* a window for all readers can clearly be seen by an examination of recent demographic trends in the United States. According to the U.S. Census Bureau 2005 estimates, 80% of the population is white with 14.4% Hispanic, 12.8% African American, 4.3% Asian, and 1% Native American. Compare these figures with the public school population, however. "Forty-three percent of public school students were considered to be part of a racial or ethnic minority group in 2004, an increase from 22 percent in 1972. In comparison, the percentage of public school students who were White decreased from 78 to 57 percent" (National Center for Education Statistics, 2006). The breakdown of racial or ethnic minority students included 16% African American, 19.3% Hispanic, 4.1% Asian, and 3.2% other. Hispanic enrollment surpassed African American enrollment for the first time in 2002.

Add to this mix the diversity resulting from immigration in the United States. Currently, "immigrants comprise over 12 percent of the U.S. population, and their children over 20 percent. If current trends continue, children of immigrants will represent at least a quarter of all U.S. children by 2010" (The Urban Institute, 2006). The surge of immigrants has contributed to another demographic trend: language diversity. English-language learners are the fastest growing group in U.S. schools today. An estimated 5,119,561 English-language learners, or approximately 10.5% of the total public school student population, were enrolled in public schools (pre-K through grade 12) in the 2004–2005 school year. This represents a 56.2% increase over the 1994–1995 figures (National Clearinghouse for English Language Acquisition and Language Instruction Educational Programs, 2006).

Moreover, the diversity, in and out of schools, extends well beyond racial, ethnic, cultural, and language boundaries. *Diversity* and *multiculturalism*, terms that would seem to indicate a focus on cultures only, are increasingly being used by educators as "umbrella" terms to encompass socioeconomic, gender, language, and religious issues, sexual orientation, and physical and intellectual ability in addition to race, ethnicity, and culture.

Thus, growing diversity, coupled with the realization that many voices had been marginalized and forgotten throughout U.S. history, has contributed to the recent emphasis on the publication of books from diverse voices and about diversity in the United States, literature that has most often been termed *multicultural literature*. Yet even with the focused efforts of publishers in the past few years, the number of books by diverse authors represents a small fraction of the total children's and young adult books published in the United States.

The Need to Represent Global Diversity in Literature

Although there has been an attempt in the publishing world of the United States to feature more diversity in the authors and themes of children's and young adult literature, the events of September 11, 2001, underscored the need for the country to "resee our nation's place in the larger world. Our world got much smaller on 9/11" (Reid, 2006, p. 10). Indeed, as Isaacs (2006) noted, "Americans have been surprised to discover that the way we see ourselves and the world isn't shared by others. Our society's values are not universal, and what we see as acts of good will aren't always taken that way" (n.p.). Our heightened awareness that we are "citizens of larger communities" (Reid, 2006) has resulted in an interest in literature from international authors and books that address themes beyond U.S. borders. One measure of this is the creation of a new booklist sponsored by the Children's Book Council and the U.S. Board on Books for Young People (a division of the International Board on Books for Young People). This booklist, which premiered for the first time in 2006, spotlighted the best children's literature from other countries that had been subsequently published in the United States. In response to their first call for submissions, the committee received 196 books and selected 42 to their list, which has as its goal to "counteract cultural stereotypes, bridge cultural gaps, and build connections" (Isaacs, 2006).

This idea of building a sense of world citizenship was also the focus of the November 2006 issue of *English Journal* "Looking Forward: Teaching English after 9/11." In an introductory essay, Younker (2006) emphasizes the importance of critical literacy in today's world. He argues that asking questions "gives us our humanity to constantly search for ways to improve society" (p. 13). He continues by offering the following questions to ponder.

- What does it mean to be a teacher in a democracy?
- What should students know and be able to do in a world that may hold more challenge than promise?
- How can we prepare students for an increasingly hostile world?

These questions represent a call for literature that can serve as a mirror that reflects *all* readers and affirms their ideas and backgrounds *and* for literature that is a window on the world. Literature is a means of building knowledge and empathy, a tool for reflection and dialogue. There has never been a more opportune moment to use literature as a bridge to understanding in our global village, to reach across the national, cultural, and religious differences that often divide us.

Exposing students to diverse literature and points of view is a first step to building bridges of understanding and developing "literate citizens in a diverse democratic society" (Banks, 2004, p. 291). Banks asserts that such citizens

> should be reflective, moral, and active citizens in an interconnected global world. They should have the knowledge, skills, and commitment needed to change the world to make it more just and democratic. The world's greatest problems do not result from people being unable to read and write. They result from people in the world—from different cultures, races, religions, and nations—being unable to get along and to work together to solve the world's intractable problems such as global warming, the HIV/AIDS epidemic, poverty, racism, sexism, and war. (p. 291)

Defining Global Literature and a Global Society

Although there appear to be strong proponents and a multitude of reasons for the inclusion of diverse literature in classrooms, there is less agreement about the terms used to refer to such literature. In general, several terms have been used to describe literature with a diverse focus, including *multicultural literature* (as previously discussed), *multiethnic literature*, *global literature*, and *international literature*. Indeed, debate often surrounds some of these terms and their definitions, as Yvonne Siu-Runyan alluded to in the Foreword of this book when she struggled to decide on the original name for the Notable Books for a Global Society booklist.

In general, *multicultural literature* is the term used to refer to literature published in the United States that portrays diverse American cultures. Often professional resources highlighting multicultural literature are divided into cultural sections related to the major cultural groups in the United States, African American, Asian American, Hispanic American, and Native American. Some definitions of multicultural literature include the criteria that the book's author is an insider to the culture depicted, while other definitions of multicultural literature may include literature written by outsiders to the culture as well as books that address diversity in terms of religion, language, ethnicity, socioeconomic status, and ability.

International literature also has conflicting definitions. On the one hand, some U.S. children's literature experts define international literature as books originally published in other countries and subsequently brought to the United States. This is the definition used by the Outstanding International Booklist Committee (Isaacs, 2006). On the other hand, international literature has also been defined as "books written and published first in countries other than the United States (both in English and translation), books written by immigrants to the United States about their home countries and published in the United States, books written by

Figure I.1. Visual Definition of Global Literature

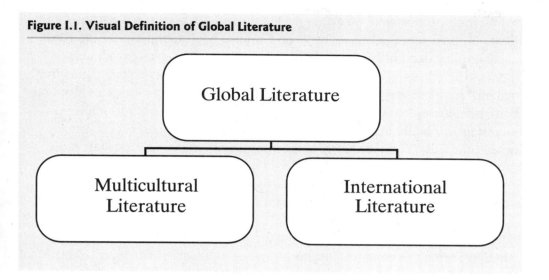

authors from countries other than the United States but originally published in the United States, and books written by American authors and published in the United States with settings in other countries" (Freeman & Lehman, 2001, p. 10). In chapter 2, Freeman, Lehman, and Scharer use the latter, broader, more inclusive definition of international literature. Given the limited number of international books (according to the narrower definition) published in the United States in the past, the broader criteria offer more books for discussion.

In keeping with the title of the Notable Books for a Global Society booklist we celebrate in this volume, we use the term *global literature* in this book. Our definition of *global literature* is a comprehensive and inclusive one, representing literature that honors and celebrates diversity, both within and outside the United States, in terms of culture, race, ethnicity, language, religion, social and economic status, sexual orientation, and physical and intellectual ability. In other words, our use of the term *global literature* includes both multicultural and international literature as depicted in Figure I.1 and all types of diversity. As such, this booklist is a rich resource for teachers at all levels.

Building Bridges

In 1977, after teaching in Colorado and Kentucky in the United States, I finally realized my dream to connect with some of the diverse characters, settings, and languages from the books I had read as a child when I moved to what was then

West Germany to teach. Soon after arriving, I had a chance to visit an American military outpost near the border between East and West Germany. At the Fulda Gap (the valley that NATO forces believed the Soviet Union might someday choose as their point of invasion), I stood a safe distance away from a high-wire fence on "our" side and looked through binoculars at an East German soldier on "their" side of an identical barrier. Between those fences lay not just a few hundred feet of land but miles of cultural and political differences. Yet, in that moment, the East German soldier and I were simply two people, perhaps with more in common than either of us could imagine.

While I did not cross the frontier between East and West that day at the Fulda Gap, I have spent the rest of my time crossing borders—geographic, language, social, cultural, and experiential ones—both real and literary. Understanding self and others is a lifelong journey, and books can help us all begin that journey. Such an exploration is critical because, as Ruggieri (2006) notes, "at the root of every conflict is a miscommunication" (p. 79). My hope is that teachers will use the resources in this book to build bridges of understanding that support their own personal growth and that encourage their students to reach across borders to see themselves and others in new ways.

REFERENCES

Banks, J.A. (2004). Teaching for social justice, diversity, and citizenship in a global world. *Educational Forum, 68*, 289–298.

Bishop, R.S. (Ed.), & Multicultural Booklist Committee. (1994). *Kaleidoscope: A multicultural booklist for grades K–8*. Urbana, IL: National Council of Teachers of English.

Freeman, E.B., & Lehman, B.A. (2001). *Global perspectives in children's literature*. Boston: Allyn & Bacon.

Isaacs, K. (2006). *It's a big world after all*. Retrieved March 6, 2007, from http://www.schoollibrary journal.com/article/CA6302985.html

National Center for Education Statistics. (2006). Participation in education. Retrieved March 6, 2007, from http://nces.ed.gov/programs/coe/2006/section1/indicator05.asp

National Clearinghouse for English Language Acquisition and Language Instruction Educational Programs. (2006). *NCELA FAQ: How many school-aged English language learners (ELLs) are there in the U.S.?* Retrieved March 6, 2007, from http://www.ncela.gwu.edu/expert/faq/01leps.html

Reid, L. (2006). From the editor. *English Journal, 96*, 10–11.

Ruggieri, C.A. (2006). Reemerging from 9/11: Teaching in a world of tragedy and terrorism. *English Journal, 96*, 79–83.

The Urban Institute. (2006, May). *Children of immigrants: Facts and figures*. Retrieved March 6, 2007, from http://www.urban.org/UploadedPDF/900955_children_of_immigrants.pdf

U.S. Census Bureau. (2006). *National population estimates*. Retrieved March 6, 2007, from http://www.census.gov/popest/estimates.php

Younker, K. (2006). Challenging roles. *English Journal, 96*, 12–13.

PART I

Diverse Perspectives in Literature

CHAPTER 1

An Analysis of the Notable Books for a Global Society, 1996–2005

Nancy L. Hadaway

"We live in one world. What we do affects others, and what others do affects us as never before. To recognize that we are all members of a world community and that we all have responsibilities to each other is not romantic rhetoric, but modern economic and social reality."
—Department for Education and Skills (2004, p. 7)

The power of literature is immeasurable. Good books help readers understand who they are and where they belong in the world. What is more, they open doors in the mind and in the heart. As Hazel Rochman (1993) asserts, "The best books break down borders. They surprise us—whether they are set close to home or abroad. They change our view of ourselves; they extend that phrase 'like me' to include what we thought was foreign and strange" (p. 9).

The possibilities inherent within literature have been brought into question in the United States, however, because the range of literature available in classrooms and libraries has not adequately or accurately reflected the diversity of all readers. Published literature in the United States, until recently, has been restricted to predominantly white middle class voices. Yet, as discussed in the introduction, readers need both a mirror to reflect their own world and a window to consider other realities—to imagine beyond self. Good books don't just reaffirm everything the reader already knows (Rochman, 1993).

As a means of broadening the range of literature offered to all readers, much attention has been focused on global literature. When we read across the boundaries of culture, race, ethnicity, gender, language, religion, social and

Breaking Boundaries With Global Literature: Celebrating Diversity in K–12 Classrooms, edited by Nancy L. Hadaway and Marian J. McKenna. © 2007 by the International Reading Association.

economic status, sexual orientation, and physical and intellectual ability, we encounter the familiar and known as well as the unknown. The impact of reading literature about one's own culture as well as that across diverse perspectives has been the focus of research projects that have documented certain transformative results. For instance, Native American students were affirmed by hearing their own voices when reading literature from their culture, voices not always included in K–12 curriculum (Glazier & Seo, 2005), while other students with limited diversity experiences developed empathy for characters of a Chinese novella (Louie, 2005). (More about this transformative potential of global literature will be explored in chapters 8 and 9.)

The potential of literature to transform, though, is dependent on the strategies used to engage students as well as the availability of literature that challenges readers causing them to question what they thought was certain (Rochman, 1993). For instance, Smith and Singer (2006) involved students in online discussion groups while reading *The Friendship* (Taylor, 1987). They reported positive results as students read and responded to the text. Over time, students moved from academic knowledge about prejudice (keeping the experience at a distance) to a more personal view of prejudice (discussing it as an event in real people's lives). Stallworth, Gibbons, and Fauber (2006) found, however, that while teachers might advocate the use of global literature, the actual use of such literature didn't necessarily occur in classrooms. One reason for this may be teachers' tendency to fall back on familiar selections in the curriculum or their unfamiliarity with global literature. Therefore, the goal of this book is to provide a resource for teacher educators and K–12 teachers with recommendations of excellent global literature, critical analysis of that literature and themes of diversity, and instructional strategies to connect books and readers. As a beginning point to those committed to the integration of global literature into classrooms at all levels, the next section introduces various book awards that target literature from diverse perspectives.

Literature With a Global Perspective

According to Bishop (1997, p. 18), a literature collection that truly reflects our global village should include books that highlight the diversity that is part of all groups. Therefore, global literature should not only reflect cultural and ethnic diversity but should also include the following representations:

- People of varying socioeconomic circumstances, occupations, lifestyles
- Differing perspectives on issues and events
- Themes that can be compared and contrasted across a set of related books

- Various genres (such as poetry, folklore, historical fiction, nonfiction, biography, realistic fiction)
- Books that span the range of literary multiculturalism
- Nonfiction that provides factual information about a people and their way of life

Beaty (1997) suggests a few other considerations, such as books with a balance of urban versus rural settings and of historical versus contemporary portrayal, detailed illustrations that avoid stereotypes, language or dialect that shows a respect for culture, and characters from different cultures that interact with one another.

As the number of published books from diverse perspectives has increased, several book awards have emerged to spotlight outstanding works by authors of color (Coretta Scott King Award, John Steptoe Award, and Pura Belpré Award) or works that accurately portray the experiences of particular groups (Americas Award, Carter G. Woodson Award, National Jewish Book Award, Sydney Taylor Book Award, and Tomás Rivera Award). Such awards serve to bring authors of color and previously underrepresented and marginalized groups to the forefront. Indeed, part of the current emphasis on multicultural literature in general, and these awards in particular, is "the perceived need to counteract a tradition of distortions, inaccuracies, and omissions of the histories, heroes, literatures, and cultural traditions of people of color" (Bishop, 1997, p. 5). However, each of these awards is focused on the presentation of cultural diversity within the United States only.

Certainly, educators can and should read across such award lists such as those previously mentioned, but they also need a collection of books considered to be outstanding and that address a wide range of perspectives from both within and outside the United States. The Notable Books for a Global Society (NBGS) booklist has this type of comprehensive focus—books that enhance understanding of people and cultures throughout the world. Each year, 25 books that honor and celebrate diversity, both within and outside the United States, in terms of culture, race, ethnicity, gender, language, religion, social and economic status, sexual orientation, and physical and intellectual ability are chosen for this booklist. (For the complete selection criteria, see the online supplement for this book found on the International Reading Association website at www.reading.org.) Thus, the Notable Books for a Global Society booklists serve as the major resource for the discussions that follow in each chapter of this book.

While each year's Notable Books for a Global Society booklist is an excellent resource for informing educators of the latest and best in global literature, the only analysis of the list is the annotated bibliography that is published each year in *The Dragon Lode*, the journal of the Children's Literature and Reading Special Interest Group of the International Reading Association in which the list appears.

Therefore, this book provides a more in-depth analysis of the major themes that cut across the books selected, such as gender, immigration, and language issues (these themes form the framework for Part II of this book). Furthermore, while teachers can select books from any year's list to be read and studied individually, they can more effectively meet the needs of students in today's diverse classrooms when they are aware of and can choose from a wide array of books that share the same theme (the chapters in Part III of this book demonstrate how to take the themes and issues in the first part of the book and to build collections of books to address instructional goals and to engage students in active inquiry).

Therefore, the remainder of this chapter offers readers a quick overview of the Notable Books for a Global Society booklists from 1996 to 2005. Readers will discover that just over half of the 249 books on the booklist address cultural groups in the United States; thus, the booklists are good source for literature that explores cultures both inside and outside of the United States. The snapshot of publishers with works that have been selected to the booklist is a great resource to build awareness of small presses that are producing excellent global literature as well as those publishers who seem to dominate the global literature niche. Further, the genre breakdown indicates that the booklists are an excellent resource for picture books, novels, and nonfiction books that can be used across the curriculum. The chapter, then, serves as an advance organizer that helps readers see the possibilities within the Notable Books for a Global Society booklists for an individual year as well as the powerful opportunities that are available in the collected booklists across 10 years.

A Categorical Examination of the Booklist

This chapter serves as a road map to the first 10 years of the booklist, exploring the following different dimensions:

- Authors
- Illustrators
- Publishers
- Genres (including fiction picture books, realistic fiction novels, historical fiction novels, nonfiction, folklore, poetry, and mixed genres)
- Cultural groups (considering not only ethnic, geographic, social, language, and religious but also physical and mental ability and sexual orientation)

This chapter's discussion of these dimensions, along with the online supplement's more detailed breakdown and discussion of different categories within the booklists from 1996 to 2005, can be used by educators to develop illustrator and author studies, genre studies, and cultural studies through literature. Using the categories from this chapter, teachers can see how easy it would be to build a text set that addresses a specific culture (for instance, books

Beyond the Mirror:
On the Importance of Global Literature

JOSEPH BRUCHAC

You can't see the world around you if you only look into a mirror. Your face fills so much of the glass that there's little room for others—who cannot do more than look over your shoulder. In fact, in a mirror, you never perceive more than half of yourself. To expand your vision, you need to turn around. Aim your gaze toward the windows to the world outside. Open your door and pass through.

There is an old saying among the Hopis: "The more you know, the less you will fear." Add to that the equally ancient truth that we all have two ears and thus are meant to hear more than one side.

It was my great good fortune when I was just out of college to be able to work for three years as a volunteer teacher in West Africa. One of the people I met was the author Chinua Achebe, whose work not only taught me a great deal about his continent but also gave me greater perspective to see my own. To fully see the place where you live, you must walk away from it. In his books, Chinua has always made great use of proverbs. I am, quite frankly, following his example throughout this brief essay.

Life, you see, is a circle. But it is so large—like the great globe that we live on—that we may think at first that it is a straight line. The literatures of other cultures show the way to the greater journey, offering adventure, experience, and knowledge. Like new friends with open hands, they guide our children, helping them recognize the ways that circle them back home again with a better understanding of others and themselves.

Books by Joseph Bruchac selected for the Notable Books for a Global Society:

Between Earth & Sky: Legends of Native American Sacred Places (1996/1997 NBGS)

Lasting Echoes: An Oral History of Native American People (1997/1998 NBGS)

The Winter People (2002/2003 NBGS)

about Africa) or to choose a specific genre and create a unit with works that portray a variety of cultures. As one example, readers will discover in the nonfiction section that the booklists had a large number of biographies, spanning many years of history as well as different cultural groups; therefore, a text set can be developed with the 28 biographies featured in the booklists, including picture books as well as chapter books, partial as well as complete biographies. In summary, yearly booklists are certainly a resource for educators, helping them to stay current, but this chapter helps teachers begin to see the ways an entire collection of global literature can be examined and used effectively to meet instructional goals, allowing them to use this information to move directly to idea generation and instructional planning.

A Look at Authors

In the booklist's first 10 years, 249 books highlighting varying people and cultures around the world were selected. Just as these books represent diverse individuals and cultures, so do their authors. And just as there are many different voices at work, some of these voices are heard multiple times. Over 180 different authors or editors are reflected, and 28 authors had two books selected to the booklist. Six authors or editors were associated with three or more titles on the booklist (see the "Authors With Multiple Works Selected" section of the online supplement for the complete list of these authors).

An author's background and its influence on the accuracy and authenticity of a work, while always an important factor, is particularly significant when considering global literature. Indeed, this is one of the most controversial issues in the field. Much debate exists over the insider versus outsider perspective, or whether a book can be considered culturally "authentic" if the author is writing outside of his or her culture. Bishop (1997) defines *authenticity* "in terms of whether or not the depiction of the characters seems accurate or rings true in relation to their physical appearance, and to their behaviors, attitudes, values, language, beliefs, their way of life—in short, their culture" (p. 16). Living within a particular culture can provide the background for addressing these issues and writing an accurate story about that culture. Indeed, Cai (2002) argues that wide reading of literature written by insiders helps to form a frame of reference to check the accuracy of global literature written by those outside the culture.

The question remains, Can authentic literature be created by individuals who are not members of the group being portrayed? Some gifted authors have managed to "get it right" with careful research, fact-checking, and even close observation and personal experience. However, Bishop (1997) argues that "the farther a writer's background, knowledge, and experiences are from the culture of the person or people about whom he or she is writing, the greater the necessity for the author to fill in the cultural gaps, the greater the effort needed to do so, and the greater the risk of mistakes" (p. 17). However, no author should be held accountable for speaking on behalf of an entire culture with a single book—the most powerful, well-written story still represents only one author, one perspective, and one story.

To consider the issue of cultural authenticity, Sanchez (2001) evaluated 20 trade books for their accuracy in portrayal of Native American people and culture. Using criteria based on the Five Great Values (Reiten, 1995), he ranked the books from 0 (lowest) to 5 (highest). The majority of the books (12, or 60%) were rated at least satisfactory. Of those 12 books, 5 were written by native authors while the remaining 7 were not. However, all native-authored books were classified with average to highest ratings; no Native American–authored book rated below average. Perhaps the ratings would have been slanted even more toward the author–culture connection had more books been native authored. This brings us to the next critical issue.

The presence of new as well as veteran authors and those from diverse backgrounds is crucial to a booklist whose goal is to spotlight global perspectives. However, while the number of diverse authors being represented has increased, it remains a small proportion of the total books published. Further, the current climate in the children's book publishing industry with megaconglomerates focused on sales and cuts in the number of publications released each year works against the emergence of many new voices. Some publishing companies, such as Lee & Low, have made a concerted effort to publish work from diverse authors and those new to children's publishing. Moreover, Front Street Books notes on their website that half of their authors have been previously unpublished.

Also problematic is the scarcity of international literature in the United States, with few translated books offered to the children's and young adult audiences in this country (see chapter 2 for more discussion on this trend). Nonetheless, the inclusion of international authors is vital to a booklist focused on a global society. Seven books published outside of the United States and translated into English were selected for the booklist (see the "International Authors With Translated Works Selected" section of the online supplement for the list of these authors and their work).

A Look at Illustrators

Illustrated books offer an opportunity to view cultural themes and groups through both the textual and visual lens. At times, the visual channel carries as much or more information and impact as the textual one, even if this is unintended (Mendoza & Reese, 2001). Consequently, just as with the author's text, cultural authenticity in illustrations is essential. Criticisms have been aimed at a number of books specifically regarding the illustrations' inaccuracies. As one example, Reese and Caldwell-Wood (1997) highlight the inconsistencies in Ted Rand's illustrations in *Knots on a Counting Rope* (Martin & Archambault, 1987), which is set in the Navajo nation but shows a mix of material culture (e.g., hairstyles and ceremonial clothing) from several different nations. Yokota (1993) has also noted several errors in Japanese costume and custom depicted in picture books published in the United States.

From 1996 to 2005 there were 116 illustrated books (includes photo-illustrated works) on the booklist. Of these, 16 illustrators had multiple works on the booklist (see the "Illustrators With Multiple Works Selected" section of the online supplement for the complete list of these illustrators and their work). A look at these artists' websites or the biographical information on dust jackets reflects the rich cultural backgrounds that they bring to the task of illustrating children's and young adult literature. Yet, while publishers strive to match illustrators with authors or works based on cultural similarities, their efforts have been complicated by the availability of authors and illustrators from comparable backgrounds.

A Look at Publishers

Authors and illustrators are key in shaping the view of our global society through their works selected to the booklist. Authors craft the stories and illustrators create the visual images paired with those stories. Publishers, however, are another critical element in the formula; they determine what projects are accepted. Moreover, in moving manuscripts forward to publication, publishers fashion the end product in the course of their role in the editing process and their decision about which illustrator (if appropriate) to match to a work.

Concern has arisen over the recent changes in the publishing industry in which independent publishers are being purchased by large, multinational corporations, creating huge publishing conglomerates. Often, the tendency of larger publishing entities has been to focus on volume sales and thus, encourage less risk taking (Reese & Caldwell-Wood, 1997; Taxel, 1997). But in 1998, Jump at the Sun, the first African American children's imprint at a major publisher (Hyperion), was launched by Andrea Davis Pinkney. A few independent multicultural presses have also emerged, including Lee & Low in New York, USA; Children's Book Press in California, USA; Cinco Puntos in Texas, USA; Fulcrum in Colorado, USA; Groundwood in Toronto, Canada; and Northland Publishing in Arizona, USA (Gangi, 2005). With the exception of Fulcrum, each of these presses was represented by books selected to the booklist from 1996 to 2005. Table 1.1

Table 1.1. Publishers Represented in the Notable Books for a Global Society Booklist (1996–2005)

The booklist reflected the activity of 31 different publishers or publishing groups. In the case of a publishing group, only imprints associated with works chosen for the booklist are noted.	Number of Books / Percentage of List
August House	1 / less than 1%
Cinco Puntos Press	1 / less than 1%
Lerner Publishing Group	1 / less than 1%
Marshall Cavendish	1 / less than 1%
National Geographic Society	1 / less than 1%
Peachtree	1 / less than 1%
Sierra Books for Children	1 / less than 1%
Tricycle Press, the children's division of Ten Speed Press.	1 / less than 1%
Albert Whitman	2 / 1%
Annick Press	2 / 1%
Candlewick Press	2 / 1%
Chronicle	2 / 1%
Northland Publishing, including the imprint Rising Moon	2 / 1%
Charlesbridge	3 / 1%
Children's Book Press	3 / 1%
Groundwood	3 / 1%
Boyds Mills Press	4 / 2%
Front Street	4 / 2%
Little, Brown, an imprint of Time Warner	5 / 2%
Henry Holt	7 / 3%
Hyperion, including Jump at the Sun imprint	7 / 3%
Lee & Low	7 / 3%
Random House, including the imprints Alfred A. Knopf, Delacorte Press, and Doubleday	9 / 4%
Holiday House	10 / 4%
Farrar, Straus and Giroux	15 / 6%
Harcourt, formerly Harcourt Brace & Company, and including the imprints Gulliver and Silver Whistle	19 / 8%
Houghton Mifflin, including the imprint Clarion Books	19 / 8%
Simon & Schuster, including Macmillan and the imprints Atheneum and Margaret K. McElderry	22 / 9%
HarperCollins, including the imprints Greenwillow, William Morrow, and Lothrop, Lee & Shepard	22 / 9%
Scholastic, including the imprints Arthur A. Levine, Blue Sky, and Orchard Books	27 / 11%
Penguin Group, including the imprints Cobblehill, Dial, Dorling Kindersley, Dutton, G.P. Putnam's Sons, Lodestar, Philomel Books, Phyllis Fogelman, Putnam, and Viking	45 / 18%

highlights the 31 publishers or publishing groups represented on the booklist with the number of books and percentage of the list for each publisher. For publishing groups, only the imprints represented on the booklist are indicated; other imprints for those publishers may exist. From a quick examination of this figure, it is obvious that the larger publishers dominated the booklist. This is not unexpected, as larger publishers have greater resources to publicize their books and supply review copies to award committees (more information about publishing trends is discussed in chapter 2).

A Look at Genres

A review of the 249 books on the booklist shows that the most predominant genre was fiction, accounting for 59% of the total books (see the "Genres" section of the online supplement for several discussions of genres and subgenres represented). The fiction selections could be further broken down into three categories: fiction picture books (23% of the total books), realistic fiction novels (21% of the total books), and historical fiction novels (16% of the total books). Nonfiction was another major genre, accounting for 22% of the total books, while folklore and poetry made up 10% and 7% of the booklist, respectively. Two mixed-genre books, combining different types of works, were also represented.

In 1997, Bishop maintained that U.S. children's literature labeled "multicultural" was not balanced in terms of genres and topics, that too large a portion was folk tales with little fiction representing the contemporary lives of Latinos, Native Americans, or Asian Americans. Bishop surveyed all published multicultural literature, and, of course, the Notable Books for a Global Society booklist is a select subset resulting from the award criteria as well as committee deliberation and attempts to balance for issues such as genre. Not surprisingly, a review of genres and subgenres of the booklist reported in Table 1.2 shows a slightly different picture. Realistic fiction novels, for instance, outstripped historical fiction novels by 5%, and the number of historical and contemporary fiction picture books was almost equal: 30 versus 27, respectively. In addition, Bishop noted that multicultural biographies were limited in all published multicultural literature, while half the nonfiction books on the booklist were biographies. The genre numbers for the booklist, however, were not broken down by insider versus outsider author. Finally, Bishop commented on the limited amount of multicultural poetry published, and over the first 10 years of the booklist that genre did have the smallest percentage of works.

Each genre presents strengths and weaknesses in terms of accurately portraying society and the diverse groups that make up our global village. Nonfiction books, for instance, present a factual foundation to help readers

Table 1.2. Genre Representation in Notable Books for a Global Society Booklist (1996–2005)

Genre	Number of Books	Percentage of List
Fiction picture book (30 with historical settings)	57	23%
Realistic fiction novel	51	21%
Historical fiction novel	41	16%
Nonfiction (34 picture books)	56	22%
Folklore	24	10%
Poetry	18	7%
Mixed genres	2	1%
TOTAL	249	100%

hopefully gain a culturally authentic view of groups and issues, whereas poetry or fiction offers affective nuances, not always present in nonfiction, that encourage personal connections. Another genre issue concerns the balance of historical versus contemporary representation of groups and issues in books. One specific example is the tendency to overrepresent Jews from a historical perspective in the context of the Holocaust. Reading across genres, then, provides a greater opportunity to increase our knowledge and move toward a deeper appreciation of our interconnected society. A discussion of balance in topics across genres is integrated throughout the remainder of the chapter. For more information about building text sets or groups of related books across genres, refer to chapter 7.

Fiction Picture Books. It is not surprising that fiction picture books accounted for a significant portion of the booklist because picture books, in general, dominate the children's book publishing industry. While not for factual instructional purposes, fiction can provide valuable insights on a culture or a group, its values, attitudes, customs as well as its ways of living, believing, and behaving (Bishop, 1997). Fifty-seven fiction picture books were selected to the booklist (see the "Fiction Picture Books" section of the online supplement for a complete list.) Over half, 30 to be exact, had historical settings, and the rest displayed more contemporary settings. Four authors had fiction picture books selected twice to the booklist: Eve Bunting, Patricia McKissack, Janet S. Wong, and Jacqueline Woodson.

Fiction picture books presented a diverse portrait of a global society spotlighting 4 continents, 20 countries or regions, and 2 major religious groups (see the "In Fiction Picture Books" section of the "Cultural Representation in Notable Books for a Global Society Booklists, 1996–2005" part of the online supplement for this breakdown). However, over half the fiction picture books reflected the United States. Within that grouping, African Americans were the focus of 42% and Chinese Americans were central to 21%. Outside North America, Asia was well represented with 16%, including stories about Afghanistan, Cambodia, China, the Hmong, Japan, Korea, and Vietnam. Africa was central to 10% of the list featuring the countries of Ethiopia, Morocco, Somalia, South Africa, and Zimbabwe. Further, books about Africa reflected a good mix of historical and contemporary settings. Conversely, picture books about Europe concentrated on historical events, with three of the four books about the Holocaust. Fiction picture books about Latin America were very limited with just one selected work, *Blanca's Feather/La Pluma de Blanca* (Madrigal, 2000/2001 NBGS), set in Mexico.

In examining fiction, Bishop (1992) describes three general approaches used to portray culture—specific, generic, and neutral. Culturally specific books, through artwork and text, offer explicit details about a particular cultural group, details that would be recognizable to members of the group portrayed. Generic books have characters that are members of different cultural groups, but there is much less cultural detail. Finally, neutral books feature diverse characters, but the focus of the book is not about multicultural or global issues. In order for readers to gain insights on significant aspects of diverse groups, then, culturally specific books are obviously the best choice. In the criteria for the Notable Books for a Global Society booklist, the focus on cultural specificity is clear. Books must be rich in cultural details, provide in-depth treatment of cultural issues, and include members of a "minority" group for a purpose other than filling a "quota." An examination of the fiction picture books selected to this list reveals this attention to culturally specific detail. For instance, in *A Song for Ba* (Yee, 2004/2005 NBGS), readers are introduced to Chinese opera, an ancient art form that these Chinese immigrants in 20th-century America are struggling to keep alive. And in *Goin' Someplace Special* (McKissack, 2001/2002 NBGS), Tricia Ann navigates segregated Nashville, USA, in the 1950s to arrive finally at the public library—one of the only places in the city that welcomes African Americans.

While it is often assumed that picture books are for younger audiences, many recently published books tackle difficult topics such as war and refugee camps, as reflected in *The Roses in My Carpets* (Khan, 1998/1999 NBGS) and *The Whispering Cloth: A Refugee Story* (Shea, 1995/1996 NBGS), or religious persecution, as in *My Name Was Hussein* (Kyuchukov, 2004/2005 NBGS). These books may be more appropriate for older readers, or the topic treatment may extend the range of grades for instructional use. For a more detailed discussion of children and war, see chapter 6, "Resilient Children in Times of War" by Linda Leonard Lamme.

Realistic Fiction. Reflecting plot, characters, and settings from current or recent times, realistic fiction was an integral part of the booklist. 51 realistic fiction novels were selected (see the "Realistic Fiction Novels" section of the online supplement under "Genres" for a complete list). Three authors had multiple books on the list: Ben Mikaelsen, Suzanne Fisher Staples, and Jacqueline Woodson.

The largest percentage of realistic fiction novels, 44%, focused on the United States, with books about African Americans leading by almost half (see the "In Realistic Fiction Novels" section under the "Cultural Representations in Notable Books for a Global Society Booklists, 1996–2005" heading in the online supplement for this listing). In contrast to the findings for fiction picture books, Latin America received more emphasis and religious diversity in realistic fiction novels. Works about Africa, Asia, and Latin America had strong showings on the booklist in the realistic fiction category. Many of the same countries highlighted in fiction picture books appeared again as the focus of realistic fiction novels including Ethiopia, South Africa, Afghanistan, and Japan, but books about Kenya, Liberia, Mozambique, Sudan, India, and Pakistan also made their way to the booklist. In addition, disability emerged as a theme in the realistic fiction novels category with three examples: *Blue Star Rapture* (Bennett, 1998/1999 NBGS), *The Truth About Sparrows* (Hale, 2004/2005 NBGS), and *Dreaming in Black & White* (Jung, 2003/2004 NBGS). Beyond reflections of culture, the booklist's titles addressed issues at the forefront of the media including the AIDS epidemic in Africa in *Chanda's Secrets* (Stratton, 2004/2005 NBGS), modern day slavery in *Dream Freedom* (Levitin, 2000/2001 NBGS), sexual orientation in *From the Notebooks of Melanin Sun* (Woodson, 1995/1996 NBGS), and the effects of political violence in *Secrets in the Fire* (Mankell, 2003/2004 NBGS) and *Tree Girl* (Mikaelsen, 2004/2005 NBGS). This trend to address pressing social issues continues with recent publications such as *I Am a Taxi* (Ellis, 2006), which spotlights drug smuggling and the cocaine trade in Bolivia, and *Sold* (McCormick, 2006), a heart-wrenching story of a 13-year-old Nepalese girl sold into prostitution.

Historical Fiction. Forty-one works of historical fiction were chosen for the booklist (see the "Historical Fiction" section under "Genres" for the complete list). Linda Sue Park and Mildred D. Taylor had two books on the lists. Park authored *A Single Shard* (2001/2002 NBGS) and *When My Name Was Keoko: A Novel of Korea in World War II* (2002/2003 NBGS), and Taylor had two books from the Logan family saga, *The Land* (2001/2002 NBGS) and *The Well: David's Story* (1995/1996 NBGS).

Compared with the cultural breakdown of realistic fiction, historical fiction selections showed no focus on Latin America and only limited attention to Africa with two books selected over 10 years (see the "In Historical Fiction Novels" section under "Cultural Representation in Notable Books for a Global Society Booklists, 1996–2005" of the online supplement for the complete breakdown). Again, the preponderance of books concentrated on the United States with 61%, followed by religion with 25%, and Europe with 18% of the list. In the subdivision of historical fiction related to Europe and religion, five books, *Daniel Half Human and the Good Nazi* (Chotjewitz, 2004/2005 NBGS), *Torn Thread* (Isaacs, 2000/2001 NBGS), *The Final Journey* (Pausewang, 1996/1997 NBGS), *Malka* (Pressler, 2003/2004), and *Sacred Shadows* (Schur, 1997/1998 NBGS), were crosslisted because they dealt with Jews during the Holocaust. While five of the eight historical fiction novels about Jews centered on the Holocaust, three others, *Journey to Ellis Island: How My Father Came to America* (Bierman, 1998/1999), *Nothing Here But Stones* (Oswald, 2004/2005 NBGS), and *The Memory Coat* (Woodruff, 1999/2000 NBGS), addressed Jewish immigration to America. Two additional books beyond these eight had a link to Jews—*A Stone in My Hand* (Clinton, 2002/2003 NBGS) about the Israeli–Palestinian conflict in Gaza City and *The Storyteller's Beads* (Kurtz, 1998/1999 NBGS), which highlighted the relationship between two refugee girls, Christian and Jewish, fleeing war-torn Ethiopia.

Historical fiction featuring diversity in the United States was weighted more toward African Americans (72%) and Native Americans (24%). The 13 books related to African Americans span over 200 years, from the American Revolution in *Hang a Thousand Trees With Ribbons: The Story of Phillis Wheatley* (Rinaldi, 1996/1997 NBGS) and *Cast Two Shadows* (Rinaldi, 1998/1999 NBGS), through the era of slavery in *North by Night: The Story of the Underground Railroad* (Ayers, 1998/1999 NBGS) and *Minty: A Story of Young Harriet Tubman* (Schroeder, 1996/1997 NBGS), to segregation and the U.S. Civil Rights movement in *Mississippi Trial, 1955* (Crowe, 2002/2003 NBGS), *The Watsons Go to Birmingham—1963* (Curtis, 1995/1996 NBGS), *The Darkest Corner* (Herschler, 2000/2001 NBGS), *Black Angels* (Murphy, 2001/2002 NBGS), and *The Red Rose Box* (Woods, 2002/2003 NBGS).

A variety of groups and historical time frames were addressed in the books spotlighting Native Americans, beginning in the early 1700s with a Mohawk raid in Massachusetts, USA, in *The Ransom of Mercy Carter* (Cooney, 2001/2002 NBGS) and moving to 1759 Québec and the struggles of the Abenaki during the French and Indian Wars in *The Winter People* (Bruchac, 2002/2003 NBGS). A look at the life among Native Americans in the 1800s was offered from the viewpoint of a half Arapaho girl in *Adaline Falling Star* (Osborne, 2000/2001 NBGS), a Choctaw boy on the Trail of Tears in *Longwalker's Journey* (Harrell, 1999/2000 NBGS), and an Ojibwa girl living near Lake Superior in *The Birchbark House* (Erdrich, 1999/2000 NBGS). Finally, in *The Year of Miss Agnes* (Hill, 2000/2001 NBGS), readers experienced village life in 1948 Alaska through the eyes of a young schoolteacher and her Athabascan pupils.

Nonfiction. Nonfiction books furnish an outstanding means of building a foundation of knowledge about our global society. Such knowledge has the potential to fuel social change (Bishop, 1997). Fifty-six works of nonfiction were chosen for the booklist; 34 of these were picture books (see the "Nonfiction" section under "Genres" in the online supplement for the complete list). Three authors, Raymond Bial, Diane Hoyt-Goldsmith, and Walter Dean Myers, had two nonfiction books for the booklist, and Russell Freedman, the well-known biographer, had three books on the list.

Although the historical fiction selections offered a "close-up" of a limited time span in history, such as the Holocaust, or a specific group within a culture, such as the Ojibwa as one Native American group, works of nonfiction had the ability to capture a "wide-angle" view with a survey of all Native American or immigrant groups, for example. Nine of the 56 nonfiction books had this broad approach. Children around the world were spotlighted in both *Children Just Like Me* (Kindersley & Kindersley, 1995/1996 NBGS) and *A Life Like Mine: How Children Live Around the World* (UNICEF, 2002/2003 NBGS). The diversity of individuals within the United States, past and present, was the subject of several books including *Lasting Echoes: An Oral History of Native American People* (Bruchac, 1997/1998 NBGS), *Children of Native America Today* (Dennis & Hirschfelder, 2003/2004 NBGS), a comprehensive history of Native Americans in *Immigrants* (Sandler, 1995/1996 NBGS), and *Tenement: Immigrant Life on the Lower East Side* (Bial, 2002/2003 NBGS). Regional culture took center stage in *Mist Over the Mountains: Appalachia and Its People* (Bial, 1997/1998 NBGS), whereas a broad view of sexual orientation was presented in *The Shared Heart: Portraits and Stories Celebrating Lesbian, Gay, and Bisexual Young People* (Mastoon, 1997/1998 NBGS). Finally, *Market!* (Lewin, 1996/1997 NBGS) offered a colorful celebration of markets around the world. Such wide-angle books can be used to provide a foundation for later historical fiction reading to increase understanding and enjoyment. One caution about wide-angle books might be that the focus on an overview of a group dilutes the cultural specificity that can lead to deeper understanding. Therefore, both narrow and wide-angle reading is a necessity.

In addition to the close-up versus wide-angle view, a careful investigation of nonfiction as a genre reveals several different kinds of factual books including travelogues, journals and diaries, photo essays, survey and browsing books, and biographies. Each type offers different ways to spotlight our global society (see the "Nonfiction Books by Format [Excluding Biographies]" section under "Genres" in the online supplement). Browsing books such as *Children Just Like Me* (Kindersley, 1995/1996 NBGS) allow readers to thumb through photographs and illustrations and sample bits of information. Counting books do not always fall into the nonfiction category; however, in *One Child, One Seed: A South African Counting Book* (Cave, 2003/2004 NBGS), readers view common objects and images drawn from the daily life of one family in the South African village of Kwazulu, Natal. Diaries and journals, on the other hand, furnish first-person accounts, making nonfiction more personal. Certainly, readers experience "lived" history after reading the entries from the diary that Japanese American Lillian "Anne" Yamauchi Hori kept with her third-grade class in 1943 in *The Children of Topaz: The Story of a Japanese-American Internment Camp* (Tunnell & Chilcoat, 1996/1997 NBGS). Biography, a literary work describing a person's life, was the most dominant format among the booklist's nonfiction works. Of the 56 nonfiction books, 28 were biographies. Biographies offer a wonderful overview of the cultural milieu within which an individual lived as well as providing insights on how a key figure might have influenced historical and cultural events.

Biographies come in a variety of formats—with partial biographies that highlight a certain portion or aspect of the person's life and complete biographies that span the course of an individual's life, although all years may not be addressed (see the "Biographies" section under "Nonfiction" in the online supplement). Partial biographies might focus on a pivotal event such as the integration of schools in *Through My Eyes* (Bridges, 1999/2000 NBGS), while complete biographies might chronicle changes over time, such as the shifting power structure of Christians and Muslims during the Crusades in *Saladin: Noble Prince of Islam* (Stanley, 2002/2003 NBGS). Biographers sometimes use a picture book format to make historical lives accessible to young and struggling readers, and 10 of the biographies on the booklist are picture book biographies. Finally, autobiographies and memoirs are biographies written by the subjects themselves. These books may be biased or more subjective than those written by impartial authors, but memoirs offer an insider perspective of culture and specific events. The first-person accounts of lifestyles, as in *Rattlesnake Mesa: Stories From a Native American Childhood* (Weber, 2004/2005 NBGS), or events such as China's Cultural Revolution in *China's Son: Growing Up in the Cultural Revolution* (Chen, 2001/2002 NBGS) or the Holocaust in *No Pretty Pictures: A Child of War* (Lobel, 1998/1999 NBGS) contribute powerful affective dimensions that more factual descriptions may lack.

Nonfiction books on the booklist covered 4 continents (Africa, Asia, Europe, and North America), 14 countries, and 4 religions (see the "In Nonfiction" section under "Cultural Representation in the Notable Books for a Global Society Booklists, 1996–2005" in the online supplement). When compared with the other genres, nonfiction offered the widest portrayal of religion on the booklist, with works highlighting five different religious groups: Christian, Jewish, Muslim, and Quaker. However, the majority of the emphasis on religion was historical. Only two books had a more contemporary focus: *One Belfast Boy* (McMahon, 1999/2000 NBGS), portraying the Catholic–Protestant conflict in Northern Ireland, and *Celebrating Ramadan* (Hoyt-Goldsmith, 2001/2002 NBGS), describing a family's observance of the Muslim religious holiday. Fifty-three percent of the books in this genre featured the United States, with 38% about African Americans and 28% about Native Americans. Outside the United States, works about Africa accounted for 7% of the nonfiction books, with 18% about Asia, and 13% about Europe. Only one work spotlighted Latin America, *The Pot That Juan Built* (Andrews-Goebel, 2002/2003 NBGS), about potter Juan Quezada, while two books touched on the Middle East, *Masada* (Waldman, 1998/1999 NBGS) and *Saladin: Noble Prince of Islam* (Stanley, 2002/2003 NBGS); all of these were historical in nature. The topic of sexual orientation was addressed in *The Shared Heart: Portraits and Stories Celebrating Lesbian, Gay, and Bisexual Young People* (Mastoon, 1997/1998 NBGS).

Folklore. Because folklore represents the knowledge and stories, traditions, and customs of a group, this genre affords one more way of viewing our global society. Folklore can provide a glimpse of what was important in a culture. Conversely, a study of folklore across cultures shows the universality of some themes. One problem with folklore, however, is that it is a window on the traditional values and mores of its creators rather than a reflection of contemporary life (Bishop, 1994). Another difficulty with published folklore is the issue of authenticity. After undergoing the many translations and revisions that are a part of crafting stories for the general public, individuals from the culture of origin may not recognize the traditional lore they grew up with (Hadaway, Vardell, & Young, 2002).

Indeed, Hearne (1993) voiced some unease that children's literature has become a primary vehicle for folklore. While the best examples should reflect a careful study of the root culture so that the language and illustrations accurately reflect the story's culture for the reader, one of Hearne's chief concerns is the lack of source notes in picture book folk tale retellings. Hearne argues that picture book creators of folk tales should include a highly visible source note with the specific source(s) of the tale along with a description for the cultural context and remarks that address any changes the author has made and a rationale for the change. And, while folklore offers an "easy multiculturalism" due to the many titles being published, teachers and librarians should search for a balance of materials representing both the historical and the contemporary (Bishop, 1994).

Of the 249 books that were selected for the booklist, 10% were classified as folklore (see the "Folklore" section under "Genres" in the online supplement). Two authors, Demi and Virginia Hamilton, had more than one book included on lists over the 10 years.

Of the 24 works of folklore over the 10 years, one was a collection of folk songs and rhymes and the others were folk tales. The folk tales included 13 individual folk tales in picture book format and 11 collections of folk tales (see the "Individual Folk Tales and Folklore Collections" section in the online supplement). Other categorizations within folklore, also represented in the booklist, were legends, pourquoi tales (tales that explain why something in the natural world is the way it is), trickster tales, and creation myths. Each of these types of folklore reflected certain defining characteristics. For instance, creation myths were used to explain the origin of the world as in the Australian tale *Animal Dreaming: An Aboriginal Dreamtime Story* (Morin, 1998/1999 NBGS) and a story from India, *In the Heart of the Village: The World of the Indian Banyan Tree* (Bash, 1996/1997 NBGS).

Like creation myths, pourquoi tales represent a culture's attempt to explain phenomena. In "How the Tiger Got Its Stripes" from *Children of the Dragon: Selected Tales From Vietnam* (Garland, 2001/2002 NBGS), readers encountered such a story. Legends chronicle characters with some basis of historical truth as in the example from China, *Fa Mulan: The Story of a Woman Warrior* (San Souci, 1998/1999 NBGS). Across the ages, the trickster tale has offered humor and hope with accounts of a small or less powerful being outwitting a larger, more powerful one. Like those in *A Ring of Tricksters: Animal Tales From America, the West Indies, and Africa* (Hamilton, 1997/1998 NBGS), Africans brought such tales to America and through their retelling were able to offer some moments of relief from the unbalanced power structure of plantation life. Finally, the pervasiveness of some themes across time and cultures was apparent with adaptations of the Cinderella story in *Raisel's Riddle* (Silverman, 1999/2000 NBGS) and "The Two Marias" from *Horse Hooves and Chicken Feet: Mexican Folktales* (Philip, 2003/2004 NBGS) as well as the variations collected in *Can You Guess My Name? Traditional Tales Around the World* (Sierra, 2002/2003 NBGS), 15 tales from around the world, each with similarities to familiar tales such as The Three Pigs or Hansel and Gretel.

The published folklore selected for the booklist reflected roots in many cultures, but folk tales from Asia and the United States were in the majority with

24% each while tales from Africa, Latin America, and Europe followed with 12% each (see the "In Folklore" section under "Cultural Representation in the Notable Books for a Global Society Booklists, 1996–2005" in the online supplement). Because the United States is a country comprising many peoples, the folklore mirrored that diversity with tales from African Americans, Chinese Americans, and Native Americans. The origins, however, could just as easily be labeled African or Chinese because these groups brought the tales to the United States as noted by the one cross-listed book, *A Ring of Tricksters: Animal Tales From America, the West Indies, and Africa* (Hamilton, 1997/1998 NBGS).

Poetry. Eighteen works of poetry were included, accounting for 7% of the lists (see the "Poetry" section under "Genres" in the online supplement). Two authors had three books of poetry, Walter Dean Myers and Naomi Shihab Nye.

The poetry included on the booklist represents not only different cultural perspectives but also diversity of format from collections of poems by a single author or by multiple authors, collections that narrowly focus on one topic, such as the poem biographies of César Chávez and George Washington Carver, or one format as in Native American riddle poems, to poem picture books and verse novels (see the "Poetry by Various Formats" section under "Poetry" in the online supplement). Poetry from multiple voices as in Naomi Shihab Nye's *The Tree Is Older Than You Are: A Bilingual Gathering of Poems and Stories From Mexico* (1995/1996 NBGS) or *19 Varieties of Gazelle: Poems of the Middle East* (2002/2003 NBGS) may offer a broader range of cultural perspectives than a collection by a single author. This is an important consideration because no one author can depict an entire culture much less the cultures of the many countries in the Middle East. However, the familiarity of one voice may be a good choice for painting a focused portrait as in Angela Medearis's examination of teen life in *Skin Deep and Other Teenage Reflections* (1995/1996 NBGS). Similar to the previous example, verse novels use one author's voice but the goal is to tell a story. Karen Hesse's *Witness* (2001/2002 NBGS) is a compelling verse novel spotlighting the Ku Klux Klan infiltration of a small town as told from the perspective of different characters. Finally, poem picture books offer an opportunity to paint a lyrical image with both text and illustrations as in Walter Dean Myers's *Harlem* (1997/1998 NBGS) or *Blues Journey* (2003/2004 NBGS).

As with folklore, poetry may provide a greater affective feel for a culture rather than detailed information. Poets, after all, paint visual images with their words and create sound tracks through the imaginative use of language. Through poetry, we may *hear* the cultural nuances such as the rhetorical style of another language as in *Maples in the Mist: Children's Poems From the Tang Dynasty* (Ho, 1996/1997 NBGS) and *Cool Melons—Turn to Frogs! The Life and Poems of Issa*

(Gollub, 1998/1999 NBGS). Thus, poetry may be an effective tool to engage students affectively. In chapter 8, Mary Napoli offers ideas about using poetry to spur global understanding.

In examining the cultural representation within poetry, 12 works reflected the United States, with half focusing on African Americans, followed by 2 on Mexican Americans and 2 on Native Americans (see the "In Poetry" section under "Cultural Representation in the Notable Books for a Global Society Booklists, 1996–2005" in the online supplement). Both the Middle East and Asia were featured in 2 poetry collections, while Africa and Latin America were the focus of one work of poetry each.

Mixed Genres. As the final category in this discussion of genre, mixed-genre books offer an opportunity to combine the best of many genres to address a theme or topic. Two books on the booklist represented mixed-genre efforts. *Earth, Fire, Water, Air* (Hoffman, 1995/1996 NBGS) was a collection of factual information, myths, stories, and poems about the four classic elements from both Western and non-Western perspectives, while *The Serpent's Tongue: Prose, Poetry, and Art of the New Mexico Pueblos* (1997/1998 NBGS) edited by Nancy Wood offered prose, poetry, autobiography, and historical narrative focused on this Native American group.

A Look at Cultural Diversity

Because the original purpose of the booklist was to celebrate and honor cultural diversity within our global society, this last section addresses dimensions of cultural diversity across the first 10 years of the Notable Books for a Global Society booklists. While some cultural analysis was conducted within each genre category in the previous section, an examination of the cultures represented across all books provides an overall picture of how well the award list met its purpose and exposes any gaps that may exist. One concern in examining cultural representation in literature is the "cultural conglomerate" notion (Yokota, 1993). Within any culture or group, there is tremendous diversity, and clustering individuals results in overgeneralization. As one example, several books about Mexican Americans are included on the lists, yet readers should not use one book to measure all Mexican Americans and certainly not all Latino Americans, a "group" that would include both native-born individuals as well as immigrants to the United States with roots in Mexico, Central, and South America as well as the Caribbean.

The dominant culture reflected in the booklists was the United States with 128 books, or more than half of the books, on the lists from 1996–2005. However, within the category of the United States, tremendous cultural diversity was represented including ethnic, cultural, and geographic origin as well as sexual orientation and religion. The major groups central to the lists were African

American with 43%, Native American with 18%, Asian American with 12%, and Mexican American with 9%. Although this cultural diversity should be applauded, the number of books for each of these major groups certainly did not reflect the demographic statistics of the United States. Latino Americans and Asian Americans far outnumber Native Americans, for instance.

Outside the United States, books about Asia represented 17% of the booklist, with China as the focal point in approximately one-fourth of those books. Next, books focused on Europe accounted for 11% of the list. However, the literature addressing a variety of countries in Europe was closely tied to the religion category with World War II and the Holocaust as the central topic of more than half these books. Religion was addressed in 10% of the books with Jews as the focal point of almost three-fourths of the books in the religion category. As noted earlier, books about Jews generally had a historical focus with the Holocaust as the central topic. Furthermore, religion as a basis for persecution and discrimination was more evident in the books than religion as a way of life. Thus, readers would not necessarily gain an overall understanding about a particular religion.

Following religion as a focus, books about Africa and Latin America weighed in with 9% and 6%, respectively. Within each of these categories, there was an excellent diversity of countries and geographic regions highlighted. The Middle East took center stage in only 2% of the booklists. Technically, the countries of the Middle East would fit into the continent (and, therefore, the category) of Asia; however, the books in this category did not always address particular countries but the general region or the religious/political overtones. The Pacific Islands and Australia were the focus of only three books, or 1%, of the booklist. Although this number of books may seem appropriate for the small land area and population of Oceania, it seems limited when one considers that this area is incredibly diverse, comprising 25,000 islands and islets of 25 nations and territories spread over millions of square miles.

Finally, the categories of sexual orientation, disability, and interracial backgrounds accounted for only 1% each on the booklist. Considering current demographic information and media attention, there is no doubt that each of these groups is underrepresented in literature for children and young adults in general.

Conclusion

Rochman (1993), in support of the transformative process of global literature, argues that "if you read only what mirrors your view of yourself, you get locked in" (p. 11). I observed this recently at a meeting where concerns were voiced about some suggested reading for middle and high school students. The apprehension was not related to mature language or adult themes in the books as is sometimes the case with young adult literature, nor was the anxiety mentioned by students but by teachers and librarians. The unease revolved around the different and difficult-to-pronounce names of characters and geographical settings as well as the positive portrayal of Islam and how Christians might perceive this. These are exactly the kinds of "challenges" that global literature should offer—a means of moving outside the comfortable world that we may live in surrounded by people, street names, and cities whose names are familiar and easy to pronounce, by major holidays that coincide with our religious and sociopolitical background, by places to go to school and to work, shop, and play in a language familiar to us. It may not be comfortable to read some books and think through other realities, yet it is crucial to our continued existence in this increasingly diverse and volatile world. Not considering the alternatives, continuing to remain locked in our own comfortable world, comes with a very high price tag.

In this chapter, the potential of global literature has been discussed along with some of the controversies—the authenticity of works by authors from within the culture versus those outside the culture, the balance of global literature across different genres, cultures, and time frames, and the limitations in terms of topics and themes explored. As a means of examining these issues, the 249 books from the first 10 years of the Notable Books for a Global Society booklist were used as a reflection of both the progress and the gaps that still exist in the area of global literature for children and young adults.

As noted in the introduction to this book, the term *global literature* has been used in this edited volume to include both multicultural literature (books about diversity within the United States) and international literature (broadly defined as books about diversity outside the United States as well as books by international authors). The latter group of books helps broaden the focus of the booklist truly making it the Notable Books for a *Global* Society booklist. While most of the chapters in the book highlight global literature, citing both multicultural and international titles, it is only fitting that one chapter be devoted solely to literature that takes the reader outside the United States. Thus, chapter 2 focuses on the importance of including international literature in classrooms to encourage global awareness.

REFERENCES

Note. Complete bibliographic citations for the Notable Books for a Global Society booklist (1996–2005) can be found at the end of the book.

Beaty, J.J. (1997). *Building bridges with multicultural picture books: For children 3–5*. Upper Saddle River, NJ: Prentice Hall.

Bishop, R.S. (1992). Multicultural literature for children: Making informed choices. In V.J. Harris (Ed.), *Teaching multicultural literature in grades K–8* (pp. 37–54). Norwood, MA: Christopher-Gordon.

Bishop, R.S. (Ed.). (1994). *Kaleidoscope: A multicultural booklist for grades K–8*. Urbana, IL: National Council of Teachers of English.

Bishop, R.S. (1997). Selecting literature for a multicultural curriculum. In V.J. Harris (Ed.), *Using multiethnic literature in the K–8 classroom* (pp. 1–20). Norwood, MA: Christopher-Gordon.

Cai, M. (2002). *Multicultural literature for children and young adults: Reflections on critical issues.* Westport, CT: Greenwood.

Department for Education and Skills. (2004). *Putting the world into world-class education: An international strategy for education, skills and children's services.* Nottingham, England: DfES Publications. Retrieved March 27, 2006, from http://www.globalgateway.org.uk/PDF/International-Strategy.pdf

Gangi, J.M. (2005). Inclusive aesthetics and social justice: The vanguard of small, multicultural presses. *Children's Literature Association Quarterly, 30*, 243–264.

Glazier, J., & Seo, J. (2005). Multicultural literature and discussion as mirror and window? *Journal of Adolescent & Adult Literacy, 48*, 686–700.

Hadaway, N.L., Vardell, S.M., & Young, T.A. (2002). *Literature-based instruction with English language learners, K–12.* Boston: Allyn & Bacon.

Hearne, B. (1993). Cite the source: Reducing cultural chaos in picture books, part one. *School Library Journal, 39*, 22–27.

Louie, B. (2005). Development of empathetic responses with multicultural literature. *Journal of Adolescent & Adult Literacy, 48*, 566–578.

Mendoza, J., & Reese, D. (2001). Examining multicultural picture books for the early childhood classroom: Possibilities and pitfalls. *Early Childhood Research and Practice, 3*. Retrieved March 6, 2007, from http://www.ecrp.uiuc.edu/v3n2/mendoza.html

Reese, D., & Caldwell-Wood, N. (1997). Native Americans in children's literature. In V.J. Harris (Ed.), *Using multiethnic literature in the K–8 classroom* (pp. 159–192). Norwood, MA: Christopher-Gordon.

Reiten, G. (1995). The five great values. In C.I. Bennett (Ed.), *Comprehensive multicultural education: Theory and practice* (3rd ed., pp. 104–107). Boston: Allyn & Bacon.

Rochman, H. (1993). *Against borders: Promoting books for a multicultural world.* Chicago: American Library Association.

Sanchez, T.R. (2001). "Dangerous Indians": Evaluating the depiction of Native Americans in selected trade books. *Urban Education, 36*, 400–425.

Smith, S.A., & Singer, J.Y. (2006). Reading *The Friendship* and talking about race. *Urban Education, 41*, 321–342.

Stallworth, B.J., Gibbons, L., & Fauber, L. (2006). It's not on the list: An exploration of teachers' perspectives on using multicultural literature. *Journal of Adolescent & Adult Literacy, 49*, 478–489.

Taxel, J. (1997). Multicultural literature and the politics of reaction. *Teachers College Record, 98*, 417–448.

Yokota, J. (1993). Issues in selecting multicultural children's literature. *Language Arts, 70*, 156–167.

LITERATURE CITED

Ellis, D. (2006). *I am a taxi.* Toronto, ON: Groundwood.

Martin, B. Jr, & Archambault, J. (1987). *Knots on a counting rope.* Ill. T. Rand. New York: Holt.

McCormick, P. (2006). *Sold.* New York: Hyperion.

Taylor, M.D. (1987). *The friendship.* New York: Dial.

CHAPTER 2

The Challenges and Opportunities of International Literature

Evelyn B. Freeman, Barbara A. Lehman, Patricia L. Scharer

"Books can make a difference in dispelling prejudice and building community...with enthralling stories that make us imagine the lives of others."

—Hazel Rochman (1993, p. 19)

This chapter focuses on the challenges and opportunities that international literature affords in opening the world to children. In the United States, there is a lack of such literature, although the potential of international children's literature to promote understanding and peace in the global community has been celebrated by many. For this reason, we have chosen to address this topic from a U.S. perspective.

Hazel Rochman (1993), whose quote opens this chapter, grew up in South Africa during apartheid and views children's literature as a way to break "barriers with the world" (p. 11). Paul Hazard, the noted French critic, also presented a strong rationale for the importance of children's literature crossing national boundaries to promote international understanding, writing in 1944 that "children's books keep alive a sense of nationality; they also keep alive a sense of [universal] humanity" (p. 146). And Mildred Batchelder, who promoted internationalism and the translation of children's books from other countries, stated in 1966, "To know the classic stories of a country creates a climate, an attitude for understanding the people for whom the literature is a heritage" (p. 34). "Sense of humanity" and "attitude for understanding"—these are essential attributes for nurturing an international perspective.

Breaking Boundaries With Global Literature: Celebrating Diversity in K–12 Classrooms, edited by Nancy L. Hadaway and Marian J. McKenna. © 2007 by the International Reading Association.

Jella Lepman, a German Jew who survived the Holocaust, dedicated herself to finding ways to promote peace and justice among children throughout the world. In 1949, she founded the International Youth Library in Munich, and in 1953 she established the International Board on Books for Young People (www.ibby.org), which now has more than 60 national sections. Lepman believed that children's literature could serve as a bridge to understanding among children around the globe. Her vision to promote international understanding and world peace through children's books is as critical today as it was then (Lepman, 1969/2002).

As teacher educators, we believe that international literature should be an integral part of a teacher education program—both for students seeking initial licensure and for teachers who return to graduate school for professional development and advanced degrees—with the intention that teachers will be inspired to share these books in K–12 classrooms. In this chapter, we describe issues related to the place of international literature in the literary canon, to teacher interest in and access to international literature, to the publication of international literature, and to suggested classroom applications.

For the purposes of this chapter, international children's literature includes the following:

> books written and published first in countries other than the United States (both in English and translation), books written by immigrants to the United States about their home countries and published in the United States, books written by authors from countries other than the United States but originally published in the United States, and books written by American authors and published in the United States with settings in other countries. (Freeman & Lehman, 2001, p. 10)

Benefits of Using International Literature in the Classroom

According to the 2000 U.S. census (found online at www.census.gov), about 75% of the population is white, 12% is black, 4% is Asian, 1% is Native American, and 13% is Latino/Hispanic. (This last group can be classified in more than one category.) From 1990 to 2000, the white population percentage declined, while all other percentages increased, most notably Asian and Latino/Hispanic, which experienced 55% and 61% growth rates, respectively. These demographics show that the U.S. population as a whole is becoming increasingly diverse, especially in urban areas, while rural and small-town areas still overwhelmingly lack diversity, with 86% of the population being white in these areas. Further, according to the American Association of Colleges for Teacher Education (1999) report, 87% of elementary and secondary schoolteachers are white. These teachers, many of whom work in seemingly homogeneous rural and small-town settings, need to be convinced of the relevance of international literature when they don't see cultural diversity reflected in their classrooms. In addition, many are often unsure of what international literature is, much less understand the need for it.

However, we argue that all teachers and students are in need of global education, particularly the aforementioned teachers. As we have already noted in the beginning of this chapter, international children's literature can play an important role in such instruction. Beyond the general goal of international understanding, there are specific benefits for children: enhancing children's language, literacy, and literary development through introduction to new terms from different languages or dialects used in meaningful contexts; meeting new narrative structures, themes, patterns, or myths; encountering new visual artistic styles in illustrations; and exposure to excellent literature. International literature also supports children's social, emotional, and moral development by broadening their perspectives, increasing their empathy for others, and dispelling stereotypes. Through international literature, children are confronted with issues that they may not have faced or new ways of exploring those topics. Such treatments and different perspectives help children to think more critically and creatively and, we hope, to be more open, sensitive, and appreciative regarding new ideas.

Additional curricular benefits include natural links to the study of geography, history, and current events. Books can offer relationships to scientific studies, such as environmental education or the impact of climate on culture. Children can learn about the history of mathematics and number systems around the world or investigate different approaches to economics and their impact on people. Teachers can help their students to learn more about the home countries of immigrants because, in the United States, all people (except possibly Native Americans) were immigrants at some point in time. Thus, children can gain appreciation for the heritage of their own family and those of others.

Given the limited access to international literature, educators might pair international books with other global literature described in this book and the Notable Books for a Global Society booklists. This approach is based upon two underlying principles. First, in general, reading books in pairs is a way of expanding insights on and perspectives about both books (Lehman & Crook, 1998), as themes, plots, characters, settings, and so forth are encountered in juxtaposition. Ideas that readers may not particularly note in one work alone may gain significance when compared with those in another book. It's important to note that the two books need not be highly similar, just that they provide readers with some interesting connections and contrasts. Thus book pairs are valuable for stimulating intertextuality.

Second, readers may sometimes have difficulty engaging with books about cultures or set in places that are very different from their own. Pairing books that feature various cultures in students' home countries with books about other countries is a means for helping children make connections with the lives of children around the world. If they can identify with or recognize the experiences of children in their home country and see how those are shared (in some ways, at least) by children in other nations, these readers may develop both more cross-cultural and international understanding and empathy.

As an example of a multicultural–international book pair activity, *Dangerous Skies* (Staples, 1996/1997 NBGS), set on the Chesapeake Bay in Virginia, USA, and *Beyond the Mango Tree* (Zemser, 1998/1999 NBGS), set in Liberia, can stimulate enlightening comparisons. Both titles are appropriate for upper elementary and middle school students. In *Dangerous Skies*, Buck, a white boy, and his best friend, Tunes, an African American girl, find their carefree friendship disrupted when they discover a corpse and Tunes is accused of murder. In *Beyond the Mango Tree*, Sarina, a white American girl, is befriended by Boima, a Liberian boy, who shows her the world beyond her safe but imprisoning home compound in direct defiance of her mother's orders.

The daily lives depicted in these two narratives offer many contrasts, and students can compare the protagonists and their friendships across racial and gender differences. The more serious issues presented in these two books will also emerge: the status and power differences between the two friends in each pair and how those change during the course of the stories, the racial and socioeconomic disparities and how those affect the friendships, and the different resolutions (and consequences) to the problems presented in each plot. Students will find many points to discuss critically, and their discussions may lead to further inquiries about the two settings and the issues raised in each account, leading to possible connections with and implications for their lives today.

Publishing Trends in Global Children's Literature

Awareness of the annual publication of children's books that represent a wide range of countries, cultures, and ethnicities is important for educators who support international understanding. Access to quality children's books from global perspectives is a complex issue involving the creators of such books, their publishers, and consumers in a constantly changing triangle within the economic context of supply and demand. Other influential factors within this issue include the availability of public funds for book purchases, political literacy initiatives, and the availability of retail outlets (see page 17 in chapter 1 for a breakdown of the different publishers represented in the Notable Books for a Global Society booklist).

To learn more about the current status of global literature for children and young adults in North America, we interviewed four publishers—three from the United States and one from Canada. The interviews were conducted informally, so we relied on a set of notes taken during each conversation to gain a general perspective of patterns and trends in publishing that may provide some insight on the status of global children's literature today in North America. These interviews with a selected sample of publishers are not intended to represent the entire industry; rather, the analysis of these conversations can provide us with ways to think about the role of the publishing industry relative to the creation of a diverse corpus of children's books available for reading in homes, libraries, and schools. (Therefore, given the informal nature of this inquiry, few quotes will be used and the publishers will not be named specifically.)

Attempts at Diversity in Recent Publishing History

One publisher described the status of children's literature 40 years ago as a time when illustrations in children's books and textbooks featured only white faces. When the need arose for a greater diversity in textbooks, publishers responded with "zipatone," a technique used to darken the physical features without changing the original artwork beyond color. This technique was not only a cost-effective solution but also a superficial response resulting in only color changes in illustration and no changes in terms of the texts. Later, in response to the demand for more books reflecting a more diverse content, publishers responded with lofty tales of faraway lands. Neither of these responses was satisfactory in the quest for children to have the kind of access to books that Rudine Sims Bishop (1982) describes with the metaphors of mirrors and windows—where children could both see themselves (as if looking into a mirror) and also learn about the lives of others (as through a window into the world).

More recently, this same publisher sees the publishing industry as moving away from global folk tales to an emphasis on contemporary stories accurately reflecting the cultures of the world and believes that publishers need to be more intentional to be sure that children's book publishing serves all children; in other words, publishers should examine manuscripts with the intent to ensure that the books selected for publication reflect global diversity, rather than leaving the global nature of their overall list to chance. His goal is that, one day, a diverse publication list will merely be incidental, the way diversity is incidental and inherent in business in a global market. However, according to this publisher, intentionality is currently needed to ensure that publishers are, indeed, serving all

An Anchor for the Wandering Heart

JANE KURTZ

AUTHOR REFLECTIONS

There are names, now, for the kind of childhood I had. I was a "third culture" kid. I was a global nomad.

All I knew as a 2-year-old was that everything was aswirl around me. Two-year-olds experiment by touching, smelling, and tasting. They can walk backward and turn pages of a book. A 2-year-old doesn't ask, "Why are we moving to Ethiopia? Will we stay there forever? Does that mean we're going to become Ethiopians?"

Those questions came later.

My family visited the United States twice while I was a child—once when I was 7 and again when I was 13. Adults said, "Isn't it amazing to meet someone who has been growing up in Africa?" Other children gaped. Almost always, someone asked, "Did you see Tarzan?"

What I wanted, then, was to learn how to be an American. Years later, though, I wanted to show people a glimpse of the beautiful country of my magical childhood.

Probably all human beings feel ignored and misunderstood. Some appear to like the sensation of fading into the shadows. Others fight to be seen. It could be argued that in the United States, the whole huge continent of Africa is practically invisible. But what I learned on the road to becoming a full-time writer and speaker is that words have power to make the invisible visible.

In 1997, I embarked on a journey of getting to know more of the continent, myself. Over the next decade, I visited and spoke in public and private schools in Ethiopia, Uganda, Kenya, and Nigeria. I gave presentations and had conversations with teachers in Botswana, Senegal, Ghana, and South Africa. As I breathed in the hot, wet, thick air of Nigeria and watched traditional dances at one of the schools, I thought again about the way people in the United States ask me, "Do you know the African language?" Nigeria alone has over 200 languages.

Those thoughts led to a collection of short stories that I edited called *Memories of Sun: Stories of Africa and America* (Greenwillow/HarperCollins, 2004). I wanted to include stories and poems by writers living in both Africa and the United States, stories that appeal to middle school and high school readers, stories both funny and sad, and stories from northern, southern, eastern, and western Africa.

Everywhere I've spoken in Africa, people have asked me, "How can we develop a reading culture in this country?" I don't know all of the answers to this

(continued)

An Anchor for the Wandering Heart (continued)

question, but I do know a good start comes when those of us in the literary community open our ears and hearts to each other.

My own heart has been stretched by Yohannes Gebregeorgis, an Ethiopian man who became a librarian in the United States and has now moved back to Ethiopia. He and I have worked together to start the first libraries and publish the first picture books for children there, a story I now tell everywhere and share on the Web.

In 2004, my own daughter and son went to Ethiopia to volunteer at the first public library for children. My son fell in love with Hiwot, the Ethiopian bookkeeper at the center, and my first grandbaby was born in Addis Ababa in 2005.

My granddaughter, too, will be a global nomad. Through all the confusions and complexities in her life, she will have something to keep her strong. She will have books.

Books by Jane Kurtz selected for the Notable Books for a Global Society:

Faraway Home (2000/2001 NBGS)

The Storyteller's Beads (1998/1999 NBGS)

the children and enabling readers to not only see themselves in books but also learn about others.

Another publisher felt that there was less discussion about global books in the industry and it was less of a "hot point" when compared to the enthusiasm of the 1990s. This publisher believes that previous interest in global books has been replaced by a "fiction boom" and the blockbuster "Harry Potter effect." Fortunately, this publisher went on to say that global books were simply a "given" on their list—that books published each year would, indeed, reflect the diversity and perspectives of the world. This position was also reflected by the Canadian publisher who felt that their list featured books reflecting global diversity. These comments might indicate that the shift from the need for intentionality to the inclusion of global literature as simply a given in the industry has already occurred.

Ensuring Authenticity

An important point, however, that one publisher made was that the strength of their list was directly related to the diversity of the authors and illustrators submitting work for consideration. This publisher spoke with concern about the limited number of authors and artists submitting work for consideration and the frustration of matching up authors and illustrators, particularly when the match is unsuccessful.

There is currently a need for an increase in the number of authors and illustrators from what Cai and Bishop (1994) called "parallel cultures." Publishers try to encourage new authors and work to match authors to illustrators but sometimes find that matches are not always successful or the number of authors and illustrators sufficient. For example, according to Bader (2003), progress in the number of African American–authored or illustrated books has been slow in the United States. Only 18 books were published by African Americans in 1985; the number peaked to 100 in 1995.

A similar concern about publishers is echoed by Andrea Davis Pinkney (2001) as she writes,

> I have worked in publishing for sixteen years. I can count the number of black children's book editors on fewer than my ten black fingers. While there is a growing interest in multiculturalism, many publishing professionals and librarians don't push themselves to expand their knowledge. This is not because they make a conscious choice to ignore other cultures. In my opinion, it is simply a matter of out of sight, out of mind—another example of "unintentional neglect." (p. 537)

Thus, the debate continues about whether the need for intentionality on the part of publishers is actually greater now or if publishers have moved beyond intentionality to the assumption that new lists will consistently reflect a global perspective.

Two publishers believed that recent books about Asian cultures were growing in numbers; however, both expressed concerns about limited growth in books reflecting Hispanic cultures. (Note: Various terms are currently in circulation describing people of Latin American–origin living in the North, Central, and South America, so we used the terms adopted by the interviewees.) One, in fact, felt that Latinos were "almost totally unrepresented," a particularly disturbing belief given the growing number of Hispanic children in the United States.

To learn more about this issue, we spoke with a publisher who specialized in books of the Hispanic tradition. This publisher cited their company's "driving force" as the goal of helping Hispanic children adjust to mainstream cultures while maintaining their cultural traditions. Many of this publisher's employees are Hispanic, and the goal of the editorial and sales staff is to become established as the experts within the industry. This will not only ensure the quality and authenticity of books they publish but will also support the efforts of other publishers who might rely on their expertise as resources to encourage the publication of authentic books about Hispanic cultures.

Economic Factors

All of the publishers discussed economic factors affecting the sales of global books. The publisher specializing in Hispanic books, for example, explained that purchasing trends are often strongly influenced by state and local policy decisions. For example, textbook adoption decisions in the United States have huge implications, particularly in states like Texas and California that have large populations of Hispanic families but also policies that state funds may be used only for purchasing textbooks and trade books appearing on approved lists (another kind of "canon"). As states vary the roles of textbooks and trade books, sales are influenced by the emphasis and approval of one over the other. Sales of children's literature drop if not on approved lists, and sales of textbooks rise with such approval.

More constant, however, are sales to libraries, as they do not appear to be influenced by policy and curricular decisions. Libraries were described as consistently working toward strong diversity in their collection; however, funds available for such purchases are often limited. In Canada, an alliance among the publishers, libraries, and parents actively works to fight funding cuts and keep libraries open.

The Fading of Independent and Children's Bookstores

The publishers also discussed important issues relative to the dwindling numbers of local bookstores specializing in children's literature. Several identified problems associated with the greater number of larger, national booksellers with sections for children and young adults in their store rather than an individual store dedicated to the sales of books for children and adolescents. In a children's specialty book store, quality books are often "hand sold" by sales staff that are knowledgeable and passionate about both the books and their customers' needs. In contrast, large bookstore chains may have limited flexibility to purchase books to meet the needs of local buyers and the expertise of the sales staff may be limited. Two publishers described buyers' significant resistance to books outside the local culture and were concerned that large bookstores purchase what they believe is easily sold with little effort to overcome customer resistance or to encourage the purchase of books from different cultures.

International Literature and Its Place in the Literary Canon

Charlotte's Web (White, 1952), *Where the Wild Things Are* (Sendak, 1963), books by Katherine Paterson, Steven Kellogg, and Chris Van Allsburg—these are frequently found on required reading lists for children's literature courses taught through teacher education programs in the United States. Classroom teachers and teacher educators choose from thousands of possible titles to select books for students to read and books to share as examples in class. These educators, consciously or unconsciously, are helping to establish and perpetuate a modern-day canon of children's literature. The concept of a canon for children's literature is a complex and controversial one that has important implications for encouraging a global perspective.

By dictionary definition, a *canon* is "an authoritative list, as of the works of an author" or "a basis of judgment, standard; criterion." Generally, a canon includes books that have stood the test of time, that are of such high literary quality that their contribution to culture is lasting and pervasive. Books included in the canon are privileged—they have won awards; they appear on the lists of recommended titles by librarians, teachers, and literary critics; they are featured in displays in book stores; they are recorded as audio books; and they are made into television specials and full-length feature films.

But questions abound about a canon. What books should be included? Who decides? By what criteria should books be selected for inclusion in a canon? How long should a book be in print before it can be considered part of a canon? As new books are added to a canon, what books should be eliminated from it?

A further complication is the perspective that canons represent political rather than literary criteria. In a chapter for Peter Hunt's *International Companion Encyclopedia of Children's Literature*, British professor Geoff Fox (1996) discusses this perspective and the following:

> tension between those who see literature as a means of handing down culture from generation to generation and those who believe that literature can foster the emotional and intellectual growth of the individual in a changing society. Those who favor the "transmission of a cultural heritage" model often wish to promote a canon of texts and authors which all should share. (p. 596)

He further asserts, "Various groups have seen themselves as excluded by attempts to impose specific books or authors upon schools: women have noted how often reading lists are dominated by male writers; ethnic minorities...believe constant vigilance is needed to ensure their literature retains a place in classrooms" (p. 596).

In the United States today, we can certainly add international literature, especially books in translation, to the list of groups that are excluded from any kind of children's literature canon. For example, the current listing of "100 Favorite Children's Books" from the New York Public Library includes only one translated book: *Anne Frank: The Diary of a Young Girl* (Frank, 1952). However, several books by authors from other English-speaking countries do appear on the list, such as books by Margaret Mahy, Philip Pullman, and Roald Dahl. On the list of "100 Picture Books Everyone Should Know," only one translated book appears, *The Story of Babar* (de Brunhoff, 1933/1960). Each country may have its own canon of literature—those treasured books that we hope all children will read and know. The Anne of Green Gables books by L.M. Montgomery are considered part of the Canadian children's literature canon but may not appear as frequently on U.S. lists. So then a further question arises, Should books from other countries be included in the U.S. canon?

Those of us committed to global perspectives, social justice, and international understanding would certainly respond affirmatively. Indeed, if we think of books considered classics in the United States, three translated books would immediately come to mind: *Pippi Longstocking* (Lindgren, 1950), *Pinocchio* (Collodi, 1944/1974), and *Heidi* (Spyri, 1880/1994). However, because of the mass marketing, movie versions, and popularity of these titles in the United States, many may not realize that these classics did not originate in the United States.

Common Challenges With Including International Literature

Even when teachers are convinced of the value of international literature, they still face common challenges with including these books in the classroom and curriculum, such as issues with access, identifying cultures and cultural authenticity, and publisher revisions to material.

Issues With Access

Although publication of books with global themes and characters still lags behind mainstream or dominant literature, scarcity of international literature is even more acute. In spite of recent trends in copublication of books from other countries, the United States still imports less than 2% of books that are translated from other languages, according to Carl Tomlinson's (1998) data from 1995. Obviously, this percentage does not include imported English-language books or books with a global focus published inside the United States, but the limited availability of international literature is easily documented by the challenge we have had with locating books for our teacher education courses.

This lack is most evident in two ways: the uneven representation of literature from different regions of the world and the limited range of genres. Some cultures, such as Latino/Hispanic and Asian (particularly Japanese and Chinese) are better represented in the available literature, perhaps because of the visibility and economic or political power of these cultures in the United States. Others, such as Indian and Muslim cultures, may be portrayed less often in the literature perhaps because of a lack of recognition of their presence in the United States. The second area in which access is lacking is the variety of literature. Some genres are much more common (such as folklore) than others (such as poetry, which often is difficult to translate).

These deficits, in turn, lead to several problems. When certain genres or regional literature are unavailable, stereotypes and misconceptions may develop. For example, too much reliance on folklore can result in the perception that other cultures are caught in the past or the period of myth and legend—almost quaint. Knowledge of a culture's folklore is important for understanding that culture, but folklore doesn't offer much insight on or information about contemporary life. Likewise, it is hard to overcome prejudices about a culture if no literature is available that portrays it. Even if a few books can be found from a culture, there is the danger of "essentializing" (Freeman & Lehman, 2001, p. 26), or mistakenly believing that the images provided in those books are representative of the entire group. For example, if readers are limited to picture books set in Tanzania, such as *My Rows and Piles of Coins* (Mollel, 1999) or *Elizabeti's Doll* (Stuve-Bodeen, 1998), they might think that all Tanzanians live in small, rural villages and gain no concept of life there in a big city such as Dar es Salaam.

Issues With Identifying Culture and Cultural Authenticity

Another major issue is identifying what books actually are from a culture. Often books do not mention the author's nationality and the story's setting or themes offer no clues, as James Stiles (2004) discovered when he was conducting a study about Australian children's literature. The books that offered no hints regarding culture he labeled "cultural chameleons"; these are books that readers might assume could happen anywhere. In addition, it sometimes is difficult to judge the authenticity of books outside one's own culture. For example, *Nory Ryan's Song* (Giff, 2000) and *Under the Hawthorne Tree* (Conlon-McKenna, 1990) are both novels about the Irish potato famine. Giff is an American of Irish decent, whose ancestors emigrated from Ireland during the famine, and she returned to Ireland to research this part of her family history. Conlon-McKenna is Irish, and her novel was highly popular in Ireland and, according to Siobhán Parkinson (2002), an Irish writer, critic, and current coeditor of *Bookbird*, "is considered *the* central work on the Famine for children" (p. 684). Until we read her insightful critique, we had no idea of the different perspectives that Irish readers might bring to

Giff's version of the story, which is far more available in the United States than is Conlon-McKenna's.

Publisher Revisions to Material

This leads to a final issue: that of accessibility to authentic literature and publishers' homogenization or sanitization of books imported from other countries. Some topics, such as references to sexual issues or bodily functions, may be acceptable in a book's home culture but taboo in another country. For example, *King & King* (de Haan & Nijland, 2000), a picture book originally published in The Netherlands, portrays a prince who falls in love with another prince, not a princess as his parents expected. The topic of sexual orientation may be benign in Holland, but it is highly controversial in the United States, and the book is not likely to be widely available here. Sometimes, however, publishers make changes simply because of what is considered to be familiar to the audience. For example, names may be changed to ones that sound less "foreign" or spellings may be Americanized. This was done in the Harry Potter series until *Harry Potter and the Order of the Phoenix* (Rowling, 2003).

Are these revisions significant? Perhaps not terribly, but they do subtly change the tone and diminish the authenticity of the books, thus hindering children's access to literature of cultures beyond their own. Such changes also demonstrate condescension toward and lack of faith in children's ability to accept and appreciate what is culturally different. And they perpetuate teachers' lack of awareness of and interest in valid international children's books and defeat the purpose of such literature to help children gain cross-cultural and global understanding. Our task as educators is to raise awareness of these issues and to continue to share the widest variety of and most authentic literature that we can. When teachers become interested and use this literature, they and their students will demand better access to it, and publishers, in turn, will respond—a topic to which we now turn our attention.

Addressing the Common Challenges

We will pose these challenges in the form of statements teacher educators and classroom teachers may ponder as they plan lessons. These statements are worded the way many teachers and teacher educators may traditionally think about their instruction. Our intention is to demonstrate how international literature can fit within the parameters of regular teaching with children's literature.

Statement 1. I want my students to be knowledgeable about award-winning books.

In the United States and other English-speaking countries, children's literature courses, K–12 textbooks, and K–12 curriculum generally feature award-winning books. Lists of awards and their recipients are included in all textbooks for college-level children's literature courses; collections of recommended booklists abound in the form of pamphlets from the American Library Association and other professional organizations; books for parents on how to select books for their children are found in bookstores; and professional books and journal articles for teachers and librarians with award-winning titles are plentiful. However, only one award in the United States specifically recognizes translated books: the Mildred L. Batchelder Award of the American Library Association. Further, many U.S. awards have specifications that the author must be living in the United States. Therefore, if educators focus on award-winning books, international books and books in translation are already at a disadvantage for inclusion, which in itself constitutes an obstacle for achieving global perspectives. The Notable Books for a Global Society booklist has included books in translation over the years, and one, *Samir and Yonatan* (Carmi, 2000/2001 NBGS), received the Batchelder Award in 2001. Two other translated Notable Books, *Asphalt Angels* (Holtwijk, 1999/2000 NBGS) and *Daniel Half Human and the Good Nazi* (Chotjewitz, 2004/2005 NBGS) were named Batchelder Honor Books.

Statement 2. I want to share books with my students that I have read and know to be of high quality.

Teacher educators and classroom teachers usually want to share books that are known to them—books they have read themselves, have studied, and have shared with children. However, in professional books and journals and at conferences that focus on children's literature, little attention is given to international books in general, and hardly any attention is paid to books in translation. Because of the lack of emphasis on international books in the United States, classroom teachers and teacher educators may not even be aware of international authors and the range of books in translation—yet some may be surprised to learn that certain books from the Notable Books for a Global Society booklist were first published in countries other than the United States. Some examples include *One Child, One Seed: A South African Counting Book* (Cave, 2003/2004 NBGS) first published in Great Britain; *Secrets in the Fire* (Mankell, 2003/2004 NBGS) translated from the Swedish by Ann Connie Struksrud, with the first English edition published in Australia; and *Anne Frank:*

A Hidden Life (Pressler, 2000/2001 NBGS) translated from the German by Anthea Bell, with the first English edition published in Great Britain.

Statement 3. There are so many books published in the United States, more than we can possibly cover in a children's literature class or in our work with children, so there would not be a need—or even room—for including international books.

This statement refers back to the earlier point about canons as political entities rather than literary ones. It represents a more narrow perspective regarding literature and children's relationship to the global community—one that is distinctly nationalistic and oblivious to how the rest of the world thinks and lives. As we explained earlier, there are compelling arguments for the importance of sharing international books in teacher education programs and in elementary and middle school classrooms.

Statement 4. I want to share international books, particularly books in translation, with my students but I can't find any.

Educators may be convinced of the value of and want to share books in translation with their students but, in fact, have limited access to them. The percentage of children's books published each year in the United States, for example, that are translated from other languages is shockingly small. Therefore, a professor or classroom teacher's ability to identify and locate international children's books from non–English speaking countries is certainly a challenge.

Steps Educators Can Take to Include More International Literature

So what next steps can be taken to include more international books in the U.S. children's literature canon? A first step may be for children's literature professionals to engage in critical discussion about the canon so that issues can become more explicit. In their text, *The Pleasures of Children's Literature*, Perry Nodelman and Mavis Reimer (2003) point out the concept of the canon "can continue to be useful, if only because it allows us to think about the implications of the idea that some books are better than others" (p. 247). They also assert,

> canons should not be fixed once and for all time for readers...canons of value, then, can be provisional categories, articulated at particular moments but subject to change as readers learn more about the meanings that matter to them. And, perhaps most importantly, thinking of canons as provisional allows us to make room for young people

to enter the dialogue about meanings and values, and the ways in which texts engender them, as full members of the community of readers. (pp. 248–249)

In the professional community, therefore, dialogue should be initiated regarding the canon and issues surrounding it.

Second, educators need to become more knowledgeable about books that are acclaimed, part of the "canon" in other countries. A starting point can be to look at the recipients of the Hans Christian Andersen Award and country nominees for that award. Also, countries around the world have their own children's book awards. The Internet provides easy access to information regarding children's literature worldwide, such as the website of the International Board on Books for Young People (IBBY; www.ibby.org), which provides information on the Hans Christian Andersen Award and links to the more than 60 national sections of IBBY, each with material about children's literature in that country.

A third step would be for educators to seek insiders' opinions about books from other countries. This should ideally be done in person, but if that is not possible these opinions can be learned through reading reviews of books from other countries written by insiders. What is an insider to a culture? In general, an insider is an individual who is a native of that culture or identifies himself or herself as a member of the cultural group. An insider may also be an individual who has lived in that country or area for an extended period of time, or who has traveled to the country or area extensively and done thorough research about its culture. The perspectives of insiders reflect an authentic understanding of that culture and enable "outsiders" to gain a benchmark against which to evaluate other literature written about that culture.

A fourth step is for professors and teachers to join IBBY or the United States Board on Books for Young People (USBBY; www.usbby.org). Through this membership, they are linked to a worldwide professional community dedicated to global children's literature. The resources and connections of IBBY provide opportunities for U.S. educators to network with others around the world working to provide literature to children.

Finally, educators need to assume an attitude of openness and a desire to embrace a wider conception of children's literature as more inclusive, extending beyond the boundaries of the United States and English-speaking countries. In this way, we can expand the notion of a children's literature canon to embrace the whole world of children's literature.

As a beginning point for educators to expand their awareness, we offer Table 2.1 with a list of 12 excellent contemporary international authors and Table 2.2 with 10 international books that are too good to miss.

Table 2.1. Notable Contemporary International Authors

Mitsumasa Anno	Tololwa Mollel
Baba Wagué Diakité	Beverley Naidoo
Niki Daly	Ifeoma Onyefulu
Cornelia Funke	Uri Orlev
Josef Holub	Mirjam Pressler
Ana Maria Machado	Bjarne Reuter

Table 2.2. Recommended International Books

Alvarez, J. (2002). *Before we were free*. New York: Knopf.

Beake, L. (1993). *Song of Be*. New York: Holt.

Ellis, D. (2001). *The breadwinner*. Toronto, ON: Groundwood.

Gregorowski, C. (2000). *Fly, eagle, fly! An African tale*. Ill. N. Daly. London: Frances Lincoln.

Holm, A. (2004). *I am David* (L.W. Kingsland, Trans.). San Diego, CA: Harcourt. (Original work published 1965 under the title *North to Freedom*)

Kodama, T. (1995). *Shin's tricycle* (K. Hokumen-Jones, Trans). Ill. N. Ando. New York: Walker.

Mahy, M. (1982). *The haunting*. New York: Simon & Schuster.

Sisulu, E.B. (1999). *The day Gogo went to vote*. Ill. S. Wilson. New York: Little, Brown.

Van der Roll, R., & Verhoeven, R. (1993). *Anne Frank: Beyond the diary* (T. Langham & P. Peters, Trans.). New York: Viking.

Yumoto, K. (1996). *The friends* (C. Hirano, Trans.). New York: Farrar, Straus and Giroux.

Conclusion

The contribution of international literature to issues of global understanding is strongly endorsed across the field of children's literature, and this potential can be greatly enhanced by studying the issues described in this chapter. First, educators must be willing to critically examine existing definitions of the canon by "reading against" the list, always looking for recently published books, translated books, and books from many countries to discuss in class. Educators must also expand their own knowledge of quality children's books. This requires a willingness to avoid the comfort of the old and familiar by celebrating the new and seeking out books with limited availability. This wide reading then forms the foundation for rich learning experiences in teacher education programs where teachers learn about quality global books for children. These books become central to classroom learning experiences about diversity and social justice. Finally, educators must also work with publishers to encourage the writing and development of books representing a growing range of cultures throughout the world. These quality books, when accessible to teachers who know how to work with their students, become the stimulus for social transformation and overcoming the barriers that divide our global society. In Section II, Themes of Diversity in Global Literature, some of the significant themes of the last 10 years are highlighted, including gender, immigration, language diversity, and children and war. The section begins with chapter 3, as Cyndi Giorgis, Janelle B. Mathis, and April Whatley Bedford examine strong females in global literature. Issues of race, ethnicity, culture, and social class cut across the discussion of gender.

REFERENCES

Note. Complete bibliographic citations for the Notable Books for a Global Society booklist (1996–2005) can be found at the end of the book.

American Association of Colleges for Teacher Education. (1999). *Teacher education pipeline IV: Schools, colleges, and departments of education.* Washington, DC: AACTE.

Bader, B. (2003). Multiculturalism in the mainstream. *The Horn Book Magazine, 79,* 265–293.

Batchelder, M. (1966). Learning about children's books in translation. *ALA Bulletin, 60,* 33–42.

Bishop, R.S. (1982). *Shadow and substance: Afro-American experience in contemporary children's fiction.* Urbana, IL: National Council of Teachers of English.

Cai, M., & Bishop, R.S. (1994). Multicultural children's literature: Towards a clarification of concept. In A.H. Dyson & C. Genishi (Eds.), *The need for story: Cultural diversity in classroom and community* (pp. 57–71). Urbana, IL: National Council of Teachers of English.

Fox, G. (1996). Teaching fiction and poetry. In P. Hunt (Ed.), *International companion encyclopedia of children's literature* (pp. 594–605). London: Routledge.

Freeman, E.B., & Lehman, B.A. (2001). *Global perspectives in children's literature.* Boston: Allyn & Bacon.

Hazard, P. (1944). *Books, children & men* (M. Mitchell, Trans.). Boston: Horn Book.

Lehman, B.A., & Crook, P.R. (1998). Doubletalk: A literary pairing of *The Giver* and *We Are All in the Dumps With Jack and Guy. Children's Literature in Education, 29,* 69–78.

Lepman, J. (1969, 2002). *A bridge of children's books.* Dublin, Ireland: O'Brien Press.

Nodelman, P., & Reimer, M. (2003). *The pleasures of children's literature* (3rd ed.). Boston: Allyn & Bacon.

Parkinson, S. (2002). Children of the quest: The Irish famine myth in children's fiction. *The Horn Book Magazine, 78,* 679–688.

Pinkney, A.D. (2001). Awards that stand on solid ground. *The Horn Book Magazine, 77,* 535–539.

Rochman, H. (1993). *Against borders: Promoting books for a multicultural world.* Chicago: American Library Association.

Stiles, J. (2004). *From chameleons to koalas: Exploring Australian culture with pre-service teachers through children's literature and international experience.* Unpublished doctoral dissertation, The Ohio State University.

Tomlinson, C.M. (Ed.). (1998). *Children's books from other countries.* Lanham, MD: Scarecrow Press.

LITERATURE CITED

Collodi, C. (1974). *Pinocchio* (E. Harden, Trans.). New York: Puffin. (Original work published 1944)

Conlon-McKenna, M. (1990). *Under the hawthorne tree*. Dublin, Ireland: O'Brien Press.

de Brunhoff, J. (1961). *The story of Babar* (M.S. Haas, Trans.). New York: Random House. (Original work published 1933)

de Haan, L., & Nijland, S. (2000). *King & king*. Berkeley, CA: Tricycle.

Frank, A. (1952). *Anne Frank: The diary of a young girl* (B.M. Mooyaart, Trans.). New York: Doubleday.

Giff, P.R. (2000). *Nory Ryan's song*. New York: Delacorte Press.

Lindgren, A. (1950). *Pippi Longstocking* (F. Lamborn, Trans.). Ill. L. Glanzman. New York: Viking Penguin.

Mollel, T. (1999). *My rows and piles of coins*. New York: Clarion Books.

Rowling, J.K. (2003). *Harry Potter and the Order of the Phoenix*. New York: Scholastic.

Sendak, M. (1963). *Where the wild things are*. New York: Harper & Row.

Spyri, J. (1994). *Heidi* (H.B. Dole, Trans.). Ill. W. Sharp. New York: Grosset & Dunlap. (Original work published 1880)

Stuve-Bodeen, S. (1998). *Elizabeti's doll*. New York: Lee & Low.

White, E.B. (1952). *Charlotte's web*. Ill. G. Williams. New York: Harper & Row.

PART II

Themes of Diversity in Global Literature

CHAPTER 3

Finding Our Stories Through Her Stories: Strong Females in the Global Tapestry

Cyndi Giorgis, Janelle B. Mathis, April Whatley Bedford

"Creating strong, believable heroes of every gender and description is an immensely valuable enterprise....The act of weaving bold new threads into our shared tapestry of story, wholly worthwhile for its own sake, may also help us to reweave the tapestry of our lives. Stories can, in surprising ways, enter into our collective consciousness, changing the very quality of our days....Through our stories we create our own choices, our own lives, our own worlds—with no limits whatsoever."

—T.A. Barron (cited in Lehr, 2001, pp. 31–32)

As illustrated in Barron's opening quote, stories have the power to make a difference in the lives of readers. The words and actions of girls and women, real and fictional, in particular can inspire readers and provide insight into the human spirit (Martinez-Roldan, 2005; Wason-Ellam, 1997). Books about successful, active, and bold female characters provide opportunities for readers of both genders to escape the stereotypes that have prevailed as to the submissive role of women in society. Across the majority of cultures and historical eras, this submissive role has included images of women who maintain the household and provide sustenance and support for the males who actively pursue historical, social, and political challenges. This image is perpetuated by the earlier lack of evidence in literature and historical texts that has frequently hidden the complex role of women as they initiate, undertake, and support social change,

Breaking Boundaries With Global Literature: Celebrating Diversity in K–12 Classrooms, edited by Nancy L. Hadaway and Marian J. McKenna. © 2007 by the International Reading Association.

political decisions, and problem solving in local, national, and global communities. As empowering stories evolve that focus on the complex and, often, dynamic role of women throughout history, they provide a more authentic look at the social roles of each gender. Therefore, stories that feature strong female characters have the potential to provide insights on gender issues across cultures and to support a developing sense of identity in young readers, both female and male.

During the past few decades, readers, writers, teachers, and scholars have articulated a need for stories about strong women in particular. Simply publishing more books with female characters who act in submissive ways might alleviate the invisibility of women in children's literature but will also perpetuate negative stereotypes. As young readers develop a sense of identity, admirable women and girl protagonists portrayed in literature have the potential to extend the female identity and a realization of their role in the global society (McCarthy, 2001). Further, "if boys read and listen to books about the experiences of females their lives are richer and their gender misconceptions are challenged" (Lehr, 2001, p. 14).

It is with a similar belief that this chapter focuses on a variety of strong, creative, and admirable female characters across the global society who use their strengths to meet life's challenges and to make their world a better place. This chapter highlights books that represent strong heroines within various genres, historical eras, and global cultures. We believe these books will engage readers in thoughtful response, critical dialogue, and greater understandings of the significant role of females across cultures. The format for these stories ranges from picture books to novels, and age appropriateness should be determined by the content and maturity of the reader.

First, the chapter examines the traits of strength exhibited by the female characters in these books selected from the Notable Books for a Global Society booklists from 1996 to 2005, specifically how these books represent females' strong sense of self, embrace of cultural roots, cleverness, ability to overcome obstacles, will to survive, and impact on society. After exploring these books with strong female protagonists and the traits that give these characters strength, Literature Response Activities demonstrate how to extend the reading of these books and assist readers in delving deeper into the characters' identities as well as their own.

Exploring Traits of Strength Exhibited by Female Characters

Exploring literature in search of the bold threads of character that Barron described in the opening quote reveals these threads to be woven tightly throughout stories of personal and cultural identity, resiliency that comes from physical and emotional stamina, and a sharp, witty intellect. Ultimately, these stories speak of the potential of these threads for individual and societal empowerment.

Strong Sense of Self

Each one of us has raised questions about our identity: Who am I? Where do I fit in? What do I believe? The most profound questions of identity often relate to an individual's perception of self. Outside influences can affect the development of both sense of self and self-esteem. Characters in the following books raise questions about who they are because of events and situations that occur in their lives. They resolve these issues by heeding the words and actions of well-intentioned family or friends, by coping with devastating circumstances, and by developing strength and determination.

Names are one way we identity ourselves. Often, names have familial connections or cultural significance. But what happens when you are a Korean child who has just moved to the United States and are struggling with assimilating into the school environment? Two booklist titles have addressed this complex issue. In *The Name Jar* (Choi, 2001/2002 NBGS), Unhei is teased by the children on the bus for her Korean name. Once she arrives at school, Unhei tells the teacher she has not yet decided on a name. To be helpful her classmates put their suggestions for a new name for Unhei into a "name jar." Even though she appreciates their willingness to help, Unhei eventually comes to realize the significance of her own name and decides that it is right for her. In the picture book *My Name Is Yoon* (Recorvits, 2003/2004 NBGS), Korean-born Yoon (which means "shining wisdom") does not like how her name looks written in English. In school, she prefers to refer to herself as "cat," "bird," and "cupcake." *My Name Is Yoon* explores the feelings of one girl as she reconciles that her identity is intact whether her name is written in Korean or in English.

Tea With Milk (Say, 1999/2000 NBGS) follows one young woman's transition from the United States to Japan. After graduating from high school, Masako ("May" to her American friends) unwillingly moves to Japan with her parents. Once there, she is homesick and rebels when her parents want Masako to learn "her own language" and learn to be a proper Japanese lady. After leaving home, Masako begins working in a department store where she meets a handsome young man, Joseph, who was educated in an English boarding school. The two become close, and when Joseph must move to Yokohama Masako chooses to go with him. Even though she is still torn between wanting to live in the United States or Japan, Joseph reassures Masako that "home isn't a place or a building that's ready made and waiting for you" (p. 30). Masako comes to realize that her sense of self isn't tied to a geographic location but rather to the individuals who have contributed to the woman she has become as she exhibits the ability and strength to make decisions about how she chooses to live her life.

Leah Hopper and her younger sister Ruth live in segregated rural Louisiana, USA, during the 1950s in *The Red Rose Box* (Woods, 2002/2003 NBGS). On her birthday, Leah receives a rose-patterned traveling case from her Aunt Olivia that contains train tickets for the family to visit her in Los Angeles, California. In California there is no sign of the racial prejudice that the Hoppers are accustomed to as a black family from the South. When the girls return home, the dramatic differences of the segregated South and privileged world of Los Angeles prompt Leah to question her life. When a trip to New York City with Aunt Olivia and Uncle Bill is arranged for Leah and Ruth, the girls are thrilled, but while they are away a devastating hurricane strikes their hometown, killing their parents. The girls are left to live with their aunt and uncle, making Leah feel the difficult pull between freedom, comfort, and her deeply felt roots. When everything in their lives has been cruelly stripped away, including the parents who helped to create their identities, Leah and Ruth must look within as they establish a renewed sense of self.

In *The Skin I'm In* (Flake, 1998/1999 NBGS), African American seventh grader Maleeka Madison must endure endless mean-spirited teasing and torment from other students about the dark color of her skin. The story focuses on the relationship between Maleeka and the rich, self-assured teacher Miss Saunders, who deals with her own issues of skin—a woman who has "got a white stain spread halfway across her face like somebody tossed acid on it or something" (p. 1). Miss Saunders constantly challenges the girl's academic and social behavior. Told in Maleeka's voice, the attitude is both genuine and alarming, as one girl struggles to gain a sense of self in spite of her mother's depression, the cruelty of "friends," and her own feelings of inferiority.

Legendary Western U.S. scout Kit Carson's sassy 11-year-old daughter *Adaline Falling Star* (Osborne, 2000/2001 NBGS) is portrayed in this fictional but moving story of loss and longing, self-discovery and hope, despair and love. After Adaline's Arapaho mother dies of cholera, her widowed father leaves her with his racist, spiteful relatives until he returns from his expedition in the Rocky Mountains. Adaline is not allowed to attend school and is forced to work as a servant. Because she is a "half-breed," part Indian, part Caucasian, Adaline is barely considered human. Using intelligence, wit, and perseverance (not to mention the companionship of a stray dog), Adaline works tirelessly to return to her home in Colorado. Osborne's lively and touching account is a work of fiction even though historical notes quote a Carson relative saying Adaline "was a wild girl."

Embrace of Cultural Roots

A number of titles selected for the booklist portray strong female characters who are members of more than one culture. Some of these girls and young women are striving to maintain the customs of a parallel culture while living within a broader mainstream society, while others are struggling to reconcile the cultural identities of their parents and grandparents with their identities as Americans. This parallels the previous discussion around identity, as culture represents a major, though not comprehensive aspect of identity. However, because of the unique issues that culture and crossing cultures present for any individual, books in this section represent a specific aspect of strength to model for young readers facing similar circumstances. The books in this category realistically convey the complexities of exploring and embracing multiple cultural identities.

In *In My Family/En Mi Familia* (Garza, 1996/1997 NBGS), Garza recounts with warmth and affection the memories of her childhood and adolescence in Kingsville, Texas, USA, near the Mexican border. This fully bilingual text, in English and Spanish, includes 13 paintings and one-page stories about everyday life in a tightly knit Mexican American community: cooking and eating traditional foods, treating childhood illnesses, celebrating holidays, and attending cultural events like weddings and dances. Astute teachers can help build young readers' understandings of the dual purposes of Garza's work—to lead Mexican Americans in a celebration of their heritage and to educate cultural outsiders about the experiences of growing up in a parallel culture within the United States. This picture book, while probably intended for upper elementary readers, may be successfully shared with readers of all ages to explore themes of family and culture.

Three picture books with related plotlines feature girls expanding their cultural roots. *Faraway Home* (Kurtz, 2000/2001 NBGS) introduces readers to Desta, a young American girl whose name means "joy" in Amharic, her father's native tongue. Desta is worried about her father's impending trip to Ethiopia to visit his ill mother. The little girl pictures her father's birthplace as wild and foreign, so far away from her own comfortable, familiar home. In lyrical, poetic language, Desta's father recounts memories of his boyhood in Ethiopia while he holds his daughter and reassures her that he will return from his journey. As Desta ponders her father's stories, she recognizes how much he must miss his country and his mother—the *emayay* (grandmother) Desta has never met. She comforts herself during their time apart by holding her father's stories in her heart.

Unlike Desta, the unnamed young girl who is the protagonist of *The Trip Back Home* (Wong, 2000/2001 NBGS) is not left at home but instead accompanies her mother from the United States to her native Korea and begins to develop her own connections to that country. In short narrative stanzas, Wong describes how the main character spends her days and nights in the company of her *haraboji* (grandfather), her *halmoni* (grandmother), and her *imo* (aunt), and the intangible gifts of family, shared memories, and a sense of place that the child receives.

In *Shanghai Messenger* (Cheng, 2005), 11-year-old Xiao Mei travels alone from the United States to Shanghai, China, as the messenger of her grandmother, who now lives in the United States and has not returned to China in many years. At first, Xiao Mei is afraid to make the long trip alone and is uncomfortable when she reaches her unfamiliar destination. However, readers learn of her eventual acceptance of and appreciation for her Chinese heritage during her summer-long visit. Xiao Mei comes to love her big, extended family "born in two countries," and she experiences firsthand the universal longing of immigrants who are rooted in two places.

All three authors wrote these books from their own experiences. Jane Kurtz grew up in Ethiopia, and her affection for her adopted homeland in Africa is evident in *Faraway Home*. Janet S. Wong, daughter of a Korean mother and a Chinese father, was inspired to write *The Trip Back Home* by a trip she took with her mother to rural Korea as a child. Andrea Cheng's trips to her Chinese husband's native country as well as childhood visits to Hungary were her inspirations. Each author sprinkles words from the native languages depicted throughout their stories, adding cultural authenticity to the texts.

A novel for adolescent readers, *Habibi* (Nye, 1997/1998 NBGS) focuses on a daughter embracing the culture of one of her parents. Liyana is a young woman coming of age in St. Louis, Missouri, when her father moves the family to his homeland of Palestine. Although her parents assure Liyana that, through this move, she and her brother will have "doubled lives," Liyana doesn't want to leave home. Nor does she immediately bond with the relatives she meets, all of whom speak a language different from her own, or accept the numerous differences between her new culture and the lifestyle she knew in the United States. She does, however, develop a forbidden friendship with Omer, a Jewish boy. Gradually, Liyana begins to embrace her Arab heritage and to form a relationship with Sitti, her grandmother, but she refuses to embrace the prejudice that would destroy her friendship with Omer. Like Liyana, Nye is the daughter of a Palestinian father and an American mother.

Project Mulberry (Park, 2005), a novel for middle-grade readers, presents Julia Song, a Korean-American coming to grips with her bicultural identity. Together with her best friend Patrick, Julia is eager to create an award-winning project for the state fair, but when her mother suggests they raise silkworms, like she did as a child in Korea, Julia is dismayed. She likes to think of herself as an all-American girl, and this project is simply too Korean. Through the development of the silkworm project, as well as through imagined conversations between Korean American author Park and her protagonist inserted between chapters of the main narrative, Julia begins to embrace her identity as both an American and a Korean and learns that prejudice can exist in all cultures.

Cleverness

Witty, intelligent, and clever females are found in stories based in oral tradition, are depicted in fictional stories, and are honored through the relating of historical events. While such examples are not new to the arena of traditional literature, focusing particularly on the wit and wisdom of female characters as described in the following books is a relatively recent occurrence in children's literature. These stories illustrate that females can be amazing problem solvers when difficult times and circumstances warrant them rising to the occasion. A creative and critically active mind as well as, at times, a humorous approach to deal with challenging situations provide a foundation for physical and emotional strength.

Every night Shahrazad begins a story, and every morning the Sultan lets her live another day—providing the story is interesting enough to capture his attention. After almost 1,000 nights, Shahrazad is running out of tales so it falls to clever Marjan, a young girl with a crippled foot, to sneak out each night to find more stories. *Shadow Spinner* (Fletcher, 1998/1999 NBGS) takes the story of Shahrazad and weaves Fletcher's own style through this familiar story of a young girl who is not only the gatherer of tales but one who suddenly becomes the center of a more surprising story than she could have ever imagined. This original story has various titles, such as "1001 Arabian Nights," and while no original manuscript has been found, it is assumed to have its beginnings between 800 and 900 B.C.

Another retelling can be found in *Fa Mulan: The Story of a Woman Warrior* (San Souci, 1998/1999 NBGS), a carefully researched interpretation of the ancient story. When Fa Mulan learns that her weak and elderly father has been drafted into Khan's army to fight the Tartars, she cleverly devises a plan to masquerade as a boy. However, she soon finds herself engaged in fierce combat with the Tartars—something no woman should do. Fa Mulan begins to study the art of war and eventually becomes skilled with the sword. As her actions and accomplishments gain fame, she is called to appear before the Khan, where she fears her true gender will be discovered.

In *One Grain of Rice: A Mathematical Folktale* (Demi, 1997/1998 NBGS), a resourceful young girl, Rani, uses her mathematical thinking to outsmart a selfish raja. The raja of a rice-growing village orders his subjects to deliver the bulk of their harvest even though the villagers are starving. When Rani returns rice grains that had fallen from the baskets laden for the raja's consumption, he offers her a reward. The brainy girl asks for one grain of rice with the amount to be doubled each day for 30 days. As the amount accumulates, Demi's lively illustrations with gold-leaf details attest to the power of doubling and the ultimate reward of good over evil.

Another story of a clever female from traditional literature is the Jewish variant of the Cinderella story, *Raisel's Riddle* (Silverman, 1999/2000 NBGS). When Raisel's grandfather, a learned scholar, dies, he leaves her with little except respect and a love for learning. The orphaned girl is forced to move from her Polish village to a large city in order to work in a rabbi's kitchen. On the night of the Purim ball, Raisel offers her own meal to an old woman who then grants her three wishes for her kindness. Silverman uses the elements from the classic tale as Raisel attends the ball, encounters the handsome young man (who is the rabbi's son), and is able to use her wit and wisdom to find true love.

The clever females found in *The Cats in Krasinski Square* (Hesse, 2004/2005 NBGS) are not from folk tales but from a little-known incident of Jewish resistance during World War II. After escaping from the Warsaw Ghetto, a young girl and her sister plot to sneak food, brought by collaborating train passengers, to those still in the Ghetto. Their scheme is jeopardized when the Gestapo learns of the plan and meets the train with dogs that will sniff out both the smugglers and the contraband food. Demonstrating courage and creativity, the girls find a way to distract the dogs and sneak the food through the Ghetto walls. Hesse's vignette, based on a true story, shares another perspective of the Holocaust and of those who risked their lives to help others.

Ability to Overcome Obstacles

Within the global tapestry are stories that speak to women's strength and perseverance when confronted by obstacles. These obstacles are found within oppressive social situations as well as ordinary life experiences that call for endurance of body and mind. Collectively, the stories provide for all readers a hopeful portrayal of achieving one's goals and dreams while each maintains a reminder of the unique ways in which these figures overcome obstacles.

Through My Eyes (Bridges, 1999/2000 NBGS) recounts the author's memories of entering a New Orleans, Louisiana, school during the era of U.S. segregation. The perspectives of an innocent child sensitively described contrast with the tumultuous angry crowd and inevitable isolation as seen in the numerous sepia photographs. Reminders of this emotional historic moment point to the strength that comes from innocence. Within this book, the inclusion of anecdotes gives tribute to a supporting community, important in overcoming obstacles.

Becoming Naomi León (Ryan, 2004/2005 NBGS) depicts the strength of a fifth-grade girl who has withstood the emotional scars of abandonment seven years earlier and now lives with her great-grandmother. Naomi's fortitude is called upon again when her mother reappears with the intent of taking her away from both the home she knows as well as separating her from her younger brother. Naomi rises above the situation when she travels with Gram to Oaxaca to find her Mexican father—a reunion that gives her not only the necessary support to defy her mother's intent but also gives Naomi a sense of heritage, family, and talent. Dealing with emotional obstacles as well as those imposed on children by self-serving adults, Naomi is a realistic character to befriend, celebrate, and admire.

At the age of 12, Sadie Wynn and her family are called upon to leave their house in Missouri, USA, to move to a shack near the Gulf Coast in Texas as a result of both the U.S. Great Depression and a drought. *The Truth About Sparrows* (Hale, 2004/2005 NBGS) tells Sadie's story as she struggles with poverty, prejudicial treatment at school, and the loss of her best friend. Sadie realizes that she must move forward, and her strength is evident not only in her personal growth but in the fortitude she represents for those around her. The rich details in this story of the Depression era serve as a reminder of the many individuals who were resilient in the face of obstacles beyond their control.

Often the innocent eyes of a child see clearly the way to remove obstacles. *The Other Side* (Woodson, 2001/2002 NBGS) in quiet simplicity tells how two young girls, one black and one white, overcome the obstacle of a fence that separates their land and their lives. Without disobeying their mothers, the two girls spend the summer visiting on the fence rather than crossing to the other side. This simple solution goes beyond the serene illustrations and story events to a profound implication for readers about addressing the obstacles that divide society at many levels—obstacles based on old beliefs and racial barriers.

Marian Anderson achieved international recognition for her voice, described by one maestro as "heard once in a hundred years." However, she was confronted with racism and injustice both in her years of professional preparation as well as where she could perform as a professional. Meeting these obstacles with dignity, Anderson stood firm in her determination to help end segregation in the arts. Her strength of character and highly recognized talent made Anderson's involvement in this movement significant, although her intent was not to be an activist. *The Voice That Challenged a Nation: Marian Anderson and the Struggle for Equal Rights* (Freedman, 2004/2005 NBGS) closes with the image of her landmark performance at the Lincoln Memorial, creating a momentous account of Anderson's place in history as a strong female.

Often fortitude is inherent in the traditions and stories that speak to the ways one's ancestors confronted obstacles. *Show Way* (Woodson, 2005) provides a unique narrative around the generations of women in the author's own family and the strength manifested through their art of quilting. Eight generations of women are represented, beginning with Soonie's great-grandmother who was sold away from her parents at age 7. She learned to make Show Ways—quilts with secret meanings that guided American slaves to freedom. Quilting becomes a connecting artistic tradition that fortifies the struggle against obstacles—from slavery to freedom to marches against segregation and, finally, to supporting Woodson's voice in sharing these stories and this art with her own daughter.

Will to Survive

Stories of overcoming obstacles are even more poignant when survival itself is the outcome of a persevering mind and physical stamina. Many titles included in this section address the role of women within war-torn countries. Often their survival is not only that of their own lives and culture but also that of others who share their experiences and communities in adverse situations.

Fireflies in the Dark: The Story of Freidl Dicker-Brandeis and the Children of Terezin (Rubin, 2000/2001 NBGS) is the inspirational but tragic story of a Bauhaus-trained woman from Prague who, when she was deported from Prague to the Terezin concentration camp, gave art lessons to the children she was told to supervise. Art was the medium through which they struggled to survive cold, hunger, isolation from their families, and the thoughts of probable death. The book shares the horrific context that documents the courage of both teacher and children. However, the illustrations and writings of the children give voice to their strength of spirit and its ultimate survival, despite the fact that only 100 people survived of the 15,000 who were taken to Terezin.

For one Holocaust survivor, memories of an idyllic childhood intruded upon by the Nazi invasion, labor, hiding, the loss of her parents, and a journey to the United States will live forever in a tapestry. Art is again shown as a means to overcome obstacles in *Memories of Survival* (Steinhardt, 2005) as the author shares the 36-panel tapestry created by her mother. Along with the fabric illustrations and captions by the artist, Steinhardt provides text to accompany her mother's art. As a young girl, Krinitz overcame the obstacles confronting her survival by disguising herself as a Catholic farmhand. However, her embroidered panels became the means for her story to survive.

Sweetgrass Basket (Carvell, 2005) shares the experiences of two Mohawk sisters at the beginning of the 20th century as they attend Carlisle Boarding School. Here, Native American children endured punishment and intimidation as they were taught menial tasks that prepared them for domestic work once they were out of school. Mattie and Sarah tell of their lives in alternating free verse, and their story is as much about preserving identity and heritage as it is physical survival. Mattie's death from exposure leaves Sarah alone in the struggle to preserve their family heritage in this sensitive story crafted from the actual experiences of the author's husband's family. This is but one account that represents the many strong Native American children whose lives were forever changed by their struggle to survive the boarding school experience.

From the tree that she climbs to enjoy the freedom of its branches and the view of sunrise, Gabriela witnesses the rape, torture, and murder involved in guerilla warfare. In *Tree Girl* (Mikaelsen, 2004/2005 NBGS), Gabi's teacher, schoolmates, and part of her family are killed. Armed with only the hope of finding a younger sister, Gabi heads north to the Mexican border to a refugee camp. Her struggle to survive encompasses not only finding her sister but helping another woman and eventually starting a school for children in the camp. The courage and determination of this young girl, amidst the atrocities of war, are based on a true account and speak to the powerful will to survive, especially if one is responsible for the survival of others.

Under the Persimmon Tree (Staples, 2005) is the story of two strong women whose paths cross as each is left alone to survive amidst the conflict in Afghanistan, one month after September 11, 2001. Najma witnesses her mother's and baby brother's deaths during an air raid after her brother and father are taken to fight for the Taliban. Nusrat is an American whose Pakistani husband is running a clinic while she holds school for a refugee camp. As each seeks news of their loved ones, Najma's search takes her to the refugee school where both women wait for loved ones and follow their hearts as they struggle to survive.

Yet another story of war-torn Afghanistan is *The Story of My Life: An Afghan Girl on the Other Side of the Sky* (Ahmedi, 2005). This autobiography brings reality to the stories of women who endure physical struggles for survival as the author shares her experience of losing her leg to a land mine. Through rich descriptions of a schoolgirl's life in Afghanistan as compared to the United States where she now lives, Farah speaks to the spirit of survival that enables her to continue following her dreams.

Impact on Society

A number of the booklist titles that feature strong women and girls portray female characters who act with courage and compassion to change their world. Across continents and historical eras, these brave females often go "against the grain" of expected behaviors for their gender or ethnicity to make the world a better place for themselves and others. Their stories prove that one person can have an impact on society and that a single act can have far-reaching effects.

Three of the books highlighted in this category focus on the power of teachers. *The Forbidden Schoolhouse* (Jurmain, 2005) is a nonfiction account of

The Magic of Story

SUZANNE FISHER STAPLES

When I was a child, I was certain my parents had brought the wrong baby home from the hospital. I was a skeptic, an experimenter, a risk-taker, while my family members were cautious people. They were definite about their thoughts and beliefs. I had wanderlust, while they valued community and home above all. And so I grew up feeling like an outcast in my own family, out of place in my own skin. It was in stories that I found characters that were just like me—people who didn't fit in, but found their way. Books like *The Little Prince*, *The Wind in the Willows*, *Little Women*, *The Prince and the Pauper* all made me feel at home in the larger world. They helped me to discover what I thought and how I believed.

Literature that crosses borders to help us gain new perspectives on the world also lets us know that we all belong. Stories about other cultures let us see that cultural differences are exciting and interesting—not irrelevant or menacing or laughable. And beneath the cultural differences we see people who are just like us—people who value family and friendship, who suffer the pain of loss and the joy of discovery.

Something magical happens when we read: The story of someone on the other side of the world becomes a part of our own story. And that changes who we are—it changes our own story. When we know the intimate details of the lives of people who live in far-off places, it's difficult to disregard them as irrelevant to us and our way of life. If you know what children in another country have for breakfast, for example, you begin to see that their stories are as important as your own stories. If you know what a mother says to her daughter while she braids her hair on a hillside, you can't disregard them if they become casualties of war.

Telling stories that leap across borders to let us see the world through the eyes of others does far more than broaden our horizons. It makes us larger people. And it may be our best hope for understanding and global peace.

*Books by Suzanne Fisher Staples selected for the Notable Books
for a Global Society:*

Dangerous Skies (1996/1997 NBGS)

Shiva's Fire (2000/2001 NBGS)

Prudence Crandall, a white teacher who began a school for black female students in Connecticut, USA, prior to the U.S. Civil War. Although persecuted, fined, jailed, and threatened with bodily harm, Prudence persevered to provide an education for young black female students at a time when few girls, particularly girls of African American descent, were deemed worthy of education. Jurmain was inspired to tell the story of Crandall, posthumously named Connecticut's state female hero, by a biography she read as a child. Meticulously researched and supplemented with drawings and photographs, this text introduces readers to one of the first women who dared to fight educational inequities in the United States.

Freedom School, Yes! (Littlesugar, 2001/2002 NBGS) describes the heroic efforts of a teacher to educate black children in the U.S. Deep South during the 1964 Mississippi Summer Project. This fictionalized portrayal, inspired by true events, dramatically recounts the dangers of attempting to teach black students in the southern United States more than 100 years after Prudence Crandall faced similar obstacles. In Littlesugar's story, Annie, a 19-year-old white teacher from the North, comes to live with Jolie and her African American family in Chicken Creek, Mississippi, to teach black children about their history. At first, the African American community is skeptical of learning about their own history from a white teacher, but they soon recognize Annie's commitment. When white community members attempt to drive Annie away by vandalizing Jolie's home and burning down a local church, Annie, her students, and their families remain steadfast in continuing the children's schooling. In both books, courage and commitment are demonstrated not only by the adult teachers but through the equally heroic efforts of their young students who fight for their right to an education.

The Year of Miss Agnes (Hill, 2000/2001 NBGS) presents readers with another inspiring teacher. Set in Alaska, USA, in 1948, this book describes the day-to-day life of the native Athabascan Indian students Miss Agnes has agreed to teach for one year. Leaving behind a comfortable existence in her home country of England for the harsh and very unfamiliar surroundings of the Alaskan "bush," Miss Agnes touches and enriches the life of every student she meets but particularly that of 10-year-old Fred, the story's narrator. Numerous cultural details capture the essence of life in this remote Alaskan village half a century ago, and the special bond between teacher and students is at the heart of the book.

Luba: The Angel of Bergen-Belsen (Tryszynska-Frederick, 2003/2004 NBGS) also focuses on the bond between a woman and a group of children, but under more dire circumstances. This true story of the Holocaust was told to Michelle McCann by Luba, a Jewish nurse from Poland who is separated from her family by the Nazis and taken to the German concentration camp of Bergen-Belsen. One night, she hears cries outside her barracks and discovers 54 Dutch children, abandoned by Nazi guards and left to die of cold and starvation. Luba not only rescues these children but endangers her own life to feed, care for, and protect them until the camp is liberated.

In the aftermath of World War II, life was still very difficult in the war-ravaged countries of Europe. *Boxes for Katje* (Fleming, 2003/2004 NBGS) is a story of friendship between Katje, a Dutch child, and her American friend, Rosie. They become acquainted when Rosie sends Katje a letter and a small box of gifts. Katje's immediate decision to share with her mother and the postman the unimaginable luxury of chocolate is noted in her thank-you letter to Rosie, and thus the two begin a correspondence that leads to ever-growing shipments of food, clothing, and other necessities from the citizens of Mayfield, Indiana, USA, to Katje's village in Holland. These gifts sustain their Dutch recipients through the harsh winter of 1945. Inspired by an actual experience of the author's mother, *Boxes for Katje* convinces readers that the actions of a child can make a huge difference in the lives of others.

To come full circle, back to the fight for civil rights in the United States, readers are treated to a detailed account of a familiar American heroine, Rosa Parks, in *Rosa* (Giovanni, 2005). Written in the lyrical language of poet Giovanni, this picture book pays tribute to the strength and quiet courage of an ordinary woman who changed the course of history. By refusing to give up her seat on a bus, Rosa Parks sparked a powerful but nonviolent movement that eventually led to the outlawing of segregation in the United States. In fact, all of the books in this category focus on ordinary females—teachers, a nurse, a seamstress, a child—who react to the contexts in which they lived in extraordinary and heroic ways.

Literature Response Activities

As readers respond to the various books about strong women around the globe, their many stories of strength, problem solving, self-identity, and perseverance can intrigue, entertain, and elicit admiration. However, returning to the idea of creating a tapestry in the opening quote by Barron, the various engagements teachers design around these books should be those that invite "weaving bold new threads into our shared tapestry of story" thus helping readers "reweave the tapestry" of their lives. Such strategies encourage personal connections with characters as well as contemplation of the various qualities that are universal and can be found within diversity of individuals within today's global community. While each book or a text set of books invites particular engagements unique to its character, situation, or context, possible response-based strategies are suggested here as examples of ways to nurture the weaving of new threads of experience with those unique personal strands that exist within each reader. The strategies here are easily adapted for all grade levels and are especially suited for elementary and middle school.

"Where I'm From" Poem Response Strategy

Many of the books in this chapter focus on issues of culture and self-identity. One strategy that addresses both is the writing of a "Where I'm From" poem (Christensen, 2001), modeled after a poem of that title by George Ella Lyon. Generally, the phrase "I am from..." leads off each stanza, but any repeating line can be used as long as it links the poem together and moves it forward. The strategy for creating a "Where I'm From" poem is supported by thinking back through one's life and then creating lists using the following ideas for inspiration:

- Generating a list of items from around the home: stacks of newspapers, Grandma's ticking clock, shelves burgeoning with books, and so on

- Listing items found in the yard: a rusty old car, a garden hose coiling like a snake, or other items that could be used to create metaphors

- Thinking about areas in the neighborhood: your best friend's house, the local grocery store, the place where everyone hung out after school

- Creating a list of relatives, especially those that can be linked to the past: Great Grandma Hazel, Cousin Elinor, Uncle Fred, and writing down their sayings

- Naming foods and dishes from family gatherings

- Remembering childhood secrets and memories

After the lists are generated, decide how to link them together in a poem. A good way to introduce this strategy is to select a character from one of the books and create a "Where I'm From" poem about that individual before striking out on your own. Depending upon the topics chosen for inclusion in students' poetry and the support provided for writing, this strategy has been used effectively by teachers of kindergarten through high school.

Appreciating Diverse Languages Response Strategy

Language is a critical component of culture, and students might choose to find out more about the languages spoken in the various cultures portrayed in the texts highlighted in this chapter. A number of these books foster appreciation of multiple languages by using words from characters' native languages (other than English) and sometimes by including a glossary or pronunciation guide of non-English phrases. Students might further their knowledge of and appreciation for

Table 3.1. Appreciating Diverse Languages Response Strategy Chart

Word	Meaning	Language	Country	Source
desta	joy	Amharic	Ethiopia	*Faraway Home*
emayay	mother	Amharic	Ethiopia	*Faraway Home*
haraboji	grandfather	Korean	Korea	*The Trip Back Home*
halmoni	grandmother	Korean	Korea	*The Trip Back Home*

multiple languages by creating a language chart listing foreign words, English translations, language and country of origin, and the book in which they are found, such as illustrated in Table 3.1. This chart can be kept in the classroom and continually expanded as more books are read by individuals, small groups, or a whole class. Again, this strategy is beneficial to students at all grade levels, but the books highlighted in this chapter that contain words or phrases from languages other than English are primarily picture books.

Oral History and Independent Research Response Strategy

The cultures and historic events portrayed in the books introduced in this chapter will naturally lead many young readers to independent research. Students might choose to research the roles of women in a culture or during the historical era related to a book in which they are particularly interested. Several of the books discussed are immigration stories or stories of bicultural individuals; these might lead readers to design and conduct oral history interviews with immigrants or people who are rooted in more than one culture. Likewise, a number of books are family stories that will spark readers of all ages to research their own family histories and share their findings through written narratives, poetry, oral storytelling, drama, or visual art.

Process Drama Response Strategy

Process drama offers students an opportunity to respond on the "edges" of the text as they create the implied text and think beyond the written word. A variety of techniques within this art form provide possibilities for students to give voice and mind to characters, to contemplate what might have been, to re-create the context of a particular book, and to make personal connections as readers contemplate the situations that called for strength in these female characters.

Readers Theatre can be a form of process drama when students create the script by combining quotes or insights from various similar characters. Readers may take one situation and create a script that might have occurred had the main character acted in different ways, or alternate the lines of script from two similar or not-so-similar strong women. In creating a compare/contrast Readers Theatre script, students are asked to think across eras or across beliefs of characters as well as to position language in empowering ways.

Tableau vivant is another potential form of process drama as it involves using one's physical positioning and facial features in response to a situation or to depict a particular event from the story. Readers might create a scene depicting the generations of women described in *Show Way*, being sure that each woman's position reflects her particular life's events as shared in the story. As many books focus on issues of equity, when using a tableau in response to text or illustrations, the reader is asked to consider the emotions of the characters and how their body language would have reflected what they felt at certain moments. You might propose a potential scenario in which the reader reflects his or her personal opinion on a topic. In response to *Through My Eyes*, a family dinner conversation might be held that could have occurred in a family the evening after Ruby entered the school. Process drama invites layers of involvement and complex thinking that nurtures understandings about people and cultures and is particularly appropriate for students in upper elementary grades and beyond.

Conclusion

In *Rosa*, Giovanni conveys the strength of Rosa Parks: "She thought about her mother and her grandmother and knew they would want her to be strong. She had not sought this moment, but she was ready for it." Learning about the legacy of significant females across historical eras and across continents is an important way to learn about our global society. However, the empowering potential of the books shared here might best be described as transforming, "changing the very quality of our days" (Barron, 2001). Books like these help prepare readers, male and female alike, to be ready for the important moments of life—moments that find them and moments they seek through their own initiative. In chapter 4 Jeanne M. McGlinn highlights an important "moment" in the lives of many newcomers to the United States—immigration. Whether immigrants sought to leave their homeland or were forced to do so, this is a defining moment in their lives. "Coming to America: The U.S. Immigrant Experience" explores the many transitions and adjustments that face the immigrant.

REFERENCES

Note. Complete bibliographic citations for the Notable Books for a Global Society booklist (1996–2005) can be found at the end of the book.

Barron, T.A. (2001). The unquenchable source: Finding a heroic girl inside a man. In S.Lehr (Ed.), *Beauty, brains, and brawn: The construction of gender in children's literature* (pp. 30–35). Portsmouth, NH: Heinemann.

Christensen, L. (2001). *Rethinking our schools: Teaching for equity and justice* (Vol. 2). Milwaukee, WI: Rethinking Schools.

Lehr, S. (2001). *Beauty, brains, and brawn: The construction of gender in children's literature*. Portsmouth, NH: Heinemann.

Martinez-Roldan, C.M. (2005). The inquiry acts of bilingual children in literature discussions. *Language Arts, 83*, 22–32.

McCarthy, S.J. (2001). Identity construction in elementary readers and writers. *Reading Research Quarterly, 36*, 122–151.

Wason-Ellam, L. (1997). "If only I was like Barbie." *Language Arts, 74*, 430–437.

LITERATURE CITED

Ahmedi, F. (2005). *The story of my life: An Afghan girl on the other side of the sky*. New York: Simon Spotlight.

Carvell, M. (2005). *Sweetgrass basket*. New York: Dutton.

Cheng, A. (2005). *Shanghai messenger*. Ill. E. Young. New York: Lee & Low.

Giovanni, N. (2005). *Rosa*. Ill. B. Collier. New York: Holt.

Jurmain, S. (2005). *The forbidden schoolhouse: The true and dramatic story of Prudence Crandall and her students*. Boston: Houghton Mifflin.

Park, L.S. (2005). *Project mulberry*. New York: Clarion.

Staples, S.F. (2005). *Under the persimmon tree*. New York: Farrar, Straus and Giroux.

Steinhardt, B. (2005). *Memories of survival*. New York: Hyperion.

Woodson, J. (2005). *Show way*. Ill. H. Talbott. New York: Putnam.

CHAPTER 4

Coming to America:
The U.S. Immigrant Experience

Jeanne M. McGlinn

"Give me your tired, your poor,
Your huddled masses yearning to breathe free,
The wretched refuse of your teeming shore.
Send these, the homeless, tempest-tost to me,
I lift my lamp beside the golden door!"

—Emma Lazarus (1883; engraved and mounted inside the Statue of Liberty in 1903)

"'Siempre lo mismo. Los pobres desperately seeking
for betterment, but often finding worse,' Papi
says. A tear slides through his voice."

—Tony Johnston, *Any Small Goodness: A Novel of the Barrio* (2001/2002 NBGS)

I
mmigration laws and immigration reform are major and often hotly debated
political topics in the United States today. According to a series of polls in the
late 1990s and early 2000, the majority of Americans want to see immigration
either stopped or limited and advocate vigorous prosecution of persons entering
the country illegally. Many disagree with amnesty programs and do not want the
government to make it easier for persons to work in the United States
(Federation for American Immigration Reform, 2006). Competing ideologies,
focused on both legal and illegal immigration, are divided between a complete
overhaul of the existing quota system versus enforcing sealed borders, increased
vigilance, and punitive laws to make America "secure." Some argue that

Breaking Boundaries With Global Literature: Celebrating Diversity in K–12 Classrooms, edited by Nancy L. Hadaway and Marian J. McKenna. © 2007 by the International Reading Association.

immigrants take away jobs from "real Americans," while others proclaim that the U.S. economy depends on the jobs that immigrants hold. Many communities that do not support immigration point to the stresses caused by immigrants on resources such as health care and welfare, while immigration advocates calculate how much immigrants contribute in taxes and in the workforce.

Many children's book authors—and in particular, Notable Books for a Global Society booklist authors of the past 10 years—have tackled this issue, with a goal to educate readers about the complex issues surrounding recent immigration, to get beyond the stereotypes attached to "legal" immigration of the late 19th and early 20th centuries, and to provide a human face to this intense debate. These authors have used a variety of genres, from picture books to historical fiction to realistic short stories, to create their stories from the tensions that exist for people who have chosen or been forced to leave their homes and countries, hoping for a safe haven, economic success, and upward mobility in the United States. They illustrate the reasons people emigrate to unfamiliar and foreign places and the difficulties of forging a new identity in a culture that often does not value their traditions or ethnicity. Table 4.1 is a list of books that address the topic of immigration.

After a brief overview of the characteristics of the U.S. immigrant population today and common misconceptions associated with immigration, this chapter will first present contrasting views on immigration as portrayed in award-winning picture books. Many depictions of the major U.S. immigration influx of the late 19th and early 20th centuries are positive in picture books, almost nostalgic, frequently glossing over the difficult social and cultural adjustments involved in immigration, while picture books about more recent immigrants more critically examine these issues. Then the chapter will analyze in greater detail the traumatic and life-changing experiences of adolescents negotiating the difficult passage into a new culture as it is presented in three novels of contemporary realistic fiction for young adults: *Tangled Threads: A Hmong Girl's Story* (Shea, 2003/2004 NBGS), *A Step From Heaven* (Na, 2001/2002 NBGS), and *Any Small Goodness* (Johnston, 2001/2002 NBGS).

The books described in this chapter are appropriate for all students but particularly for middle-grade readers. Picture books can provide a quick introduction to issues surrounding U.S. immigrant experiences and serve as a catalyst for discussion. The chapter concludes with Literature Response Activities that involve developing pro and con arguments on the immigration debate by drawing on the reading of the novels and limited Web research as well as personal response activities, which require readers to reflect on their connections to the characters in the novels.

Table 4.1. Books About Immigration in the Notable Books for a Global Society Booklist, 1996–2005

Year Selected	Title and Author
1996	*Immigrants* by Martin W. Sandler *An Island Like You: Stories of the Barrio* by Judith O. Cofer *The Whispering Cloth: A Refugee Story* by Pegi Deitz Shea
1997	*When I Left My Village* by Maxine Rose Schur
1998	*When Jesse Came Across the Sea* by Amy Hest
1999	*Journey to Ellis Island: How My Father Came to America* by Carol Bierman *Marianthe's Story: Painted Words/Spoken Memories* by Aliki
2000	*The Memory Coat* by Elvira Woodruff *Streets of Gold* by Rosemary Wells
2001	*Esperanza Rising* by Pam Muñoz Ryan *Faraway Home* by Jane Kurtz *The Upside Down Boy/El Niño de Cabeza* by Juan Herrera
2002	*Any Small Goodness: A Novel of the Barrio* by Tony Johnston *Oranges on Golden Mountain* by Elizabeth Partridge *A Step From Heaven* by An Na *Uncle Rain Cloud* by Tony Johnston
2003	*The Color of Home* by Mary Hoffman *Dead Man's Gold and Other Stories* by Paul Yee *Good-Bye, 382 Shin Dang Dong* by Francis Park and Ginger Park *Tenement: Immigrant Life on the Lower East Side* by Raymond Bial
2004	*My Name Is Yoon* by Helen Recorvits *Tangled Threads: A Hmong Girl's Story* by Pegi Deitz Shea
2005	*Escape From Saigon: How a Vietnam War Orphan Became an American Boy* by Andrea Warren *Nothing Here But Stones* by Nancy Oswald

U.S. Immigration Today and Common Misconceptions

One of the pervasive myths about immigrants today is that they are quite different from the immigrants who arrived in America at the early part of the 20th century (Justice for Immigrants, 2005). The majority of immigrants from the late 19th and early 20th centuries came from eastern and southern Europe, while more than half of the 33.5 million foreign-born persons in the United States today (53.3%) were born in Latin America and 25% in Asia (Larsen, 2004). However, aside from the countries of origin, there are more similarities between these two groups than differences. A report describing the foreign-born population of the United States in 2003 (based on data collected by the U.S. Census Bureau in the Current Population Survey) shows that the foreign-born population stands at 11.7%, a number that is very close to the 15% from the earlier immigration influx (Larsen, 2004).

While earlier immigrants tended to settle in the north and east, today's immigrants tend to live in all parts of the United States, although people born in Latin America and Asia have mainly settled in the western United States, which has the largest concentration of foreign-born persons (Larsen, 2004). Today's immigrants, like earlier immigrants, settle in urban neighborhoods where they can speak their native languages, create businesses, and interact with other persons of their ethnic background. They are generally younger than the native population, live in larger households, and are unlikely to graduate from high school (Larsen, 2004).

Earlier immigrants worked in low-paying and labor-intensive jobs, such as factories or mining. They were often accused of taking jobs from native citizens and driving down wages because of their willingness to work for low pay. Today's U.S. immigrants tend to work in service occupations, while native-born workers tend toward management or professional skills occupations (Larsen, 2004). Thus, members of the foreign-born population tend to earn less than the native population, and many live at the poverty level (which is determined by comparing the total family income with poverty thresholds determined by the government for the size and composition of a family). The situation is even worse for noncitizens; Larsen (2004) reports that 16.6% of this population lives at poverty level, compared with 11.5% for the native population. According to census data, "Foreign-born noncitizens were twice as likely to be poor as foreign-born naturalized citizens, whose poverty rate was closer to that of the native population" (Larsen, 2004, p. 7). (For more information or statistics about U.S. immigrants and policies affecting them, please see the website of the Office of Immigration Statistics at http://www.dhs.gov/ximgtn/statistics/index.shtm, which is maintained by the Office of Policy of the U.S. Department of Homeland Security.)

Earlier U.S. immigrants were vilified by native citizens; they were accused of seeking only their own economic advantage, refusing to learn English, and being a drain on social services. In fact, the laws governing immigration quotas came about during the 1920s as a reaction to the racist attitudes of the time. A similar reaction to immigrants today is evident from a survey of U.S. public opinion polls. For example, one common misconception is that immigrants threaten U.S. workers. A poll taken in December 2005 by *CNN/Gallup/USA Today* (reported by the Federation for American Immigration Reform, 2006) showed that 60% of respondents believe that "illegal immigrants" are driving down wages and that 52% felt the same way about "legal immigrants." Many also claim that immigrants do not pay taxes and have come to the United States for welfare. However, all of these assertions have been rejected in multiple studies collected by the National Immigration Forum (2005). For example, a paper from the Congressional Budget Office (2005) on "The Role of Immigrants in the U.S. Labor Market" shows that immigrants are an important source of workers who continue to meet the demands for labor as the aging baby boomers (persons born between World War II and the Vietnam War) leave the workforce for retirement, creating huge vacancies in skilled jobs and professions. Although immigrants might take away some low-paying jobs from native workers, their presence can also be seen as an incentive to encourage *all* U.S. citizens to get an education, which will enable them to get a higher paying job. Another study, conducted by Northeastern University and reported in *The Washington Post*, indicated that without immigrant labor the record economic expansion of the 1990s would not have occurred (Cohn, 2002). In addition, the study concludes that most immigrants contribute more value in taxes than they consume in community services and resources.

Though a report from the Department of Homeland Security Office of Immigration Statistics (2005) indicates that most immigrants enter the United States legally, another common misconception is that most immigrants cross the border illegally, so the words *illegal* and *immigrant* are generally used in polls about immigrants and immigration policy. A report on recent polls illustrates this conflation of the terms *illegal* and *immigrant* (Federation for American Immigration Reform, 2006), as most of the polls ask respondents for their reaction to "illegal immigration" in the United States. However, according to statistics from the Department of Homeland Security, 75% of immigrants have legal permanent status, and of the remaining 25% nearly half overstayed temporary visas, so the majority of immigrants have entered the country legally and are documented. This fact suggests that the persistence of equating "illegal" with "immigrant" is done for a political purpose, to build anti-immigration sentiment. As indicated earlier, this is no different from the reaction to earlier immigrants.

Contrasting Views on U.S. Immigration Examined in Picture Books

Behind these numbers, polls, and statistics are the human issues of immigration. Immigration occurs as a result of significant factors that "push" people away from their homes and "pull" them toward the opportunities they believe will be available in a new country. Many people who are seeking economic improvement, civil rights, or freedom from persecution see the United States as a place to start over and to pursue dreams for advancement. However, at the same time, they also suffer losses—they must break the ties of family, language, and culture. The difficulties of surviving in a foreign land separated from the supports of family and all familiar associations, being an outsider—both physically and culturally, and facing racism adds a dimension of personal suffering and anguish to the better life that immigrants seek. For some immigrants, these difficulties melt away as economic success and education lead to a blossoming of their aspirations, while for others the dream proves much too illusive. Some of the booklist titles dealing with the U.S. immigration movement of the late 19th and early 20th centuries focus on the positive side of this equation, while others present a much more complex picture of the ambiguous feelings of immigrants, dealing with their sense of loss and alienation.

America as the Promised Land: The Nostalgic View of Immigration

The mythic story of the journey to America—the promised land—for millions of immigrants at the end of the 19th century is retold in two picture books and one work of nonfiction. *When Jessie Came Across the Sea* (Hest, 1997/1998 NBGS) romanticizes the reality of harsh working and living conditions for immigrants. On the day she leaves her home, Jessie, a 13-year-old orphan, is promised "America! Good things await you there" (n.p.). True to this idealized vision of America, difficulties melt away or are nonexistent for Jessie. After an effortless passage through Ellis Island, Jessie works as a seamstress in a Lower East Side tenement while learning English and saving her money. Soon her hard work pays off and she is able to buy a ticket for her grandmother's passage. This story's happy ending evokes nostalgia for the immigrant experience while it teaches the values of hard work and upward mobility.

Similarly evoking the promise of America is *Streets of Gold* (Wells, 1999/2000 NBGS), which is based on the memoir of Mary Antin (1912), *The Promised Land*. For Mary's family of Russian Jews, America holds the promise of freedom to practice their religion. Her father tells her, "They don't care what religion you are there.... No Czars who give you bad dreams, no secret police who tell us where we can go or what we can't do" (p. 14). Happily reunited with their father, the family settles into a tenement in Boston where they soon find that the reality doesn't match the "bricks of gold" they had been promised. However, the promise of education sustains them. On Mary's first day of school, her father tells the teacher that she is taking his children "into the kingdom of heaven" (p. 32). As her English improves, Mary writes a 35-verse poem on George Washington, a tribute to her love of America and its freedoms, which is printed in the *Boston Herald*. Wells's story, however, glosses over the losses suffered by immigrants. For instance, Mary does not regret losing her name or language so she can "fit in."

Tenement: Immigrant Life on the Lower East Side (Bial, 2002/2003 NBGS), a work of nonfiction, also presents a nostalgic version of the immigrant experience. Bial uses documentary photos depicting cramped and squalid living conditions, crowded working conditions in slum neighborhoods and sweatshops, but he counters these images with descriptions of the promise of economic prosperity and betterment awaiting immigrant families. For example, next to a sketch of a street scene on the Lower East Side, Bial writes, "Despite their daily hardships, they [immigrants] enjoyed visiting with one another on the busy street" (p. 44). Next to a photo of a sweatshop, Bial asserts, "by working long and hard, men managed to support their families and working women proved themselves to be 'brave, virtuous, and true'" (p. 36). While admitting that immigrants were "haunted by cold, poverty, and disease" (p. 41), Bial maintains that such rigors were part of a "test" by which immigrants showed that they had the skills and endurance to survive and prosper in America. Thus, Bial uses his account of immigrant life to promote the romanticized ideal of the "level playing field," where all that is required of anyone is hard work and all have equal opportunity for success. With his emphasis on the "fond memories" of immigrants, Bial shortchanges the enormous difficulties they faced in an alien land.

Struggles for Survival: A Critical Lens on Immigration

Unlike the authors who focus on the promise of America, other writers explore the feelings of loss and alienation experienced by immigrants who miss their homes and are struggling to adjust to new customs and language. In *Good-bye, 382 Shin Dang Dong* (Park & Park, 2002/2003 NBGS), 8-year-old Jangmi leaves her home in Korea for a new home in Massachusetts, USA. She is homesick and wonders if she will ever feel comfortable in this strange place. Being greeted by neighbors and meeting a girl her age helps, but Jangmi knows it will take time to adjust. Sitting beneath her new maple tree, she thinks, "Maybe I would come to love it as much as our willow tree back home in Korea. But not today" (n.p.). Another picture book, *My Name Is Yoon* (Recorvits, 2003/2004 NBGS), confronts similar problems of adjustment. Yoon does not like America because everything is different and she is alone. But one day a girl in her class reaches out to her. Now with the encouragement of her parents and new teacher, Yoon begins to see that "Maybe different is good, too" (n.p.).

While these two young children experience some alienation, adults often encounter greater difficulty through immigration experiences, suffering a loss of identity and self-respect as they struggle to learn new behaviors and language. They often react in anger when they must rely on their young children to translate for them and fear that they are losing their authority in the family. In

Uncle Rain Cloud (Johnston, 2001/2002 NBGS), Carlos, who is in the third grade, dreads market day and teacher conferences with his Uncle Tomas, who cares for him while his parents work long hours. Tomas is angry that he can't speak English and because the few English words he knows, "sounded ugly—like all of 'el Blah-Blah,' English" (n.p.). Only at night, when he can speak in his native tongue, does Uncle Tomas relax and tell Carlos the mythic and intricate stories of Mexico's gods. One night when he is particularly upset, Uncle Tomas refuses to tell Carlos a story. Finally he admits, "These days I am not myself. My *maldito* pride—I feel like a broken-winged bird. A thing that just flops around. You speak for me, a grown man, because...I am...afraid to speak English" (n.p.). Carlos tells his uncle that he has the same fears of being teased about his English, but he has to keep trying. When Uncle Tomas realizes his nephew's courage, he decides to put aside his own fears so that they can help each other and learn from each other. Carlos helps his uncle pronounce English words, and Uncle Tomas teaches him the stories of his Spanish ancestors. Uncle Tomas's realization of loss as well as gain gives the reader a realistic idea of an immigrant's experience.

Realistic Portrayals of the Lives of Modern Immigrants

The themes of these picture books—the promises and frustrations of coming to America and the struggle to hold on to cultural identity and traditions against the equal pressure to forge a new identity—are presented most clearly in three books: *Tangled Threads* (Shea, 2003/2004 NBGS), *A Step From Heaven* (Na, 2001/2002 NBGS), and *Any Small Goodness* (Johnston, 2001/2002 NBGS). These realistic novels use a similar pattern to tell their stories: the dreams and promises of coming to America, the initial reactions upon arrival (including both happiness and frustrations), the adjustment period of trying to find a place in the new culture and the resulting conflict, and finally a resolution for the main character who is able to change and thrive or fails to adjust and rejects the new homeland.

Finding a Haven

Tangled Threads, which is the continuation of the picture book *The Whispering Cloth: A Refugee Story* (Shea, 1995/1996 NBGS), shows how some immigrants are able to create a safe space in the United States where they can continue many of their cultural traditions while beginning to adjust to American values. Mai, a 13-year-old Hmong orphan and refugee from Laos, is eager to emigrate to America, which represents all her hopes and dreams for family, happiness, and freedom from a "land of war, land of prisons, land of lies" (p. 41). Mai suspects that America is very different from anything she has ever known; nevertheless, she is confident that she will be able to handle it all. She dreams that she "will jump over every skyscraper and drive a car—real fast on the highways" (p. 14). Mai's anticipation is in stark contrast to her grandmother's reluctance to "leave this land of our ancestors" (p. 41). For her America is a place of danger and loss, where everything moves too fast and the natural is overcome by the artificial. Because she fears that in such a place she will not "belong," she has secretly been delaying their departure from the refugee camp in Thailand. Mai's parents were killed by the Pathet Lao after the Vietnam War, but her uncle and his family emigrated to the United States years before.

At first, Mai and her grandmother are disappointed. Settled in their new apartment, they find that their family has been changed by their lives in America. Her cousins have new American names—"Heather" and "Lisa"—and her uncle no longer follows the traditional religious beliefs. Mai is confused when she sees her cousin's flagrant disregard for her father and outright rebellious behavior, which is so out of character with Hmong values of obedience and respect for elders and parents.

It's not long before Mai is drawn into a conflict between the traditional values that have governed her life so far and the choices that would let her assimilate into the American culture. She wants to be a good Hmong girl, but at the same time she is intrigued by American values, which invite independence, individuality, and self actualization. And, almost immediately, Mai finds herself in conflict with her grandmother, who wants to enforce the traditional values and control everything that Mai does. However, in moving to America and relying on Mai, her grandmother has lost her authority. She cannot speak the language and she is afraid of all the new things they experience. When Mai sees her grandmother's fears and realizes that she has lied about leaving the refugee camp, she rebels. She wants to confront her but is stopped by her sense of respect for elders. She says, "I didn't have the courage, and that made me feel ashamed. I behaved like the obedient Hmong girl I had always been" (p. 142). Unable to resolve this conflict, Mai takes control in other ways—by translating only as much as she wants, by defying her grandmother's dictates against joining the Christian church.

These conflicting feelings could lead to alienation, but Mai has a safety net: She and her grandmother have settled among family and Hmong friends. Despite changing in some ways, such as joining a new religion and consulting U.S. doctors, they also prize their culture and traditions. When Mai learns some traditional dances with Hmong friends, she realizes how special these dances are for her grandmother. When she sees her grandmother's smile, she says, "I felt shame again. In the past seven months I had done little to make my grandmother smile" (p. 169). Mai realizes that her grandmother hasn't been able to make the same transition that she has and that for her it has been just too much change too fast. Mai also realizes the sacrifice her grandmother made in order to give Mai new opportunities. Most importantly, she sees the wisdom of her grandmother's choices, which are actually a great gift. During those years in the camp, Mai mastered the art of Pa'ndau, traditional embroidery, which still connects her with her dead parents. Mai thinks "If Grandma had brought me to America five years sooner, I never would have learned to embroider so well. I might never have felt the spirits of my parents" (p. 172).

After her grandmother's sudden death from heart failure, with the support of her community, Mai finds deep respect for her grandmother. She vows to hold on to the rich traditional ways of the Hmong: the ancestor worship that lets her feel the spirits of her dead parents; the 13-day period of mourning and the soul-releasing ceremony that will give rest to her grandmother's spirit; her needlework that puts her in touch with her parents and grandmother; and the New Year's dance of the ball toss, which is a community courting ritual and celebration. She feels great pride as Hmong from all over the Northeast gather to celebrate, and she thinks that if her grandmother had experienced this celebration she "would have seen that we could live here without giving up everything Hmong" (p. 216). She resolves that there must be a way to be both Hmong and American and is determined to celebrate the richness of both.

Breaking the Ties That Bind

Young Ju and her family in Na's *A Step From Heaven* go through many of the same experiences as Mai, but their journey brings a totally different resolution. Unlike Mai, who is a refugee, Young Ju's family leaves Korea for economic opportunity in the United States (*Mi Gook*): "Apa says that in Mi Gook everyone can make lots of money" (p. 13). The parents' naïve expectations are reflected in 4-year-old Young Ju's thoughts of America. Promises of opportunities make her parents happy. Young Ju thinks, "Mi Gook is the best word. Even better than sea or candy" (p. 13) and "Mi Gook must be in heaven" (p. 15). But slowly she senses that things will be different. She is saddened to learn that she will have to leave her friends and her house and that she has to change to be accepted in America. Young Ju is frightened when her mother takes her to a "beauty shop" where her soft, straight hair is turned into "ugly toy-man hair" (p. 22). Most difficult of all, she must leave her beloved grandmother.

Young Ju's first days at school are confusing and frightening. Her teacher appears to be a giant, like an old witch who eats bad children, and her father changes her name, introducing her as Young "to keep it simple" for the

Race Matters

JANET S. WONG

AUTHOR REFLECTIONS

I was married in 1990 in Naples, Florida. My soon-to-be husband, Glenn, and I went to the county clerk's office to get our marriage license. We filled out the form, waited for the license to be typed, got the license, and walked to the elevator. Waiting there, I noticed an error. The license read, "Groom-Race: Caucasian; Bride-Race: Caucasian." I am half-Chinese and half-Korean. We marched back into the office to tell the (Caucasian) clerk that she'd made a mistake. "You can just white-out the 'Cauc' part," I told her. "Then it will say 'Asian'—which is what I am." I smiled and pointed deferentially to her mistake, looking very much the stereotypical agreeable Asian female. She looked at me quizzically and said, "But, honey—you're one of the white races!"

We tried once more to persuade her to make the change but failed, so Glenn and I left the office chuckling to ourselves. We thought it was mildly funny. We wondered why it mattered, to know the races of a bride and groom. We guessed that the clerk (or the county) was against interracial marriage, and perhaps changing my race made our union seem less "objectionable." My mother-in-law thought it was humorous, too, if rather peculiar. Then I talked to my father. He was not amused. He was insulted. He insisted that I have the mistake corrected. "She thinks she's doing you a favor, making you white," he said. "And she's not."

Why do we need literature with a global perspective? To remind nonwhite readers that they don't need the "favor" of being made white. To show the clerk's grandchildren—and in fact all children—that the world is not just black and white, as so many have been taught. To make all children curious and fascinated and humored and saddened by people with Norwegian and Vietnamese and Guatemalan and Iraqi and Hopi and Ethiopian and English faces and names and stories. To make German Americans in Atlanta want to eat Chinese food for dinner on the Fourth of July, once they've stuffed themselves with burgers and hot dogs at lunch. To make the grandson of an Irish farmer say, "I would never have thought so, but life on a Korean farm seems just like home."

Recently I was in a restaurant with my son, waiting for our check, but our server was nowhere in sight. I flagged down another server and asked him to find our server for us. "What does he look like?" he asked. I said, "He's black." My son was appalled at my political incorrectness. I defended myself saying, "But he *is* black! What was I supposed to say, the tall skinny one?" (There were at least three tall, skinny guys, and only one African American.) My son did not answer; he just

(continued)

Race Matters (continued)

frowned at me. But I maintain that I did nothing wrong: Race was a relevant fact because it was the most obvious way to describe our waiter.

We need to become comfortable with who we—and others—are, describing ourselves neutrally by our race and ethnicity the way someone might use "tall" or "red-haired" or "in the blue shirt" or "the writer," but also recognizing when race is not the best description. In a crowd of non-Asian women, I could be described best and most easily as the Asian one; but in a crowd of thin women, you should call me the chubby one; and in a crowd of chubby Asian females, I am the short one with the flat shoes, the plain one with no makeup, the one who waves her hands around when she talks, the children's poet dressed all in black.

Books allow us to reconstruct reality and reflect on what really matters. Books, in their depth and complexity, help us get under the skin of a character and into the guts of story. Under the skin and into the guts: if we see each other that way often enough, eventually we cannot help but become a more compassionate, intelligent, respectful society, a society where race and all other physical differences really are secondary. When this happens, perhaps race will no longer matter. For now, though, it does matter. So if any of you happen to find yourself being turned into something that you are not, speak up for what is right.

Books by Janet S. Wong selected for the Notable Books for a Global Society:

The Trip Back Home (2000/2001 NBGS)

Apple Pie 4th of July(2002/2003 NBGS)

Americans. Not understanding English, Young Ju constantly fears she is disobeying the teacher, who will punish her.

The parents' anticipation, like Young Ju's, soon turns to disappointment as they find their dreams unfulfilled. Her father is unhappy that the family is obligated to his sister and her husband and that they have no privacy. He is disappointed in his jobs as a gardener and office cleaner. At least in Korea he had his own boat. His pride is hurt because he can't provide for his family in the way that he wants and he lashes out at his wife, blaming her for being dissatisfied.

As they are facing these difficult adjustments, the one thing the family values most of all is their Korean identity. Young Ju's father wants her to learn English, but he also insists that she speak Korean at home so she won't forget who she is. When the family celebrates the arrival of a baby son, Park Joon Ho, Young Ju's place in the patriarchal family order is made clear to her. Boys are superior to girls; they will get to do and be anything they want. Young Ju ponders, "Why does he get to be president? I am the one who is stronger and bigger" (p. 41). Young Ju's father has set expectations about his own role as the authority in the family, and he wants to train his son to act in a prescribed way. He physically punishes his son for "whining like a girl" and denigrates his love of art, wanting to teach him hard lessons about what is required of a "man."

It is this notion of Korean manhood and identity that deepens the father's self-hatred. He senses that he is losing control of the family because he cannot speak English. When he takes Young Ju to the Department of Immigration to get a work permit, he is frustrated that he has to follow her lead. He demands that she translate what is said and he gets angry when she interrupts him. Moreover, he feels like a failure because he cannot provide more for the family. His disgust is heightened when his mother dies and he cannot afford to attend her funeral in Korea. He drinks and physically attacks his wife for considering him "worthless."

Adding to their disappointment is the parents' sense that their children are changing, "becoming too American." They are afraid of the harmful influence of American friends. Young Ju's questions show that she is being influenced by American ways. A good Korean girl would never question her parents, while "American girls do not study, they are boy-crazy, and they do not think of anyone but themselves" (p. 105). For her part, Young Ju is embarrassed by her family, their lack of material possessions, but most of all by their tension and anger. She wonders why her parents can't act like the parents of her American friend: "Why can't Apa barbecue and ask Uhmma if she needs help? Or Uhmma tease Apa and then lightly kiss him on the cheek to make sure he knows she was only kidding?" (p. 110).

Living outside of the Korean community, Young Ju's parents have few resources to cope with their problems until the mother decides to join a local Korean church where they can meet other people like themselves. Attending services with her children for the first time, the mother is uplifted by the ceremony and fellowship, which gives her hope. But her husband is so estranged that he avoids speaking to anyone in the congregation and refuses to see any connection between his experiences and that of other Korean immigrants.

With no outlets, the father's frustrations turn into anger, self-destructive actions, and eventually abuse of his family. In his need to prove that he is still the head of the family, he refuses to be questioned and he deals out harsh punishment when he thinks he is losing control of the children. Catching Young Ju in a lie about an American friend, he beats her and then turns on her mother, blaming her for the children's disobedience. This is his breaking point. His sense of self and manhood is so threatened that he decides he cannot continue to live in America. After he is arrested for spousal abuse, he abandons the family and decides to return to Korea. It is then that Young Ju's mother makes a decision that is unlike anything expected of a Korean wife. She decides to stay in America to give her children opportunities to study, to become strong and independent. So even though the mother has appeared to be the most pliant, she has been changing, finding a way to move beyond her traditional role to more independence and a belief in her ability to make a new place for herself and her children in America.

In this novel Na shows that the journey of emigrants to a strange land is difficult and can be emotionally damaging. Young Ju's parents come to America with hope for economic advancement, but the cost is too high for her father when it threatens his identity. Only years later, as she is preparing to leave for college, does Young Ju begin to understand her father. Seeing some old photos for the first time, she realizes that her mother came from a wealthier class than her father, which created the tension in their marriage. She senses how he felt when he was unable to provide more for his family, and she thinks that she didn't really know him. In another picture she can't recognize herself as a toddler in her father's arms playing in the waves. Young Ju's mother says he was so different then, that he was a dreamer just like Young Ju. She wants Young Ju to remember who she is. She says, "You come from a family of dreamers" (p. 152). She could be speaking for all immigrants who dream and imagine new beginnings in America. For some the promise is fulfilled, but some break under the strain.

Creating a New Identity

In Johnston's novel *Any Small Goodness*, the Rodriguez family adjusts to the new culture of the United States in a different way than the two families in the novels just explored. The Rodriguezes are not content to live in a separate community in which they re-create the culture of their homeland like Mai and other Hmong families. At the same time they are not broken by the conflict between their self-identity and the challenges of living in the United States like Young Ju's father. Instead Johnston shows how a strong sense of self fostered within a loving family enables these immigrants to celebrate who they are as well as discover the values of the new culture.

The Rodriguez family comes north from Mexico to Los Angeles, California, because the father needs better work. For them, this is no promised land but a scary place, a place of darkness. They fear the barrio with its dangerous gangs. Arturo compares gangs to "those saber-toothed tigers in pits of tar, kids get sucked into them" (p. 13). Los Angeles is "home to movie stars and crazies and crazy movie stars" (p. 8).

The book highlights a major problem of becoming "gringo-ized," of forgetting who you are. The first step happens in school when the teacher changes the children's Mexican names into Americanized versions. So "Arturo" becomes "Arthur." This happens to all the children: "There's Jaime and Alicia and Raul. Presto change-o! With one breath of teacher-magic, they're James and Alice and Ralph" (pp. 9–10). While the kids pretend that they don't care, that their new names make it easier to fit in, they also feel "erased." They have become someone else and they miss their old selves. Arturo's family hates his new name, especially his *abuelita* (grandmother) who says that this name "burns in my ears like poison" (p. 12). She knows that if Arturo allows his name to be taken away from him he will lose his identity and his connection to all the generations of his family. Hearing his grandmother's whispered prayer that he will recognize this consequence, Arturo has a sudden change of heart. He says, "What a *menso*-head I am.... To give up my name. It's to give up my family. To let myself—all of us—be erased to chalkboard dust" (p. 18). He and his friends make a pact to reclaim their names and their self-identity.

Arturo has this powerful support and example of self-respect from his family, and he also discovers examples of loving behavior in his new community. Mr. Leo Love, who lives on the edge of the barrio, rescues the family cat from his avocado tree despite his allergies and fear of heights. Arturo is also inspired by Coach Tree, his name for the former National Basketball Association player who coaches the local barrio school's team, not for money, just "for love only" (p. 45). Arturo also learns about Leona Scott, an African American woman and piano prodigy, who could have been a celebrity but chose to teach piano to kids in the barrio. She wanted to fulfill a promise that she had made to her teacher that she would pass on her talent to others. Arturo feels a special attachment to his school librarian, Ms. Cloud, who inspired his love of reading by helping him find books that speak to him. He hopes he can become a "book-warrior" like her some day.

These nurturing and creative behaviors contrast with the destructive acts of gang violence and intimidation, which bring fear and hopelessness into the community. These acts are so destructive that Arturo thinks that it isn't worth creating anything when it will just be destroyed. When his family is attacked in a drive-by shooting, Arturo becomes angry and distrusts everyone, even the police who investigate the crime. But the kindness of one officer acts as an antidote. Arturo's father says, "In life there is *bueno* and there is *malo*. If you do not find enough of the good, you must yourself create it" (p. 103). Arturo is able to take these words to heart, to choose kindness over anger. He and his friends create the "Green Needle Gang" to perform anonymous acts of kindness for the poor in the community. Arturo doesn't change who he is, instead, he recreates himself by drawing on the examples of those he meets in his new community. In his identity, he arrives at a new synthesis, a new American way.

Literature Response Activities

Following are several activities that encourage students to respond to the novels as well as engage in research and critical thinking about the issues of immigration. These activities can be adjusted to meet the needs of particular grade levels or individual groups of students.

Self-to-Text Reader Connections

In order to enable students to make connections with the experiences of the characters, ask them to write a letter addressing the main character in one of the contemporary realistic novels discussed in this chapter. The letter should have two main parts. First, students should tell the character what they admired about how he or she handled situations depicted in the novel. Then, students should write about connections they see between their life experiences and those of the characters.

Before beginning this writing, it would be useful to have students brainstorm about their connections to the main character with whom they feel the most empathy. This will give the student a bank of ideas to use when composing a letter.

Constructive Controversy Debate on U.S. Immigration

Immigration is a controversial issue that can lead to polarized and emotional responses. In order to engage students with the immigration experience and help them evaluate positive and negative responses to immigration, they can participate in a "constructive controversy" debate. In this debate they will argue first for one side and then the other. After engaging in this activity, students will think critically about the arguments on both sides of this issue. They can draw on their reading of these novels to think about the fears and difficulties experienced by immigrants and how they adjust or don't adjust to the challenges they face.

To begin, present your students with a controversial statement to debate, such as "Immigration is very positive for the United States," or "Immigrants are a strain on the communities in which they live." Divide students into small groups to prepare for the debate and assign them to argue either for or against. Then, ask students to brainstorm ideas by drawing on their reading of the novels and their personal experiences. Next, direct students to websites that offer both pro-

and anti-immigration arguments to generate facts for the side they have been assigned. The following are some suggested websites:

- Federation for American Immigration Reform at http://www.fairus.org
- Justice for Immigrants at http://www.justiceforimmigrants.org
- National Immigration Forum at http://immigrationforum.org

Once students have completed their small-group work, they are ready to work with other groups that have studied the same side.

The following list outlines the structure of the debate:

1. Divide the class in half according to the position, pro or con, that they will argue. Give students time to confer to generate a list of their best arguments and to designate several students who will present their consensus.
2. Once the debate begins, each side will have three minutes to present their arguments.
3. After both sides have presented, send students back to their small groups to discuss the arguments they have heard and to prepare to argue the opposite side.
4. Sides reconvene to organize their arguments, following the same format as earlier.
5. After both sides have presented, send students back to their small groups to confer about the strongest arguments they have heard, pro and con.
6. Discuss with the whole class what arguments they have chosen on both sides of the issue. Ask students if the argument is rational or emotional and how they can tell. Ask them what information helped create a strong argument for their position.

Influencing Pro-Immigrant Action

Immigration numbers and quotas are two sides of an issue frequently debated, but too often the personal stories of immigrants are lost. Now that students have read the novels and witnessed the immigration experiences of characters in the novels, they are in a unique position to describe the stresses experienced by immigrants, especially school-age children, in the United States. Using the novels as a resource, ask students to brainstorm all the difficulties faced by immigrants in schools as described by the authors. If possible, you may invite persons who have recently become U.S. immigrants into the class for a conversation about their experiences as students in public schools. You may direct students to look at websites about your school system that indicate the demographics of your schools and the teachers in the system.

Then, based on their review of the novels and research into local statistics, ask the students to write a letter to the school newspaper, principal of their school, or local board of education, describing the needs of immigrant students as they understand them and the ways in which schools can better meet the needs of diverse students. You may choose to have students share their individual letters in order to create a group or a whole-class letter that the class will actually send.

Conclusion

The books on immigration discussed in this chapter explore the difficult and ambiguous feelings of people who leave their homelands to begin life in a new land of promise. Some immigrants remember the experience with nostalgia even though it was incredibly difficult. Novels and picture books that depict the exodus of European immigrants at the end of the 19th century and beginning of the 20th century generally fall into this category. Recent novels tend to present a more complex assessment of immigration. Authors show that when people leave their homelands, adjustments are never easy and that some individuals decide that the price of living in America is too great. By exploring these complex reactions, authors give readers, preservice teachers, classroom teachers, and adolescents an opportunity to live through the experience and to feel firsthand the cost of a dream. In chapter 5, "Language Diversity in the United States and Issues of Linguistic Identity in a Global Society," Nancy L. Hadaway and Terrell A. Young explore in greater detail one particular aspect of adjustment: language.

REFERENCES

Note. Complete bibliographic citations for the Notable Books for a Global Society booklist (1996–2005) can be found at the end of the book.

Antin, M. (1912). *The promised land.* Boston: Houghton Mifflin.

Cohn, D. (2002, December 2). Immigrants account for half of new workers: Report calls them increasingly needed for economic growth. *The Washington Post.* Retrieved March 6, 2006, from http://www.immigrationforum.org/DesktopDefault.aspz?tabid=176

Congressional Budget Office. (2005) *The role of immigrants in the U.S. labor market* Retrieved March 26, 2007 from http://www.cbo.gov/ftpdocs/68xx/doc6853/11-10-Immigration.pdf

Department of Homeland Security Office of Immigration Statistics. (2005). *Temporary admissions of nonimmigrants to the United States in 2004.* Retrieved March 6, 2006, from http://uscis.gov/graphics/shared/statistics/index.htm

Federation for American Immigration Reform. (2006). *Public opinion polls on immigration.* Retrieved March 6, 2006, from http://www.fairus.org

Justice for Immigrants (2005) *Myths* Retrieved March 1, 2006, from
   http://www.justiceforimmigrants.org/myths.html
Larsen, L.J. (2004). *The foreign-born population in the United States: 2003* (Current Population
   Reports P20-551). Washington, DC: U.S. Census Bureau.
Lazarus, E. (1883). The new colossus [manuscript poem]. In *A century of immigration, 1820–1924*.
   Retrieved March 19, 2007, from http://www.loc.gov/exhibits/haventohome/haven-century.html
National Immigration Forum. (2005). *Immigrants and the economy*. Retrieved March 6, 2006, from
   http://www.immigrationforum.org

CHAPTER 5

Language Diversity in the United States and Issues of Linguistic Identity in a Global Society

Nancy L. Hadaway, Terrell A. Young

"A different language is a different vision of life."
—Federico Fellini (cited in ThinkExist.com Quotations, 2007, n.p.)

An estimated 6,000 to 7,000 languages are spoken around the world today (Crystal, 2000), and approximately 200 of these are designated as "main" languages as they have a million or more speakers (O'Neil, 2006). The United States, while predominantly an English-speaking country, also features a diverse representation of languages with almost 400 different languages spoken nationwide (Shin & Bruno, 2003). This language diversity may be most visible in U.S. schools, where English learners are the fastest growing population. About 3.9 million public school students were reported to be limited English proficient (LEP) in 2001, a number that nearly doubled in less than a decade (Kindler, 2002).

While the United States has become an increasingly diverse nation in terms of language backgrounds, the question of whether linguistic diversity is valued and accepted is open to debate. How are immigrants that speak a language other than English viewed? Do Americans regard language diversity as a resource to nurture and maintain at the same time building English-language development? How does America's stance on linguistic diversity and our own personal ability (or inability) to interact in other languages influence our relationships in a global society? Reflecting on the importance of language diversity in the United States as a microcosm of what is happening in our global society helps us begin to understand the language loss and "language death" (Crystal, 2000) that are

Breaking Boundaries With Global Literature: Celebrating Diversity in K–12 Classrooms, edited by Nancy L. Hadaway and Marian J. McKenna. © 2007 by the International Reading Association.

occurring at a rapid pace. UNESCO (2005) has even published an online *Atlas of the World's Languages in Danger of Disappearing*, which is available at www. unesco.org/webworld/babel/atlas.

This chapter considers the aforementioned questions and concerns through an analysis of recent children's and young adult books that address issues of language diversity in the United States and its impact on linguistic identity in a global society. Books from the Notable Books for a Global Society booklists from 1996 to 2005 that address language diversity, as well as other topically related books that speak to language diversity, will be examined. After a historical overview of language diversity in the United States, the chapter first offers examples of books with information about other languages and bilingual books in several formats. Then, the chapter considers language diversity from a personal perspective, spotlighting literature about children and adults who have moved to the United States and are in the process of learning English or about individuals who are trying to reconnect with their linguistic roots. Finally, the chapter suggests a variety of Literature Response Activities, applicable for grades K through 12, that will help educators integrate the topic of language diversity and linguistic identity into classrooms.

Most of the books highlighted in this chapter are picture books that can be used to affirm the many adjustments encountered by English learners, and these books can also be used to build awareness among younger monolingual English speakers of the transitions required in learning a new language. In addition, the concerns addressed in picture books and novels about language diversity offer an introduction to complex issues that can be used as discussion points for older students in middle school and high school as well as with professionals in K through 12 schools or in teacher education. Consequently, educators can use this chapter not only to discover examples of children's and young adult literature that speak to language diversity for use in K through 12 classroom instruction but also for their own professional development to learn about the process and issues involved in language acquisition.

A Historical Overview of U.S. Language Diversity

From the beginning, language diversity has been a way of life in America (Crawford, 1999). Yet through its history America has had an inconsistent love affair with multilingualism. Early immigrants worked to maintain their home language and supported legislation enacted in more than 12 states mandating bilingual education in Swedish, Danish, Norwegian, Italian, Polish, Dutch, and Greek. (See chapter 4 for more detailed discussion of immigration in the United States and booklist titles that can be used for exploring this topic in the classroom.) After the swell of immigration from 1890–1920, however, restrictive national immigration quotas with literacy requirements were enacted, and many states passed laws forbidding foreign languages in schools and mandating English-only instruction. Students were often punished for using their home language, as illustrated in the nonfiction picture book *Harvesting Hope: The Story of Cesar Chavez* (Krull, 2003/2004 NBGS). When young César Chávez broke the rule about speaking English only, "a teacher hung a sign on him that read, I am a clown. I speak Spanish" (n.p.). The prohibition on speaking other languages also applied to teachers who could be fined, fired, or lose their teaching certificate for using a language other than English on school grounds (Crawford, 1999).

During this same time, Native Americans were often encouraged or forced to send their children to government-run boarding schools such as the Carlisle Indian Industrial School (1879–1928) so they could "unlearn their Indian ways." At school, the children were forbidden to speak their native languages, situations poignantly described in picture books such as *Bright Path: Young Jim Thorpe* (Brown, 2006) and *Home to Medicine Mountain* (Santiago, 1998) and also touched upon in the novels *Sweetgrass Basket* (Carvell, 2005) and *Code Talker: A Novel About the Navajo Marines of World War II* (Bruchac, 2005).

World War II deepened language divisions even more, and language difference was viewed as suspect. Cynthia Kadohata's novel *Weedflower* (2006) sensitively depicts the fear among Japanese Americans after the bombing of Pearl Harbor. Readers feel Sumiko's pain as her aunt demands that all vestiges of the Japanese language—magazines, newspapers, even the notebooks that Sumiko uses to practice Japanese—be burned.

After World War II, the launch of Sputnik triggered concerns about weaknesses in the U.S. educational system and sparked a renewal of interest in an academic curriculum including foreign-language instruction. Then, in 1965, the Bilingual Education Act was signed into law to assist growing numbers of non-English–speaking schoolchildren. The most recent U.S. census figures report a non-English language spoken in 18% (or one in six) U.S. households (Shin & Bruno, 2003). This is a level of linguistic diversity not seen in the United States since the immigration surge of the late 19th and early 20th century. Thus, immigration (as discussed in chapter 4) and language diversity have moved to the forefront of the U.S. media, and, echoing the reactions to language diversity and immigration in the past, there have been renewed calls for English-only restrictions and the passage of legislation enforcing these restrictions, such as California's Proposition 227 that stresses the need for students to be taught primarily in English. Some U.S. citizens feel that the increase in language diversity in the United States has led to a resistance among immigrants to learn English and to assimilate into mainstream culture, though demographic research shows a different trend, as immigrants are making the transition to English and heritage language loss is occurring more rapidly than ever before (Crawford, 1999).

Despite the push to restrict non-English–language usage, many Americans view the study of a foreign language in a positive light. In a national survey by the American Council on Education (2005), over 85% of the respondents indicated that knowledge of a foreign language was important. Moreover, as a result of leadership by the American Council on the Teaching of Foreign Languages, 2005 was designated as the Year of Languages in the United States. Nevertheless, when speakers of other languages become U.S. immigrants, the heritage, or home, language is seen as an obstacle, a negative factor in the process of assimilation and acquisition of English.

Promoting Awareness of Language Diversity Through Literature

Outside the United States, spoken English has a wide geographic distribution, particularly in terms of electronic communication. Still, English is a distant third among the most common languages in the world. Mandarin Chinese has almost three times the number of native speakers, and Hindi has several million more than English (O'Neil, 2006). Such statistics underscore the need to consider a broader view of language in the curriculum.

Bilingual and Interlingual Books

Despite the historical and more recent resistance to language diversity in the United States, one indication of movement toward awareness and acceptance is literature published for children and young adults that introduces, reinforces, or informs readers about other languages. For instance, in the United States, there has been an increase in the number of bilingual books published for children in a variety of formats (Ernst-Slavit & Mulhern, 2003) from those with the complete text in two languages, such as *In My Family/En Mi Familia* (Garza, 1996/1997 NBGS), to those published in different versions, one book for each language, such as *Too Many Tamales* (Soto, 1993) and *¡Qué Montón de Tamales!* (Soto, 1996), as well as books in English interspersed with words and phrases from another language, such as *Confetti: Poems for Children* (Mora, 1996/1997 NBGS). While the majority of books with complete text in two languages are English/Spanish, many other languages are being used in children's literature, as reported in the first Bilingual Books for Children Booklist from the Association for Library Service to Children (2005). This list of books of high literary quality published from 1995 to 1999 included selections in Chinese, Hopi, Inuktitut,

Japanese, Khmer, Korean, Russian, Swahili, Thai, Tibetan, Vietnamese, and, of course, Spanish.

The 249 Notable Books for a Global Society booklist selections from 1996–2005 clearly reflect the recent increase in the publication of bilingual books

"Words Free as Confetti"

PAT MORA

"Come words, come in your every color." When I wrote these words, the first line of the poem "Words Free as Confetti" (from *Confetti: Poems for Children*, 1996/1997 NBGS), I was thinking of the wonder and variety of my tools as a writer. Since I'm a bilingual writer, I was also thinking of how blessed I feel to be able to sort through and select words with different sounds and textures. *Bird* and *pájaro* may mean the same feathered creature, but each word enters us in a different way.

In the poem for teens "Ode to Pizza" in *My Own True Name* (2000), I included the word for *cheese* in 16 languages. What fun! Culture is embedded in language. Sharing words, like all sharing, creates a connection, in this case, a bridge constructed of letters. How we need bridges and connections in our blue planet on which we zip off e-mails, often to people like us in educational and economic level, and yet may have trouble relating to fellow community residents who don't look or act or sound like us.

When wisely used, open books-open worlds-open hearts. Those of us who knew bookjoy as children, know how far we traveled and learned—not only facts like the plush clothes worn by royalty long ago; we felt how Anne Frank was like us, a girl full of longing. We became more human.

One in five children in our country speaks a language other than English at home. Our "global society" exists outside and inside our country. *Confetti*, now out in Spanish as *Confeti: Poemas Para Niños* (2006), celebrates Mexico, the Southwest desert, and customs and values found there. I chose the title because children delight in the freedom of tossing colored bits of paper. Words and literacy are also liberating. Sharing our pleasures helps unite our human family.

Book by Pat Mora selected for the Notable Books for a Global Society:
Confetti: Poems for Children (1996/1997 NBGS)

(see this book's online supplement on the International Reading Association's website at www.reading.org for a complete listing of bilingual books included on the booklist). This collection of books includes 66 works: 6 bilingual books with complete text in English/Spanish, 4 bilingual books with separate versions in English and Spanish, and 56 interlingual books. The interlingual books reflected tremendous language diversity with 27 different languages. Some books used more than one language other than English, as was the case with *No Pretty Pictures: A Child of War* (Lobel, 1998/1999 NBGS), which had German, Polish, and Swedish integrated into the text. Spanish was the predominant language among bilingual books on the Notable Books for a Global Society booklists, but other languages included Amharic, Arabic, Chamoru, Chinese, Farsi/Dari, French, German, Hebrew, Hindi, Japanese, Korean, Maasia, Polish, Sanskrit, Spanish, Swedish, Tamil, Vietnamese, Yiddish, and 7 Native American languages: Abenaki, Ojibwa, Quiche, Athabascan, Lakota, Kwakwala, and Iñupiaq.

Certainly, bilingual books can be a positive reflection of the linguistic diversity of the classroom. For English learners, bilingual books support English acquisition by connecting the new language with the more familiar home language. In addition, for children who are already literate in their first language, these books offer exposure to their new language in meaningful formats, ones that affirm children's cultural backgrounds and that might possibly encourage language maintenance not just a transition to English only. However, bilingual books are not just for culturally and linguistically diverse students: It is beneficial for all students to be given opportunities to see the diversity of languages in the United States. Although students are sometimes aware of the prevalence of Spanish in the United States (almost 80% of English learners in school are native Spanish speakers [Kindler, 2002]), they may be completely unaware of the many other languages used in their community or state.

As a word of caution, some criticisms have been leveled against bilingual books (Edwards & Walker, 1995; Walker, Edwards, & Blacksell, 1996). For instance, the presentation on the page may give one language precedence or higher status through the order of appearance as well as differences in font size, boldness, or spacing between lines, difference in type quality between the scripts (such as a non-Roman versus Roman alphabet), and differences in directionality (e.g., English is read from left to right, Urdu is read from right to left). Finally, translations may be plagued by literal renditions that lack the flow of the native language as well as by incorrect lexical constructions; unclear phrases; awkward expressions; and grammatical, spelling, or typographical errors (Schon, 2004). Rather than quickly embracing any bilingual book for classroom use, teachers unfamiliar with a particular language should consult colleagues who are native speakers of the language, seek out book reviews online and in professional journals, or become familiar with the recommendations of experts such as Isabel Schon, who regularly publishes recommended lists of books in Spanish (for example, see her list of recommended books in Spanish on the American Library Association's website at www.ala.org/ala/booklist/speciallists/speciallistsand features1/SpanishBks.htm).

Learning About Languages

While bilingual books showcase language by telling the same story in more than one language, they do not directly inform the reader about language. Another way of gauging awareness and support for linguistic diversity is to look at books that specifically address language. Though children's and young adult titles on this topic can be hard to come by, there are some excellent books that can be used to expand reader awareness. *People* (Spier, 1980), though not wholly devoted to the topic of language, is still an outstanding example. Spier devotes four pages of this picture book on diversity to language, noting that "there are 201 main languages spoken on earth...not to mention the countless variants and dialects spoken by smaller groups" (n.p.). In addition, he shares that the deaf can communicate through sign language, and the hand signs for each letter of the alphabet are provided. Finally, a stunning two-page spread illustrates the many writing systems around the world with 40 examples of different alphabets and scripts from Greek to Japanese—a powerful reminder of linguistic diversity in print. *Scripts of the World* (Bukiet, 1993) offers an overview of writing systems with five types highlighted: Chinese, Latin, Indian, Arabic, and Cyrillic. It may also help to discover the many words in English that have been borrowed from other languages—"*camel* from Hebrew, *piano* from Italian, *zero* from Arabic" (*The Journey of English*, Brook, 1998, p. 43). When the Normans invaded England in 1066 and conquered the Anglo Saxons, French became the language of government adding such words as *authority*, *council*, *crown*, *empire*, *judge*, *jury*, *liberty*, *mayor*, *parliament*, *prince*, *tax*, *treaty*, and *treasurer* to the English lexicon (p. 20). Also, "over half of American states' names are from Native American languages. Alabama, Alaska, Connecticut, Idaho, Massachusetts, Oklahoma, and Tennessee are just a few of them" (p. 36).

Finally, it is important to acknowledge the many languages around the world that exist in spoken form only and the work of individuals who keep languages alive by creating a written form of the spoken words of a group. Crawford (1999) highlights the critical nature of language loss in Native American communities, noting "one-third of indigenous tongues have disappeared since the coming of Columbus" (n.p.). Further, extrapolating from recent declines among speakers of Navajo, Crow, Hualapai, Choctaw, and Tohono O'odham, Crawford cautions that "virtually all Native American languages could be extinct within two or three generations" (n.p). And so the publication of *Sequoyah: The Cherokee Man Who Gave His People Writing* (Rumford, 2004) was especially timely. Sequoyah was responsible for creating the Cherokee syllabary, thus giving that language a written form. This bilingual biography in English/Cherokee tells the story of Sequoyah and how his work allowed the printing of materials in Cherokee, as a result ensuring the survival of that language.

Exploring Themes of Linguistic Identity in Literature

While bilingual and language books provide a window to view linguistic diversity, books about the personal cultural and linguistic adjustments involved in learning a new language are another important resource for considering our global society. Reading books that touch on the themes discussed in this section—the discomfort of learning a new language, the length of the acquisition process, or the emotional impact of language loss or struggling to maintain one's home language—help educate *all* students, not just English learners, about language diversity. Most of the books cited in this section are picture books that reflect contemporary immigration and language-learning situations of young children in the elementary grades, but their experiences mirror those of older students and can certainly be used to introduce and discuss issues of language learning across the grade levels. Moreover, some of the authors, such as Aliki, Juan Felipe Herrera, and Amada Perez, were immigrants and English learners themselves, and these books, though not autobiographical, nonetheless depict events from their own lives. Finally, it is important to note that while many good examples of the language-adjustment process are presented in the books in the chapter, none of them describes a full assimilation or acculturation.

Adjustment to a New Language and Culture

Every day, families move across geographic boundaries and must adopt a new language for daily interactions at school and at work. In the United States, where other languages are not historically a mandatory part of many curricula, the general public often expects these learners to be "up and running" with their new language in a relatively short period of time. Moreover, a belief exists "that [individuals] can discard their old cultural values [and languages] and replace them with new ones as easily as they throw away old shoes and get a new pair" (Igoa, 1995, p. 44). These are unrealistic expectations, no matter what the language or geographic setting. Language and culture are inextricably connected.

For English learners, entering school and interacting with teachers and peers in an unfamiliar language at the same time they are learning a new language and concepts across the curriculum is a frightening and frustrating experience. Igoa (1995) identifies six stages of adjustment that provide an excellent lens to examine children's and young adult books that attempt to portray this process. This section highlights these stages—mixed emotions, excitement and fear, curiosity, culture shock, assimilation, and feeling grounded—through an examination of children's and young adult literature that reflects issues that may occur in the language-acquisition process. Educators can use these stages as a guide when working with English learners and can use the suggested books to help affirm English learners and to foster understanding of language difference and language acquisition among native-English–speaking peers.

In the first stages of adjustment, children feel mixed emotions about moving to a new country or going to school. In the bilingual picture book *My Diary From Here to There/Mi Diario de Aquí Hasta Allá* (Pérez, 2002), we meet Amada, who is anxious amidst her family's excitement about their move from Mexico to Los Angeles, California, USA. She uses her diary to share her worry that she won't be able to learn English. Different from taking a foreign-language class for one period a day, Amada is about to walk into a school where every class is conducted in English. She will be expected to learn not only a new language but also new concepts in that language.

The next stage of adjustment is characterized by excitement or fear. In *La Mariposa* (Jiménez, 1998), we meet Francisco, whose initial excitement about beginning first grade in the United States ends abruptly when he boards the bus and doesn't understand the new language he is hearing. His fear only escalates in school where he doesn't understand the teacher, and then at recess he is admonished for speaking Spanish to a classmate.

Once children enter school, a natural curiosity may take hold as they try to adjust to their new environment. In the picture book *I Hate English!* (Levine, 1995), Mei Mei has just moved from Hong Kong and she does not want to learn English. After a long period of refusing to speak at school, she is eventually paired with a tutor who takes her for a walk through Chinatown and allows her to just listen. Once Mei Mei is allowed this comfort zone, she begins to talk to her tutor to make sense of her new surroundings.

Over time, the conflict between the new environment and the child's existing set of rules leads to culture shock, and children feel a sense of depression, confusion, and isolation as they experience a new language and culture. This sense of isolation is spotlighted in several books. After moving to Iowa, USA, from India, *Blue Jasmine's* 12-year-old protagonist, Sheema, struggles with American English and customs, noting, "I was always the outsider listening in" (Sheth, 2004). Again, this sense of isolation is shown in the picture book *One Green Apple* (Bunting, 2006). Farah, a young Muslim immigrant, feels alone and unwilling to risk speaking in this new language. She notes that "I am tight inside myself" (n.p.). Even writing one's name in a new language can evoke sadness as in *My Name Is Yoon*. Yoon doesn't like the way that her Korean name looks in English. "I did not like YOON. Lines. Circles. Each standing alone" (Recorvits, 2003/2004 NBGS).

As children grow accustomed to their new environment, they begin to experience some assimilation or acculturation. Assimilation into the classroom and school routine can be fostered by caring teachers who provide support to English learners. *The Upside Down Boy/El Niño de Cabeza* (Herrera, 2000/2001 NBGS) and *The Color of Home* (Hoffman, 2002/2003 NBGS) offer examples of teachers who help children work through their communication difficulties and adjustment issues with music and art activities in the classroom. In a note from the author, Herrera dedicates his book to Mrs. Sampson, the third-grade teacher, "who first inspired me to be a singer of words, and most of all, a believer in my own voice" (n.p.).

Finally, children move into the mainstream culture and they feel more "grounded." In *I Love Saturdays y Domingos* (Ada, 2002/2003 NBGS), the reader encounters a young girl who successfully navigates two language worlds—one with her paternal grandparents in English and the other with her maternal grandparents in Spanish. Because this young girl must have grown up in a bilingual home, her situation doesn't necessarily portray the adjustments of immigrants who must learn English from the beginning in school. As a point of contrast with the more contemporary depictions of language adjustment already presented, in *Streets of Gold* (Wells, 1999/2000 NBGS) Mary, an immigrant in the late 19th century, appears to be firmly grounded in her new world, willing to exchange her name as well as her home language for English in school. Unfortunately, this book offers a limited and unrealistic portrait of the language-adjustment process with little struggle to learn the language presented. Moreover, it reflects the often-heard assertion of past immigrants—"I learned English without any help, so why shouldn't today's immigrants do so as well?" Teachers might use books such as this to compare the differences in attitudes toward language adjustment in the United States over time and point out contradictions.

Again, none of the books highlighted in this chapter describes the complexities and full extent of assimilation or acculturation experiences. Most books tend to leave the "story" at some sort of initial resolution of the issues related to language adjustment. Yet the time to reach this beginning assimilation point may be lengthy. In *La Mariposa* (Jiménez, 1998), for instance, Francisco takes a full year to begin to gain confidence.

Issues Involved in Children's Language Acquisition

As Igoa's stages illustrate, cultural adjustment takes time and work, but the process of actual language acquisition may be even more time-consuming. After a semester or so in a bilingual or English as a second language class, children may appear to have an adequate mastery of the language, but often they really have mastered only some basic conversational or survival skills. What students need for success in school is formal listening, speaking, reading, and writing skills related to academic content (Cummins, 2003). The road to that level of language proficiency for the English learner may take five years or more (Thomas & Collier, 1995). All the while, their English-dominant peers are continuing to push forward, learning new concepts without the additional responsibility of learning them in a new language. Therefore, children experience a complex range of issues with content learning and the development of their identities, some of which are explored in literature.

Taken as a whole, there are few examples of literature that realistically depict the long and difficult process of language acquisition. Readers see the beginning of the process as children first encounter the discomfort of fitting into a new language environment, but they are rarely taken past that point. Moreover, the movement is toward English with little mention of maintaining and fully developing literacy in the home language or of sharing the home language to help expand the world of English speakers. As educators, we must consider what these books communicate to us as well as to English learners and their monolingual English-speaking peers.

Discomfort With Using a New Language. When Juanito (*The Upside Down Boy/El Niño de Cabeza*, Herrera, 2000/2001 NBGS) speaks English, "his tongue feels like a rock." This is understandable when one considers the process of first-language acquisition. Children learn the sounds of their own language naturally, but as they grow older it becomes more difficult to learn the sounds that are not part of the home language. Therefore, they handle the new sounds and structures by using knowledge of the home language, often resulting in mispronunciation and accented speech. Language learning also requires the speaker to take risks by making hypotheses about how the new language works and testing these out, which leads to occasional errors. Sadly, children at school (and adults as well) can be insensitive at this point in the language-acquisition process. As a result, English learners may be teased and, consequently, withdraw, as depicted in the poem "Invisible" from *My Name Is Jorge on Both Sides of the River* (Medina, 1999). Jorge feels so uncomfortable in the classroom that he wishes to become invisible.

It's very safe

being invisible,

I'm perfect!

I can't make mistakes

—at least

nobody sees them,

so nobody laughs. (p. 8)

The Gradual Process of Learning a New Language. To add to the frustration level, the progression toward fluency and proficiency in a new language is often slower than most learners would like. In the preproduction phase, most learners need a "silent period," such as that adopted by Mei Mei in *I Hate English!* (Levine, 1995), in order to listen to the language and become acclimated to the new sounds and structures. This can be a confusing period, as the learner sorts through a great deal of "noise" to comprehend the basics. Yet very little, if any, of that comprehension can be expressed. This is clearly described through the inner voice of Farah while on the class field trip in *One Green Apple* (Bunting, 2006).

> Our teacher gathers us around her. She talks to the class. Then she looks at me in a kind way. "One," she says. She touches an apple, then picks it. "One," she says again. I am to take only one, as the other students have done. I nod. I want to say, "I understand. It's not that I am stupid. It is just that I am lost in this new place." But I don't know how to tell her. (p. 12)

After days or months in an initial preproduction or "silent period," children move to the stage of early production with survival vocabulary and very basic sentence structure (Hadaway, Vardell, & Young, 2002). In the bilingual (English/Korean) picture book *Aekyung's Dream* (Paek, 1988), for instance, Aekyung is able to speak only limited English after six months in America, and she must continue to face her classmates' teasing. To complicate things further, some older immigrant children are placed at grade levels below their chronological age because of limited English proficiency. Such is the case in *Don't Call Me Slob-O* (Orgel, 1996). Slobodan, a recent immigrant, is placed two grade levels below his age, so in addition to his struggles with a new language he must also deal with the differences in age and maturity of his classmates.

Finding Creative Ways to Communicate. During this time of language emergence, English learners sometimes find creative means to communicate across language barriers. In so doing, they begin to conquer their fears and lack of confidence and continue to develop language. Several children's books offer examples of this process. As previously noted, *The Upside Down Boy/El Niño de Cabeza* (Herrera, 2000/2001 NBGS) and *The Color of Home* (Hoffman, 2002/2003 NBGS) both describe how young boys are able to "speak" English through their artwork. *Marianthe's Story: Painted Words/Spoken Memories* (Aliki, 1998/1999 NBGS) presents "two" stories. In the first, told in third-person narrative, Mari's adjustments to America are described, and though Mari is not able to speak English she learns that art can transcend her language difficulties to some extent. Then, when the reader flips the book over, Mari tells about her home country and why she came to America in first-person narrative. In addition to art, drama can be an effective tool for communicating across language boundaries. In *In English, Of Course* (Nobisso, 2003), Josephine wants to tell her new classmates all about her home in Naples, but she hasn't acquired enough English to do so. Instead, she chooses to tell the class about a visit she once paid to a farm—an easier oral communication option at her English proficiency level. Josephine uses her limited knowledge of English with teacher support and then supplies the rest of the meaning by acting out the sequence of events through creative nonverbal dramatics. In this way, she is able to share and become part of the class.

Serving as Interpreters for Adults Who Speak Their First Language. Once children move beyond initial communication barriers and develop their English, they are often called upon to serve as interpreters for adults in their environment. While functioning in this role can build confidence in language ability, it can also be a heavy responsibility for a child. In *I Speak English for My Mom* (Stanek, 1989), Lupe helps her mother in almost every aspect of daily life—shopping in stores where Spanish is not spoken, going to the doctor for check-ups, and attending parent–teacher conferences. *Speak English for Us, Marisol* (English, 2000) is another picture book example illustrating the important role of interpreter that children serve in the neighborhood outside the family circle.

Losing Touch With Home Language and Culture. The picture book *I Hate English!* (Levine, 1995) depicts the inner struggle of Mei Mei, a young immigrant. As she begins to acquire more English, she worries that she will lose touch with her native heritage, culture, and language. These are real concerns for children (and families). On one hand, parents exert pressure for their children to learn English, so they can be a part of this new home. Yoon, for instance, works hard to please her parents by learning an unfamiliar language (*My Name Is Yoon*, Recorvits, 2003/2004 NBGS). Conversely, once children move toward English, they often move *away* from their home language, failing to develop that language fully, which can build barriers in communicating with the family and neighborhood setting, on visits back home, or with extended family members. Several picture books illustrate how family members communicate across the linguistic hurdle. In *Dear Juno*, Juno and his Korean grandmother use nonverbal symbols such as drawings and objects in their correspondence with each other (Pak, 1999). And in *Sitti's Secrets* Sitti and her Palestinian grandmother invent their own language with signs and hums and claps (Nye, 1994).

Recapturing Linguistic Roots. Loss of the home language comes quickly, often by the second generation. Some children are fortunate enough to be able to visit relatives and learn about their cultural and linguistic roots. Such is the case in the book *Shanghai Messenger* (Cheng, 2005), written in free verse, as 11-year old Xiao Mei travels to Shanghai to spend the summer with Uncle Hai Tao's family. There she learns about wontons, tai chi, and her mother's native language, Mandarin. A similar portrait is painted in the picture book *The Trip Back Home* (Wong, 2000/2001 NBGS), recalling a young girl's trip to Korea with her mother to visit her grandparents and aunt. In this story, the young girl shares her language by bringing an alphabet book in English that she and her aunt can read together. To reciprocate, farewell gifts include an original poem written in Korean to take back home to America. In *Uncle Rain Cloud* (Johnston, 2001/2002 NBGS), readers encounter a small glimpse of language maintenance as Uncle Tomas teaches nephew Carlos the stories of his ancestors, in the hopes of helping him hold on to his Spanish-language heritage.

Recapturing linguistic roots by moving from English back to the home language of the parent is a less common theme. Nevertheless, *Tea With Milk* (Say, 1999/2000 NBGS) presents Masako, who graduates from high school in America and unwillingly moves to Japan with her parents and rebels at her parents' urging to learn "her own language." Liyana in *Habibi* (Nye, 1997/1998 NBGS) is unhappy when her father moves the family from St. Louis, Missouri, USA, to his homeland of Palestine, and she must forge a relationship with relatives, all of whom speak a language different from her own.

Sharing Language Roots. Another undeveloped theme is sharing language roots. English learners have much to contribute, not only in telling about their home country, as in *Marianthe's Story: Painted Words/Spoken Memories* (Aliki, 1998/1999 NBGS), but also in sharing their home language. English learners are a wonderful resource; they could share much to enrich the understanding of their monolingual English-speaking peers. Readers do glimpse a bit of this process in *Tomás and the Library Lady* (Mora, 1997) as Tomás and the librarian reach out to one another and teach one another some basic English and Spanish words and phrases. And *Say Hola, Sarah* (Giff, 1998) introduces readers to Sarah whose friend, Ana Ortiz, helps Sarah with her Spanish project.

Adults and Language Learning

Although the language-learning experience for children can be frustrating and frightening, adults allow more latitude to children in terms of language use. There is an expectation that children have not "finished" learning the language, as adults expect them to make some errors. For adults, on the other hand, the ability to speak a language, and to do so competently, plays a substantial role in how well they perform critical daily activities such as grocery shopping and banking, communicating with public officials and service providers, and interviewing for and carrying out jobs successfully. The importance of language use to adults is clearly indicated by the U.S. census designation "linguistically isolated": "A linguistically isolated household is one in which no person aged 14 or over speaks English at least 'Very well'" (Shin & Bruno, 2003). So even if a child under 14 speaks only English, a household will still be categorized as linguistically isolated. In the United States, "In 2000, 4.4 million households encompassing 11.9 million people were linguistically isolated" (Shin & Bruno, 2003).

Learning a language as an adult is difficult. Inhibitions seem to increase with adolescence, and these inhibitions limit learning—in particular, the willingness to undertake the trial-and-error process of learning a language. For adults, limited English proficiency means a different kind of awkwardness than it means for children, such as problems finding work and sometimes taking work that is more menial than their education level or work experience from the home country might indicate. In *A Step From Heaven* (Na, 2001/2002 NBGS), the language barrier after immigration results in several low-paying jobs for Young Ju's father, and he becomes bitter and abusive to his wife and daughter. Eventually, the father returns to Korea, leaving the family in America.

Adults may begin to feel helpless and useless, especially when their children must navigate everyday life events. Uncle Tomas in *Uncle Rain Cloud* (Johnston, 2001/2002 NBGS) "feels like a broken-winged bird" because he knows only a few words of English and his nephew, Carlos, must translate at a teacher conference and help him shop at the supermarket. Moreover, adults may experience a feeling of estrangement from their children as youngsters enter school and become more and more a part of an English-speaking world. "Elena," a poem from *My Own True Name* (Mora, 2000, p. 40), poignantly portrays a mother whose children "go to American high schools./They speak English./At night they sit around/the kitchen table, laugh with one another." Her closing line clearly shows the widening gap between her and her children: "I stand by the stove and feel dumb, alone." The feelings of separation that arise as family members acquire English often lead to conflict within the family as children adopt American cultural ways as well as language.

For adults, the price of language difference can be quite steep. They have less time and sometimes less structured support to learn the necessary English in order to participate fully in the adult world of work and caring for a family in their new environment. In addition, the differences in children's and adults' ability to use their new language can create not only a communication barrier but also a cultural division. Thus, educators need to be aware of the many affective as well as linguistic difficulties that students' parents may experience.

Literature Response Activities

Through literature, readers can gain an appreciation for language diversity and the issues surrounding language acquisition and language use. To draw readers further into the themes and topics highlighted in this literature, there are a variety of reader-response strategies that teachers might choose and use in grades K through 12. Educators' most important goal should be to find the best books to share in classrooms that develop awareness and understanding of the diversity of languages used to communicate in the global community and the role that language plays in self-identity and self-concept.

Visual Displays Celebrating Language Diversity

Teachers can celebrate the language diversity at the school, district, or community level in many ways. Classrooms can create a community snapshot by locating local businesses, churches, billboards, or other publicly displayed items written in other languages and taking snapshots of these to create a graphic display in the classroom. A variation of this linked to real-world print would be to have students bring food labels, pamphlets, the front pages of newspapers, or other texts in different languages and fashioning a bulletin board with those. An extension on this activity is to explore how English has been borrowed by the languages of other countries. Also, librarians can join the celebration and create a display of bilingual or interlingual books.

Mapping Language Influence in U.S. Geography

As noted on page 99, many geographical names were borrowed from Native American languages. To reinforce the influence that many languages have had on English place names and geographical vocabulary, the class can research geographical names and terms that were borrowed from another language. A website such as www.xmission.com/~amauta/images/namestate.pdf is a helpful resource. A running list can also be kept on a class word wall (see Table 5.1 for a possible format) as students encounter new examples in different units of study.

Table 5.1. Mapping Language Influence in U.S. Geography

Geographical Name/Term	Language of Origin	Meaning
Alabama	May come from Choctaw	Thicket-clearers or vegetation-gatherers
Alaska	Corruption of Aleut	Great land or that which the sea breaks against
Colorado	Spanish	Ruddy or red
Sangre de Cristo Mountains	Spanish	Literally the "blood of Christ" in reference to the red glow on the mountains from the setting sun
Canyon	Spanish	Deep gorge

If the specific meaning or story behind the name is not known, students might even write fictionalized stories about the naming event. For instance, the Brazos River in Texas, USA, is supposedly named for *los brazos de Dios* (or "the arms of God"). In groups, students can brainstorm the conditions or events along the way that led explorers to name the river and then write their own versions to share with the class. An extension of this activity is to have students research the influence of other languages on countries outside the United States.

Mapping Language Diversity

Teachers can assign different time periods to groups of students who then research immigration statistics for that era along with the languages that these individuals brought to America. To delve further into this topic, students can also find out where these immigrants have settled in the United States and how this group may have shaped language or life in that area. As an extension, students can write fictionalized journal entries about the language adjustment of one immigrant child or teen from their group. To help create an authentic voice for these entries, students will need to investigate the similarities and differences in the languages.

Another extension for learning about geography and language diversity is to map where languages are spoken throughout the world. It is surprising to note the many countries that speak French beyond the borders of France, for instance. Or, as noted earlier, English is one of the most widespread languages used in the world, an official language in 52 countries (O'Neil, 2006).

Read-Alouds and Read-Alongs

Teachers can invite the parents of English learners or other community members who are fluent in another language to read aloud to their class, and a bilingual book with versions in two languages or with text in both languages can be spotlighted. As a class activity, the teacher can select bilingual or interlingual poetry, create a transparency of the poem, and lead the class in a read-along. Different poetry performance or choral reading techniques can be used (for example, assigning Spanish words and phrases to student volunteers who have been coached by parents or community members and then having them chime in at the appropriate place in the read-along).

Conclusion

The examples of books shared in this chapter illustrate that a basic introduction to the idea of language diversity and linguistic adjustment is present but not fully developed. The reader is exposed to only part of the story, and much of the emphasis is on the current social and educational philosophy that pervades the United States: English learners need to make the transition to their new language as quickly as possible. While we would certainly support the goal that immigrants learn English so that they can participate fully in work and school, play and service in their new environment, we contend that much is lost by ignoring the linguistic heritage that individuals bring to the process of learning English. The United States has long had the reputation of monolingualism, denying the importance of learning other languages or encouraging dual language development. However, fear and intolerance of differences, whether they be language, religion, or worldviews, can be a divisive element in society and may even lead to conflict or war, as discussed in the next chapter on "Resilient Children in Times of War."

Therefore, let us celebrate and educate students about language diversity. After all, language is more than just the sounds and symbols used to convey meaning; there is an affective component to language as well. Language is the "pliable adhesive" we use to "bind together nations, communities, societies, groups, and personal relationships. Through language, we give voice to ideas, dreams, despairs, hopes, fears, memories of yesterday, visions of tomorrow" (Andrews, 1993, p. xv).

REFERENCES

Note. Complete bibliographic citations for the Notable Books for a Global Society booklist (1996–2005) can be found at the end of the book.

American Council on Education. (2005). *Public experience, attitudes, and knowledge: A report on two national surveys about international education*. Retrieved July 13, 2006, from http://www.acenet.edu/AM/Template.cfm?Section=Activities&TEMPLATE=/CM/HTMLDisplay.cfm&CONTENTID=6045

Andrews, L. (1993). *Language exploration and awareness: A resource book for teachers*. Mahwah, NJ: Erlbaum.

Association for Library Service to Children. (2005). *Bilingual books for children booklist*. Retrieved June 7, 2006, from http://www.ala.org/ala/alsc/alscresources/booklists/bilingualbooks.htm

Crystal, D. (2000). *Language death*. Cambridge, MA: Cambridge University Press.

Crawford, J. (1999). *Heritage languages in America: Tapping a "hidden" resource*. Retrieved June 6, 2006, from http://ourworld.compuserve.com/homepages/JWCRAWFORD/HL.htm

Cummins, J. (2003). Reading and the bilingual student: Fact and friction. In G. Garcia (Ed.), *English learners: Reaching the highest levels of English literacy* (pp. 2–33). Newark, DE: International Reading Association.

Edwards, V., & Walker, S. (1995). *Building bridges: Multilingual resources for children*. Clevedon, UK: Multilingual Matters.

Ernst-Slavit, G., & Mulhern, M. (2003). Bilingual books: Promoting literacy and biliteracy in the second-language and mainstream classroom. *Reading Online, 7*(2). http://www.readingonline.org/articles/art_index.asp?HREF=ernst-slavit/index.html

Igoa, C. (1995). *The inner world of the immigrant child*. Mahwah, NJ: Erlbaum.

Kindler, A. (2002). *Survey of the states' limited English proficient students and available educational programs and services, 2000–2001 summary report*. National Clearinghouse for English Language Acquisition and Language Instruction Educational Programs.

O'Neil, D. (2006). *Language and culture: An introduction to human communication*. Retrieved March 25, 2007, from http://anthro.palomar.edu/language/language_1.htm

Schon, I. (June, 2004). *Caveat emptor/Inferior translations*. Presentation at the Summer Institute, Barahona Center for the Study of Books in Spanish for Children and Adolescents, San Marcos, CA.

Shin, H.B., & Bruno, R. (2003). Language use and English-speaking ability: 2000. *Census 2000 Brief*. U.S. Census Bureau. Retrieved June 5, 2006, from http://www.census.gov/prod/2003pubs/c2kbr-29.pdf

ThinkExist.com Quotations. (2007). *Federico Fellini quotes*. Retrieved April 25, 2007, from http://thinkexist.com/quotes/Federico_Fellini/

Thomas, W., & Collier, V. (1995). Language minority student achievement and program effectiveness. *California Association for Bilingual Education Newsletter, 17*(5), 19, 24.

UNESCO. (2005). *Atlas of the world's languages in danger of disappearing*. Retrieved March 25, 2007, from http://www.unesco.org/webworld/babel/atlas

Walker, S., Edwards, V., & Blacksell, R. (1996). Designing bilingual books for children. *Visible Language, 30*, 268–283.

LITERATURE CITED

Brook, D. (1998). *The journey of English*. Ill. J. Zallinger. New York: Clarion Books.

Brown, D. (2006). *Bright path: Young Jim Thorpe*. New Milford, CT: Roaring Brook Press.

Bruchac, J. (2005). *Code talker: A novel about the Navajo marines of World War II*. New York: Dial.

Bukiet, S. (1993). *Scripts of the world*. Cincinnati, OH: AIMS International.

Bunting, E. (2006). *One green apple*. Ill. T. Lewin. New York: Clarion Books.

Carvell, M. (2005). *Sweetgrass basket*. New York: Dutton.

Cheng, A. (2005). *Shanghai messenger*. New York: Lee & Low.

English, K. (2000). *Speak English for us, Marisol*. Ill. E. Sanchez. Morton Grove, IL: Albert Whitman.

Giff, P.R. (1998). *Say hola, Sarah*. Ill. D. DiSalvo-Ryan. Milwaukee, WI: Gareth Stevens.

Jiménez, F. (1998). *La mariposa*. Ill. S. Silva. New York: Houghton Mifflin.

Kadohata, C. (2006). *Weedflower*. New York: Atheneum.

Levine, E. (1995). *I hate English!* Ill. S. Bjorkman. New York: Scholastic.

Medina, J. (1999). *My name is Jorge on both sides of the river*. Ill. F. Vandenbroeck. Honesdale, PA: Boyds Mills Press.

Mora, P. (1997). *Tomás and the library lady*. Ill. R. Colon. New York: Knopf.

Mora, P. (2000). *My own true name: New and selected poems for young adults*. Houston, TX: Arte Publico.

Mora, P. (2006). *Confeti: Poemas Para Niños*. New York: Lee & Low.

Nobisso, J. (2003). *In English, of course*. Ill. D. Ziborova. New York: Gingerbread House.

Nye, N.S. (1994). *Sitti's secrets*. Ill. N. Carpenter. New York: Four Winds Press.

Orgel, D. (1996). *Don't call me Slob-O*. New York: Hyperion.

Paek, M. (1988). *Aekyung's dream*. San Francisco: Children's Book Press.

Pak, S. (1999). *Dear Juno*. Ill. S. Hartung. New York: Viking.

Pérez, A.I. (2002). *My diary from here to there/Mi diario de aquí hasta allá*. Ill. C. Gonzalez. San Francisco: Children's Book Press.

Rumford, J. (2004). *Sequoyah: The Cherokee man who gave his people writing*. New York: Houghton Mifflin.

Santiago, C. (1998). *Home to Medicine Mountain*. Ill. J. Lowry. San Francisco: Children's Book Press.

Sheth, K. (2004). *Blue Jasmine*. New York: Hyperion.

Soto, G. (1993). *Too many tamales*. New York: Putnam.

Soto, G. (1996). *¡Qué Montón de Tamales!* New York: Putnam.

Spier, P. (1980). *People*. New York: Doubleday.

Stanek, M. (1989). *I speak English for my mom*. Ill. J. Friedman. New York: Albert Whitman.

CHAPTER 6

Resilient Children in Times of War

Linda Leonard Lamme

"I dream of giving birth to a child who will ask, 'Mother, what was war?'"
—Eve Merriam (Maggio, 2004)

We rarely think of children when hearing news reports about war because the focus is typically on the soldiers who are fighting or the overall destruction incurred, yet children do live and die in the midst of these horrendous conflicts. In the past 10 years, over 2 million children have died in wars, and 6 million have been injured (Hartnett, 2000).

Children in the middle of wars develop an amazing array of survival techniques, growing, changing, and even helping other children. They encounter a wide range of challenges and often respond in ways far more mature than their ages would indicate. The goals of this chapter are to describe children's experiences in war as depicted in the Notable Books for a Global Society booklist from 1996 to 2005 (see Table 6.1 for a list of the books discussed), to examine the degree to which these stories and themes within them reflect the actual war experiences of children, and to present Literature Response Activities for sharing these books across the curriculum in social studies, art, writing workshop, bilingual education, and current events studies

It is difficult to determine at what age or grade level war stories are appropriate. Children who live in violent neighborhoods can read and understand these stories at much earlier ages than children who have little exposure to violence. The novels are most appropriate for grades 5 and above, while the picture books about war are more benign than the novels and therefore more appropriate for a wider audience. *Nim and the War Effort* (Lee, 1997/1998 NBGS) and *Boxes for Katje* (Fleming, 2003/2004), in particular, can be shared with children of any age. The other picture books are appropriate for children in grades 3 and higher.

Breaking Boundaries With Global Literature: Celebrating Diversity in K–12 Classrooms, edited by Nancy L. Hadaway and Marian J. McKenna. © 2007 by the International Reading Association.

Table 6.1. Notable Books for a Global Society (1996–2005) Books on Children's War Experiences

War	Year(s) of War	Title, Year Published, and Year Selected	Author	Genre
French and Indian War	1759	*The Winter People* (2002/2003 NBGS)	Joseph Bruchac	Novel
World War II	1940–1945	*The Children of Topaz* (1996/1997 NBGS)	Michael O. Tunnell and George W. Chilcoat	Informational Book
		Nim and the War Effort (1997/1998 NBGS)	Milly Lee	Picture Book
		When My Name Was Keoko (2002/2003 NBGS)	Linda Sue Park	Novel
		Boxes for Katje (2003/2004 NBGS)	Candace Fleming	Picture Book
Korean War	1950–1953	*Peacebound Trains* (1996/1997 NBGS)	Haemi Balgassi	Picture Book
		My Freedom Trip (1998/1999 NBGS)	Frances Park and Ginger Park	Picture Book
Palestinian/ Israeli Conflict	1988	*A Stone in My Hand* (2002/2003 NBGS)	Cathryn Clinton	Novel
Afghanistan Civil War	1989–2001	*Parvana's Journey* (2002/2003 NBGS)	Deborah Ellis	Novel
War in Kosovo	1998–1999	*Sweet Dried Apples* (1996/1997 NBGS)	Rosemary Breckler	Picture Book
		Girl of Kosovo (2001/2002 NBGS)	Alice Mead	Novel
Guerilla Warfare in Guatemala	1960–1996	*Red Midnight* (2003/2004 NBGS)	Ben Mikaelsen	Novel
		Tree Girl (2004/2005 NBGS)	Ben Mikaelsen	Novel

This collection contains books that describe war experiences in ways that inspire and teach important lessons. The authors who created these authentic portrayals of children's experiences in seven different wars conducted extensive interviews with children, family members, or friends with war experiences; conducted extensive research for the story; or lived through a war experience themselves. Alice Mead (*Girl of Kosovo*, 2001/2002 NBGS) visited the children of Kosovo on several trips between 1974 and 1999, going to schools, talking with parents, and spending time in their villages. Deborah Ellis traveled to Afghan refugee camps in Pakistan for *Parvana's Journey* (2002/2003 NBGS). Pegi Deitz Shea visited the Ban Vinai refugee camp in Laos to interview residents for *The Whispering Cloth: A Refugee Story* (1995/1996 NBGS) and *Tangled Threads: A Hmong Girl's Story* (2003/2004 NBGS). While writing *A Stone in My Hand* (2002/2003 NBGS), Cathryn Clinton traveled to Palestine, interviewed Palestinians living in the United States who had come from both the West Bank and Gaza, and did extensive research. Ben Mikaelsen's travels throughout Latin America and his interactions with witnesses to the violence in Guatemala led to *Red Midnight* (2003/2004 NBGS) and *Tree Girl* (2004/2005 NBGS). Rosemary Breckler based *Sweet Dried Apples: A Vietnamese Wartime Childhood* (1996/1997 NBGS) on the experiences of a close friend. Michael O. Tunnell and George W. Chilcoat created *The Children of Topaz: The Story of a Japanese-American Internment Camp* (1996/1997 NBGS), the only nonfiction book discussed in this chapter, from museum archives and from the diaries of the third-grade students of Lillian Yamauchi Hori in the World War II "relocation" camp in Utah, USA.

Several authors either lived through wars or had family members who did. Millie Lee based her World War II *Nim and the War Effort* (1997/1998 NBGS) on an incident from her own childhood in the Chinatown section of San Francisco, California, USA. Haemi Balgassi dedicates *Peacebound Trains* (1996/1997 NBGS) to his mother, Hyun Suk Rowe, who told him about her rooftop ride on a peacebound train. Frances and Ginger Park's *My Freedom Trip: A Child's Escape From North Korea* (1998/1999 NBGS) is drawn from their mother's story of escape from North Korea. *Boxes for Katje* (Fleming, 2003/2004 NBGS) is drawn from the post–World War II experiences of author Candace Fleming's mother, whose family participated in sending care boxes to families in war-devastated Europe.

Some of the stories blend personal history and research. *When My Name Was Keoko: A Novel of Korea in World War II* (Park, 2002/2003 NBGS) is based on Linda Sue Park's family history during the Korean War as well as extensive historical research. For *The Winter People* (Bruchac, 2002/2003 NBGS), Joseph Bruchac, himself part Abenaki, researched the history of his people.

Many of the books contain nonfiction information framing the story. Alice Mead explains some history of Balkan ethnic divisions without which the story of the Albanian *Girl of Kosovo* (Mead, 2001/2002 NBGS) would be hard to understand. *Parvana's Journey* (Ellis, 2002/2003 NBGS) ends with an author's note explaining the war in Afghanistan. In an afterword to *Red Midnight*, Ben Mikaelsen explains that the soldiers committing the violence in the story were supported and armed by the U.S. government to fight against communist guerillas. These reference features are useful to put the stories into context. War stories describe children in a variety of roles. Children may hide their age or gender to become soldiers. Children may become refugees. Characters in these books are observers, victims, rescuers, resistors, or are deserted and must fend for themselves. Often older children care for younger ones, assuming adult roles. War has many different effects on children, sometimes involving ethnic conflicts, which evoke irrational hate that children rarely understand. They may lose friendships and become fearful. It is often the children in these stories who stand up for what is right despite the actions of biased or fearful adults.

Reading these books will expand students' knowledge of the world. Anyone reading the stories of these children cannot help but admire and be inspired by their resilience in the midst of great hardship. Students will find excellent role models in these pages and will undoubtedly be moved to learn more about the cultures and conflicts involved. They will also become more aware of the plight of civilians and children in any armed conflict, so that someday they may make a real difference in the world as children become adults with a better understanding of the tragedy of war.

Children's Experiences With War as Reflected in Literature

The first section of this chapter shares stories about children who are forced to mature rapidly. Some live through bombing; others experience the death of a parent. The second section discusses family upheaval caused by fathers going to war as well as families fleeing from a war zone and being placed into refugee camps or internment camps. In the last section, the books depict heroic children who, in the face of extreme hardship, set out on their own to find family members, support resistance efforts, or endure discrimination. Some children withstand extreme hunger, endure the death of parents and relatives, or help other children. Together these themes present the diversity of children's war experiences.

Innocence Lost

When children and their families are immersed in war, young people quickly lose their innocence and are required to behave with far more maturity than their ages. For example, 11-year-old Zana in *Girl of Kosovo* (Mead, 2001/2002 NBGS) faces many trials, including the death of her father and brother as well as suffering a serious injury to her leg when her house is bombed by Serbs. When it is a Serbian doctor who saves Zana's life, she realizes that ethnic hatred is pointless and that human kindness crosses cultural borders.

In *Parvana's Journey*, 13-year-old Parvana has grown up in a sheltered intellectual family in which she has become an avid reader (Ellis, 2002/2003 NBGS). After she digs a hole and buries her father, her book learning offers few of the survival skills required to live in the vast Afghan desert, skirting both mine fields and soldiers, in search of her mother. Parvana assumes an adult role as she rescues and cares for an orphaned baby and is joined by Asif, age 9, and Leila, age 8, also orphans. By the end of the story, Parvana has changed from a naïve bookworm to a mature caretaker of young children whom she has saved from starvation.

Children of the World—Becoming Authors of Their Lives

BEN MIKAELSEN

AUTHOR REFLECTIONS

Growing up as a child in Bolivia, South America, gave me a perspective not shared by many American children. By the time I was 10 years old, I had been through three revolutions, walked to school stepping over dead bodies, had seen a man shot to death only feet away, and watched my first execution. I didn't appreciate, then, how wrong these events were or how this was only the tip of an iceberg of crimes committed against the indigenous Mayan population. As a child, I could never have understood the fear in which they lived their lives nor could I have appreciated the class, race, or gender differences that guided these oppressive events. Years later during volunteer work in Guatemala, I heard stories from many more who, as children, had seen the rape, torture, and massacre of every human being they had ever known. I realized that tens of thousands of indigenous Guatemalans had met the same fate—systematic genocide. Their many recollections made my personal experiences pale in comparison, and to know that my own country, the United States of America, had played a key role in allowing the massacres filled me with shame as a citizen.

As an author visiting hundreds of schools around the United States each year, I began to realize how limited was the perspective and exposure of most U.S. children to these world events. The average American child failed to even understand who refugees were, much less share an empathy for their plight. It had always struck me as tragic when the memories of horrific historic events, such as the Holocaust, are diminished by time. But there seemed to me something even more tragic when events such as the massacres in Guatemala were omitted and not even taught in U.S. schools because of the nation's complicity. The ultimate tragedy of this omission being the abandoning of our principles.

(continued)

Children of the World—Becoming Authors of Their Lives (continued)

AUTHOR REFLECTIONS

Despite the tragedies, I've seen in the faces of young people in Central and South America a resilience that is nothing short of a miracle. What has always haunted me from my research south of U.S. borders is the sense of helplessness that is shared by those who still remember the loss of everyone they ever loved. No future child should ever be made a victim or be made to feel as helpless as their parents were during those past tragedies. The single lesson I wish so desperately to teach children with my writing is that they are not helpless citizens on this planet. They are the "authors of their own lives." Through education, they have the power to control their reality as surely as they control the events of some story they write on a piece of paper.

There are those who would consider these admonitions as unrealistic, but I for one believe in the power of our children to change the world. I loved a saying I saw in a school recently: "If you want to change the world for a year, plant rice. If you want to change the world for 10 years, plant trees. But if you want to change the world for a lifetime, educate a child." This is my dream. I wish to help give hope to the children of the world, and I wish to give children in the United States an empathy for those less fortunate than they are. Not simply to be good Samaritans, but because empathy is a necessary step if we are to ever have world peace and truly appreciate freedom.

Books by Ben Mikaelsen selected for the Notable Books for a Global Society:
Red Midnight (2002/2003 NBGS)
Tree Girl (2004/2005 NBGS)

Living amid bombing is a terrifying war experience that can move children from fear to a determination to survive. In *Sweet Dried Apples* (Breckler, 1996/1997 NBGS), the young Vietnamese child narrator hears "constant roaring in the sky. Booming noises echoed from far off" (n.p.). In the beginning, she doesn't understand what the roaring and booming noises of the Vietnam War are. Toward the end of the story, she is fully cognizant that when "the night suddenly became bright with fire," bombs were detonating and people were being killed. Similarly, the child in *Peacebound Trains* (Balgassi, 1996/1997 NBGS) explains that the familiar sound of distant gunfire "chilled their hearts" as she and her family escaped from Seoul during the Korean War. "The night skies were crimson from the bombs, and we spent many black hours crouched in the basement" (p. 21).

Family Upheaval and Separation

In several booklist titles, families are torn apart during war and some children become orphans. The separation experiences in these books involve travel in search of family members, relocation to avoid battles or to escape oppression, and incarceration. Families separate when men go to war and women have to fend for themselves, sometimes traveling to refugee camps. In these books, war has a devastating effect on the family as an institution.

Violence is a way of life in Gaza in 1988 in *A Stone in My Hand* (Clinton, 2002/2003 NBGS). Eleven-year-old Malaak spends her free time on the roof with her birds as she pines for her father who left to find work in Gaza city and died in a bus bombing. Her angry brother wants to join the Islamic Jihad and hangs out with boys who carry stones in their pockets to hurl at soldiers. Her family seems to be falling apart.

In several of the picture books, a pattern emerges of fathers leaving for battle, while bombing in the villages forces grandmothers, mothers, and children to walk long distances to refugee camps. *Sweet Dried Apples* (Breckler, 1996/1997 NBGS) begins when a young girl's father leaves to fight in the Vietnam War and her family joins the stream of refugees walking to the coast where they board a boat for America. In *Peacebound Trains* (Balgassi, 1996/1997 NBGS) Yuh-bo is awakened in the middle of the night to quickly gather a few belongings and walk silently with her family in the icy cold to the peacebound train, which is crammed with people trying to escape North Korea. At the train, her father refuses to board and instead will enlist in the military, saying it is his duty. In a similar story, *My Freedom Trip* (Park & Park, 1998/1999 NBGS), Soo's guide, Mr. Han, takes her at night by train and then by foot over a mountain, until early the next day they reach the river, where her father waits on the other side. Soo's mother never is allowed to leave, so the family is permanently separated. These stories depict how refugee children are bewildered, afraid, and distressed as their families are torn apart.

Family upheaval also occurs in stories of occupation when children see their homeland changed and their friends, family, and neighbors tortured, repressed, incarcerated, or murdered. Two novels describe the Japanese occupation of Korea in World War II. In *When My Name Was Keoko* (Park, 2002/2003 NBGS), 10-year-old Keoko and her 13-year-old brother, Tae-yul, see rules gradually tighten and food become scarce, causing Tae-yul to join the military because families with sons in the military receive larger rations. Similarly, in *Year of Impossible Goodbyes* (Choi, 1991) 10-year-old Sukan and her mother suffer through both the Japanese military rule and the subsequent Russian invasion before they escape to find her father in South Korea.

During the French and Indian War, when British and Stockbridge Indians raid and torch the small town of St. Francis in the novel *The Winter People* (Bruchac, 2002/2003 NBGS), 14-year-old Saxo is wounded and his widowed mother and sisters are captured. Yet Saxo is determined not to abandon hope of seeing his family again, even if he must accept help from an enemy soldier.

In the United States, many Japanese American families were interned behind barbed-wire fences during World War II. Teacher Lillian Yamauchi Hori and her third-grade students kept a classroom diary from May to August 1943. Michael O. Tunnell and George W. Chilcoat published that diary along with their commentary and black-and-white archival photos of the desert relocation camp in Topaz, Utah, in *The Children of Topaz* (Tunnell & Chilcoat, 1996/1997 NBGS). Among topics like baseball and Boy Scouts the children write about people being shot by a guard. And one family is torn apart when the son joins the United States Army to escape the internment camp while the rest of the family must remain incarcerated.

Two picture books share the horrors of the Vietnam War from the perspective of refugee children. *The Whispering Cloth* (Shea, 1995/1996 NBGS) and *Sweet Dried Apples* (Breckler, 1996/1997 NBGS) create visual and textual images of the devastation of war and the subsequent escape of grandparents and grandchildren because parents are dead or away in the army. Family members support one another even when they are being pulled apart by the war.

Resilience and Resistance

For most of the children depicted in these books, war is about survival. For example, children walk for miles in long lines of refugees through the forests of Thailand and Vietnam to reach the coast in *Sweet Dried Apples* (Breckler, 1996/1997 NBGS). A similar refugee situation awaits Gabriela in *Tree Girl* (Mikaelsen, 2004/2005 NBGS) after she witnesses the destruction of her village. With her parents dead, she takes charge of her younger siblings and joins the refugees struggling to reach Mexico. Such children must be enormously stoical because food is scarce and they are not in the best of health.

However, some of these books depict brave children who not only survive but also resist the enemy. Some are smart and creative in how they handle horrible situations. Keoko's older brother, Tae-yul, in *When My Name Was Keoko* (Park, 2002/2003 NBGS) joins the Japanese military to learn how to fly and receives training to become a kamikaze pilot, with the intention to give up his life for the resistance. Before Tae-yul leaves under the cover of night, he delivers messages to his uncle who is printing an underground newspaper. Keoko saves an elderly neighbor by rushing to get her when the siren blows for the daily accounting. Moreover, Parvana, age 13, in *Parvana's Journey* (Ellis, 2002/2003 NBGS), disguises herself as a boy for her journey across war-torn Afghanistan and helps three other children as she travels. Finally, in *Tree Girl* (Mikaelsen, 2004/2005 NBGS), once Gabriela arrives at a refugee camp she helps two elderly women and starts a school.

In many wartime situations, occupying armies try to suppress the cultural identity of the people they have conquered. For example, in *When My Name Was Keoko* (Park, 2002/2003 NBGS) and *Year of Impossible Goodbyes* (Choi, 1991), the Korean language is banned and Korean national symbols destroyed during the Japanese occupation of Korea. The children are given Japanese names. Only at home by candlelight do Keoko and Sookan dare to practice Korean reading and writing in resistance to the law of the land. Moreover, when Korean families are told to uproot all of the Sharon trees, the national trees of Korea, Keoko's family burns most of the trees in their yard but hides one in a bucket in their barn to replant after the war. In *Girl of Kosovo* (Mead, 2001/2002 NBGS), Zana reunites with her Serbian neighbors, even though they are now considered to be the enemy, the night before they are forced to flee from their home.

In both *Nim and the War Effort* (Lee, 1997/1998 NBGS) and *Boxes for Katje* (Fleming, 2003/2004 NBGS), children take initiative to support families affected by war. Nim defies her family's rules and goes beyond the borders of her Chinatown neighborhood in San Francisco, California, USA, to find newspapers to support the U.S. war effort during World War II. Rosie, a young girl from Indiana, rouses her entire community to donate basic supplies, such as sugar, to be sent to Katje in a town in the Netherlands that has been devastated during World War II.

Disobeying the rules of an occupying country is a sign of resistance. These books show children who reclaim their identity and stubbornly go underground with their culturally linked behaviors while putting on a brave face to survive. Children from war fronts across the world rally in support of their counterparts facing oppression.

Literature Response Activities

The picture books discussed in this chapter make wonderful read-alouds at the elementary school level because they are sure to generate responses and questions that might benefit from teacher facilitation. When stories like these are read aloud, children have time to process the information during reader response in a supportive classroom climate. In middle and high school, these books fit into history lessons about wars because students will then learn about world history in a personal and meaningful way, viewing wars from the vantage point of the participants and their families, rather than just studying dates and who won and lost the conflict. Also, by reading these books and participating in the following literature response activities for various subject areas across the curriculum, students can learn conflict resolution skills and an ethic of activism to combat the horrors of war.

Using War Stories for Bilingual Education and Cultural Appreciation

Because wars are typically caused by ethnic and cultural uprisings, an important use of war stories can be to study ethnic conflict. Language is an essential element in the occupation stories. Only at home do children in *When My Name Was Keoko* (Park, 2002/2003 NBGS) and *Year of Impossible Goodbyes* (Choi, 1991) speak their native language. In school and in public, they are forced to speak Japanese. In *When My Name Was Keoko*, Keoko uses her knowledge of Japanese to teach her elderly Korean neighbor how to count to 5 so that she won't get into trouble during the daily inspections where people are lined up and must count in Japanese. Korean writing is pictured in *My Freedom Trip* (Park & Park, 1998/1999 NBGS). Most of the other books have phrases or words from other languages interspersed with the English text.

Therefore, these books make an excellent resource for bilingual-education teachers and second-language teachers, who can use them to demonstrate how important language is to identity as well as the potential of bilingualism to avert conflict. Classroom teachers can invite community members such as international students into the classroom to talk about their culture and speak with the students, perhaps teaching them some words or phrases.

Connecting the Literature to Science and Nutrition Studies

The families in these books struggle to keep their cultural traditions despite the upheaval caused by war. One problem is the lack of traditional foods: The enemy cuts off the availability of rice in the Korean War, diverting the food to the army and requiring Koreans to change their staple diet. In *The Children of Topaz* (Tunnell & Chilcoat, 1996/1997 NBGS), the Japanese American families struggle to eat the food that is provided for them. Food is scarce in times of war, which can be a primary cause of illness and death in the civilian population. Therefore, as a part of a health and nutrition unit, these books can provide insight on the food staples of Asian cultures and the importance of nutrition. Students could create food webs to show nutrition information on the food staples from different cultures. Similarly, *Sweet Dried Apples* (Breckler, 1996/1997 NBGS) can be connected to a science unit on herbs and herbal medicine. In this book, Ong-Noi, a grandfather and village herb doctor, gives away his herbal remedies and comes back home to die before the family departs to escape the Vietnam War. Because herbal medicine is becoming more common in America and other countries, students can read this book while studying herbal medicine as a part of a culture-inclusive science curriculum.

Social Studies Unit on War and the Military

After teachers distribute these books about war for students to read and discuss, students can create timelines, find the actual locations in the books on a world map, or look for nonfiction books and other resources about the same war. These activities ground discussion about war in both time and place. Students can also read, view, and listen to taped interviews with U.S. veterans at www.loc.gov/vets/ or invite veterans into the class to talk about their war experiences and answer students' questions. Groups of students can conduct research on different wars and present their findings to the class. Teachers might have students interview their family members to determine if they or any of their ancestors fought in wars and what their experiences were.

Once students have historical background and personal connections to war experiences, they can apply that to a current events study on war. The Warchild website (found online at www.warchild.org) is an excellent resource on efforts to help children of war today. The following are some possible activities.

- Identify locations of current conflict on a globe or world map.
- In groups, research conflicts using archived newspaper and Web sources. Discover when the conflict began, who is involved in the conflict, and the causes of the conflict.
- Develop a timeline of significant battles or events in the war or conflict.
- From news sources, create a list of war events over a period of several weeks.
- Chart the number of casualties and the cost of the war over time.

Several booklist titles involve characters that join the military. Students who have family members in the military may relate to stories like *Peacebound Trains* (Balgassi, 1996/1997 NBGS). After Yuh-bo's husband, Harabujy, shepherds his family on the long journey to board the train carrying people to the coast, he grips his wife's hand and says, "Yuh-bo, you and the children must ride this train" (p. 32). He explains, "I must go and do my part in this war, as a soldier. It is my duty, Yuh-bo" (p. 32). As mentioned previously, Keoko's older brother, Tae-yul, in

When My Name Was Keoko (Park, 2002/2003 NBGS) joins the Japanese military. The descriptions of Tae-yul's training provide insights on what military training is like and could be interesting to American students who have family members in the military or who might consider military life in the future for themselves.

Students may wish to write and send packages to soldiers who are currently serving in war zones (information about one such effort can be found online at http://anysoldier.com). At the same time, they can read *Nim and the War Effort* (Lee, 1997/1998 NBGS) and *Boxes for Katje* (Fleming, 2003/2004 NBGS), which describe the World War II relief effort. Nim collects newspapers for a school newspaper drive to support the soldiers, and Rosie collects items like soap to send to a town in the Netherlands that was devastated during World War II. Today's students and their teachers can locate war relief agencies, especially those involving children. They can recycle cans and bottles for cash, hold garage sales, or raise money in other ways to support children who live in war zones, just as Nim and Rosie did. They can collect books or necessities to send to children in refugee camps.

Writing Workshop

Writing is a wonderful way to learn and to process emotional information, so it is natural that writing would provide an excellent vehicle for students to respond to books about war. The writing curriculum can take many different forms that might be organized around a daily writing workshop (Ray, 2002).

Stories about war often show children being uprooted from their homes and families. Many students will relate to such experiences because of divorce, job relocation, migrant work, or other contemporary issues. *Sweet Dried Apples* (Breckler, 1996/1997 NBGS) depicts a family of refugees boarding a boat for America. In *Peacebound Trains* (Balgassi, 1996/1997 NBGS), Yuh-bo, Sumi's grandmother, reminisces about not wanting to leave her beautiful house and gardens or her mother's antique chests when her family is forced to leave North Korea.

In these books most people escape at night. Children are awakened and must quickly gather what belongings they can carry so that the family can escape in the shelter of darkness. Babies are strapped to the backs of older children or parents. Many of today's students may not have to suffer such extreme hardships physically, but emotionally they can relate to the disruptive experiences in their family and school lives. Students might collect data on today's displacement issues by researching immigrants or refugees, or they can write about displacement issues in the books or their own displacement experiences.

These titles can encourage the writing of oral histories. After reading several, have students find out how the authors wrote the books. Students can interview people or conduct research in archives. Teachers might suggest that students interview veterans about their experiences, transcribe the interview, have it checked for accuracy by the person interviewed, and put the transcription into an oral history archive.

Writing plays a significant part in several of these books. For example, Parvana keeps a journal in *Parvana's Journey* (Ellis, 2002/2003 NBGS) while Rosie sends notes in her box of rations to the Netherlands in *Boxes for Katje* (Fleming, 2003/2004 NBGS). The children in the Japanese American internment camp kept diaries in *The Children of Topaz* (Tunnell & Chilcoat, 1996/1997 NBGS). Like Keoko's uncle in *When My Name Was Keoko* (Park, 2002/2003 NBGS), students can produce a newspaper that informs people about war and its impact upon a society, or they might write letters to the editor of their local newspaper regarding ways to reduce violence, promote peace, and aid victims of wars. These are writing activities that can be replicated easily in any classroom.

Current Events Study on Homelessness and Hunger

The images of hunger and homelessness are stark in some of these stories. Parvana and three other homeless children wander across Afghanistan nearly starving, until they finally find shelter and food in a refugee camp in *Parvana's Journey* (Ellis, 2002/2003 NBGS). In several other books, women and children travel to refugee camps while their brothers and fathers serve in the military. These stories accurately depict the displacement and sadness of being homeless.

According to the National Coalition of the Homeless (2006), more than 800,000 people in the United States face homelessness on any given night in February, and many of those are families with children (p. 2). Reading books about the homeless fosters students' sensitivity to the issue and provides examples of ways that they can support the homeless population in their own town. Students also can seek out organizations aiding the homeless and find out how they, too, can support those efforts. More importantly, students can study the causes of homelessness and do projects on what can be done to rectify the situation.

Creating Picture Book Art

Art teachers and classroom teachers alike will find a treasure trove of art in the picture books about war. In *The Whispering Cloth* (Shea, 1995/1996 NBGS) Mai and her grandmother walk miles to a refugee camp in Thailand. To reduce their boredom and to make a tiny bit of money for food, they practice the traditional craft of *pa'ndau* stitchery. Students might learn quilting or create small stitchery squares for a class wall hanging. Deborah Kogan Ray creates rice paper images for the illustrations in *My Freedom Trip* (Park & Park, 1998/1999 NBGS). Students would enjoy creating art with rice paper, too, or other crafts that are mentioned in these books.

The painted illustrations include expressive art with emotional overtones that contribute significantly to the stories. Studying the use of color, texture, and style to increase emotional resonance can enhance an art curriculum on painting. Deborah Kogan Ray creates three distinct scenes in her Vietnamese setting of *Sweet Dried Apples* (Breckler, 1996/1997 NBGS). At the beginning of the story are lush green forests depicting the serenity of the Vietnamese landscape, followed by barren, ashen war scenes, and dark, foreboding water scenes with the refugee boat. In *My Freedom Trip* (Park & Park, 1998/1999 NBGS), Debra Reid Jenkins's oil paintings depict Soo's frightening escape and journey to freedom, highlighting only her face. Yangsook Choi creates similar brown tones in her oil paintings of Nim's gathering of newspapers in *Nim and the War Effort* (Lee, 1997/1998 NBGS). Students can experiment with color to achieve rich tones for their artwork.

The portrait of Nim's grandfather pinning small crossed flags of China and the United States onto her blouse at the beginning of *Nim and the War Effort* (Lee, 1997/1998 NBGS) is similar to the paintings of Chris Soentpiet in *Peacebound Trains* (Balgassi, 1996/1997 NBGS). Within the story, the illustrator paints darker, more somber pictures with the characters' portrait-like faces highlighted and uses art to enhance flashbacks. The depictions of people's faces in light with the surrounding background dark might offer an introduction to portraiture.

Conclusion

This collection from the Notable Books for a Global Society booklist depicts with clarity the harshness of war in the eyes of children. Through experiencing battles, injuries, and relocation, their childhood innocence is lost. They are forced to assume mature roles while their families are torn apart. Children of war are survivors whose stories are emotional and uplifting to read. The novels are well researched and well written, giving a clear voice to the characters. The illustrations include beautiful art with emotional overtones that contribute significantly to the picture book stories. These are the kinds of books that readers cannot put down.

REFERENCES
Note. Complete bibliographic citations for the Notable Books for a Global Society booklist (1996–2005) can be found at the end of the book.

Hartnett, S. (Ed.). (2000). War on children. *CBR News*, *32*, 5. Retrieved March 24, 2007, from
http://www.healthlink.org.uk/PDFs/cbrnews32.pdf

Maggio, R. (2004). *Women's reflections on war*. Retrieved March 22, 2007, from
http://www.mindfully.org/Reform/2004/Women-Reflections-War1mar04.htm

National Coalition for the Homeless. (2006, June). *How many people experience homelessness?*
(NCH Fact Sheet #2). Washington, DC: National Coalition for the Homeless. Retrieved March
24, 2007, from http://www.nationalhomeless.org/publications/facts/How_Many.pdf

Ray, K.W. (2002). *What you know by heart: How to develop curriculum for your writing workshop*.
Portsmouth, NH: Heinemann.

LITERATURE CITED

Choi, D.N. (1991). *Year of impossible goodbyes*. Boston: Houghton Mifflin.

PART III

Strategies for Using Literature to Promote Global Awareness

CHAPTER 7

Keys to Global Understanding: Notable Books for a Global Society Text Sets

Carolyn Angus

> "A story can be a powerful teaching tool. In folktales told far and wide,
> characters may gain wisdom by observing a good example or by
> bumbling through their own folly. A story's plot may inspire listeners to
> reflect on personal actions, decision making, or behavior. An entertaining
> story can gently enter the interior world of a listener. Over time, a tale
> can take root, like a seed rich with information, and blossom into new
> awareness and understanding."

—Heather Forest (1996, p. 9)

What Forest (1996) has to say about wisdom tales in her introduction to *Wisdom Tales From Around the World: Fifty Gems of Story and Wisdom From Such Diverse Traditions as Sufi, Zen, Taoist, Christian, Jewish, Buddhist, African, and Native American* can be adapted to express the value of books that have been selected for Notable Books for a Global Society booklists since 1996. These notable books can be powerful teaching tools, serving to engage students in reading, conversation, research, and writing. Whether fiction or nonfiction, the books may inspire readers to reflect on personal actions, decision making, or behavior. These well-written books can gently enter the "interior world" of a listener or reader and serve as keys to global awareness and understanding.

Breaking Boundaries With Global Literature: Celebrating Diversity in K–12 Classrooms, edited by Nancy L. Hadaway and Marian J. McKenna. © 2007 by the International Reading Association.

Using Text Sets for Studying the Notable Books for a Global Society, 1996–2005

One way of using the Notable Books for a Global Society booklists in classrooms is to develop text sets. Text sets are groups of books that are conceptually related in some way (Short & Harste, 1996). Short and Harste point out that "when readers read two or more texts that are related in some way, they are encouraged to share and extend their understandings of each text differently than if only one text had been read and discussed" (p. 537). It is important that all students have the opportunity to take part in reading and discussing the books in a text set. All students can do this if teachers accommodate for all levels of reading ability and interests among students when selecting books from different genres and including picture books, short stories, and other printed materials as well as novels and informational books in text sets.

As students share information about their reading and discuss the topics or themes of text sets, they begin to make intertextual connections: text-to-self, text-to-text, and text-to-world, as Goss (2003) illustrates with her suggestions for using a literature cluster of books that promote peace. It is text-to-world connections that are particularly important as teachers work to provide learning experiences that promote greater understanding of global issues. Using the 2005 Notable Books for a Global Society booklist as core titles and drawing from previous lists, this chapter offers several text sets, including clusters of books that are related by theme or topic, an author study, a grouping of short stories, and an extensive web of smaller text sets of folk literature. This chapter also provides suggested Perfect Pairs—pairs of books that are related in some way and in which one of the books in each pair is a 2005 booklist selection.

Heroes of the Holocaust

The Cats in Krasinski Square (Hesse, 2004/2005 NBGS) tells the story of two sisters, who, with the help of some abandoned cats, outsmart the Gestapo to smuggle food to Jews in the Warsaw Ghetto during World War II. This picture book can be used over a wide range of grades to introduce a text set of fiction and nonfiction books about private citizens who jeopardized their own safety to help others survive during World War II (see Table 7.1 for a list of suggested books that could be used as part of this text set). One picture book that could be combined with *The Cats in Krasinski Square* is *The Butterfly* (Polacco, 2000/2001 NBGS), a fictionalized account of the resistance activity of Marcel Solliliage, a member of the French underground. In this book, a young girl's mother hides a Jewish family in their basement during the Nazi occupation of France. Two nonfiction books that could be used are *A Special Fate: Chiune Sugihara, Hero of*

Table 7.1. Text Set: "Heroes of the Holocaust"

Title	Setting	Genre
Brothers in Valor: A Story of Resistance by Michael O. Tunnell (2001/2002 NBGS)	Hamburg, Germany	Historical Fiction
The Butterfly by Patricia Polacco (2000/2001 NBGS)	Choisi-le-Roi, near Paris, France	Picture Book
The Cat With the Yellow Star: Coming of Age in Terezin by Susan Goldman Rubin with Ela Weissberger (2006)	Terezin, Czechoslovakia	Informational Book/Biography
The Cats of Krasinski Square by Karen Hesse (2004/2005 NBGS)	Warsaw, Poland	Picture Book
Escaping Into the Night by D. Dina Friedman (2006)	Norwogrodek, Poland and western Belorussia	Historical Fiction
Fireflies in the Dark: The Story of Friedl Dicker-Brandeis and the Children of Terezin by Susan Goldman Rubin (2000/2001 NBGS)	Terezin, Czechoslovakia	Informational Book/Biography
A Hero and the Holocaust: The Story of Janusz Korczak and His Children by David A. Adler (2002)	Warsaw, Poland	Informational Book/Biography
Luba: The Angel of Bergen-Belsen by Luba Tryszynska-Frederick as told to Michelle R. McCann (2003/2004 NBGS)	Bergen-Belsen, Germany	Informational Book/Biography
Passage to Freedom: The Sugihara Story by Ken Mochizuki (1997/1998 NBGS)	Kaunas, Lithuania	Informational Book/Biography
Resistance by Janet Graber (2005)	Normandy, France	Historical Fiction
Sky: A True Story of Resistance During World War II by Hanneke Ippisch (1996)	Holland	Informational Book/Biography
A Special Fate: Chiune Sugihara: Hero of the Holocaust by Alison Leslie Gold (2000/2001 NBGS)	Kaunas, Lithuania	Informational Book/Biography

the Holocaust (Gold, 2000/2001 NBGS) and *Passage to Freedom: The Sugihara Story* (Mochizuki, 1997/1998 NBGS). *A Special Fate* is a biography of Chiune Sugihara, who, as a Japanese consul in Lithuania, saved the lives of thousands of Jews by issuing them visas during World War II despite orders by the Japanese government not to do so. *A Passage to Freedom*, an informational picture book illustrated by Dom Lee, tells the story of this 1940s event from the viewpoint of Chiune Sugihara's 5-year-old son, Hiroki.

This "Heroes of the Holocaust" text set also includes accounts of adults helping children living in concentration camps. *A Hero and the Holocaust* (Adler, 2002) is a picture book biography of Dr. Janusz Korczak, the director of a Jewish orphanage in Poland, who went with the children into the Warsaw Ghetto and then, although offered freedom, chose to accompany them to Treblinka death camp. *Luba: The Angel of Bergen-Belsen* (Tryszynska-Frederick, 2003/2004 NBGS) is a biography of Luba Tryszynska-Frederick, who saved the lives of more than 50 abandoned Dutch children she discovered in an empty field behind the barracks of Bergen-Belsen concentration camp in the winter of 1944–1945. *Fireflies in the Dark: The Story of Friedl Dicker-Brandeis and the Children of Terezin* (Rubin, 2000/2001 NBGS) tells the story of Friedl Dicker-Brandeis, a Czechoslovakian Jew, who helped children live through the horrors of imprisonment at the Terezin concentration camp by teaching them art. *The Cat With the Yellow Star: Coming of Age in Terezin* (Rubin, 2006) is about the concentration camp experiences of Ela Weissberger, who, in 1942 at the age of 11, was sent to Terezin. Ela studied art with Friedl Dicker-Brandeis and performed in the children's opera *Brundibár* as the cat. After reading *The Cat With the Yellow Star*, teachers may want to share with students the picture book *Brundibar* (Kushner, 2003), based on the Czech opera.

For older students, the text set could be expanded to include accounts of young people involved in wartime resistance movements in German-occupied Europe. *Sky: A True Story of Resistance During World War II* (Ippisch, 1996) tells how teenager Hanneke Eikema joined the Dutch resistance movement and was later arrested and sentenced to life imprisonment by the Germans. In *Resistance* (Graber, 2005), a 15-year-old girl comes to understand why her widowed mother endangers the family by involving them in the French Resistance in German-occupied Normandy. *Brothers in Valor: A Story of Resistance* (Tunnell, 2001/2002 NBGS) is the fictional account of the experiences of three German teenagers, members of the Mormon Church, who risk their lives by organizing an anti-Nazi movement in Hamburg. In *Escaping Into the Night* (Friedman, 2006), 13-year-old Halina Rudowski escapes from the Polish ghetto and joins a secret underground forest encampment where Jews are offered protection.

After reading and discussing some of these books about the ways individuals participated in resistance activities during World War II, older students can expand their understanding of the different forms of resistance by exploring Internet resources, such as the websites of the Simon Wiesenthal Center's Museum of Tolerance, the United States Holocaust Memorial Museum, and the Center for Holocaust Studies, for other personal histories of resistance.

Fostering a Global Outlook

MICHAEL O. TUNNELL

AUTHOR REFLECTIONS

Well-written books that express multicultural themes or are international in their origin or outlook may have a profound effect on readers, young and old. By promoting a global viewpoint, they especially can assist young readers in understanding that members of the human family have more similarities than differences.

Today, many of us have a growing awareness and concern about including all cultures and nationalities as equal members of the world's family. "Parallel cultures" is the term sometimes used to describe the goal of according "equal status" to all of the world's populations. However, we are far from achieving this ideal. Quality children's and young adult books may serve to help our new generations see people living in far-flung parts of the globe, or even in their own city, in this more equitable light.

Xenophobia is in part responsible for our worldwide inability to live together in peace. Parents and society may purposely or inadvertently program children to mistrust, fear, or even hate certain groups of people who are unlike them. According to Thomas Sobol (1990), teaching children at an early age "about the [positive] differences and similarities between people will not singularly ensure a more gentle and tolerant society, but might act as a prerequisite to one" (p. 30).

Literature can be one of the most powerful tools for combating the ignorance that can breed xenophobic behavior. As Nancy Hansen-Krening (1992) points out, "for decades experienced educators have reported success stories about using children's literature to broaden attitudes toward people from a variety of cultures" (p. 126). Indeed, studies have indicated that students' prejudices have been reduced because of reading and discussing good books embodying global perspectives.

Perhaps the following words from renowned author James Baldwin best sum up the potential power of books to make our planet a better place: "Literature is indispensable to the world.... The world changes according to the way people see it, and if you alter, even by a millimeter, the way a person looks at reality, then you can change it" (cited in Sims, 1982, p. 1).

Books by Michael O. Tunnell selected for the Notable Books for a Global Society:

Brothers in Valor: A Story of Resistance (2001/2002 NBGS)

The Children of Topaz: The Story of a Japanese-American Internment Camp coauthored with George W. Chilcoat (1996/1997 NBGS)

Folklore Collections From Around the World

Three Minute Tales: Stories From Around the World to Tell or Read When Time Is Short (MacDonald, 2004/2005 NBGS) is an extensive collection of very short stories that are perfect for sharing, either by telling or reading aloud. The inclusion of notes on the stories, suggestions for telling them, and a list of additional sources make this book a good centerpiece for a "Folklore Collections From Around the World" text set. Teachers can gather some of the books MacDonald lists in her "More Short Tales for Telling" bibliography from which students can select stories to read or tell. As stories are shared, students will learn about the rich cultural diversity of traditional tales as well as the universal nature of folk tale themes. Older students may be interested in learning about the folk tale "motif-indexes" cited by MacDonald and in reading some of the variants she mentions in her notes for the tales.

Teachers may want to share folklore from collections of longer stories that are rich in cultural detail, too. Reading a few tales aloud encourages students to read other stories in the books on their own. Collections of folklore that have been selected for Notable Books for a Global Society booklists from 1996 to 2005 are included in Table 7.2.

Here in Harlem

Here in Harlem: Poems in Many Voices (Myers, 2004/2005 NBGS) makes a good starting point for an author study on Walter Dean Myers. As he states in the introduction to *Here in Harlem*, the voices heard in the poems are those of people Myers has known or whose lives have touched his. Students can practice reading their favorite poems from the book and then hold dramatic readings of the poetry. Following Myers's pattern of celebrating voices of his hometown, some students may want to write poems from the perspectives of different people in their hometowns after interviewing neighbors about what it is like to live there. Some books to consider when developing a text set of Myers's books with a Harlem connection suitable for use with middle school and high school students are listed in Table 7.3. After students have read some of Myers's poetry, short stories, and fiction, teachers may want to share excerpts from *Bad Boy: A Memoir* (Myers, 2001) with them so that they can gain a better understanding of how Myers's childhood in Harlem influences his writing for children and young adults.

Harlem Stomp!

Harlem Stomp! A Cultural History of the Harlem Renaissance (Hill, 2004/2005 NBGS) can be the core book of a text set on the Harlem Renaissance. *Harlem Stomp!* is filled with details of the rich cultural life of Harlem in the 1920s,

Table 7.2. Text Set: "Folklore Collections From Around the World"

Title	Origin
Between Earth & Sky: Legends of Native American Sacred Places by Joseph Bruchac (1996/1997 NBGS)	Native American
Can You Guess My Name? Traditional Tales Around the World retold by Judy Sierra (2002/2003 NBGS)	13 countries
Children of the Dragon: Selected Tales From Vietnam retold by Sherry Garland (2001/2002 NBGS)	Vietnam
Echoes of the Elders: The Stories and Paintings of Chief Lelooska edited by Christine Normandin (1997/1998 NBGS)	Native American (tribes of the Northwest Coast of North America)
Her Stories: African American Folktales, Fairy Tales, and True Tales by Virginia Hamilton (1995/1996 NBGS)	African American
Horse Hooves and Chicken Feet: Mexican Folktales selected by Neil Philip (2003/2004 NBGS)	Mexico and Southwestern United States
Mysterious Tales of Japan by Rafe Martin (1996/1997 NBGS)	Japan
A Ring of Tricksters: Animal Tales From America, the West Indies, and Africa by Virginia Hamilton (1997/1998 NBGS)	African American, West Indies, and Africa
Three Minute Tales: Stories From Around the World to Tell or Read When Time Is Short by Margaret Read MacDonald (2004/2005 NBGS)	Many countries
Walking the Choctaw Road: Stories From Red People Memory by Tim Tingle (2003/2004 NBGS)	Native American (Choctaw)

Table 7.3. Text Set: "Here in Harlem"—Selected Texts by Walter Dean Myers

Title	Genre
The Autobiography of My Dead Brother (2005)	Realistic Fiction
Bad Boy: A Memoir (2001)	Biography
The Beast (2003/2004 NBGS)	Realistic Fiction
Harlem (1997/1998 NBGS)	Poetry/Picture Book
Here in Harlem: Poems in Many Voices (2004/2005 NBGS)	Poetry
145th Street: Short Stories (2000)	Short Stories
Street Love (2006)	Realistic Fiction

including some of the prose, poetry, song lyrics, art, and photography of important African American figures of the period. Based upon their interests, students can learn more about these individuals and, in the style of *Harlem*

Stomp!, create an oral or visual presentation of their contributions. *Shimmy Shimmy Shimmy Like My Sister Kate* (Giovanni, 1996) is a good resource. In this collection of poems, Nikki Giovanni adds comments about the individual poems and provides background material on the Harlem Renaissance. Table 7.4 includes books for a "Harlem Stomp!" text set that focuses on some major figures of the Harlem Renaissance.

Seeing Beyond Color

Face Relations: 11 Stories About Seeing Beyond Color (Singer, 2004/2005 NBGS) includes short stories about teenagers struggling with identity, interpersonal relationships, and prejudice by popular authors such as Joseph Bruchac, Naomi Shihab Nye, Jess Mowry, Rita Williams-Garcia, and M.E. Kerr. Reading aloud short stories from *Face Relations* is a good way to get middle school and high school students talking about issues with which they, too, must deal and introduces them to authors whose books invite young people to embrace diversity. To encourage independent reading, teachers can display and initiate book talks about some of the books by authors whose short stories are featured in *Face Relations* or in the collections of short stories listed in Table 7.5.

Table 7.4. Text Set: "Harlem Stomp!"

Title	Genre
The Entrance Place of Wonders: Poems of the Harlem Renaissance edited by Daphne Muse (2005)	Poetry
Free to Dream—The Making of a Poet: Langston Hughes by Audrey Osofsky (1996/1997 NBGS)	Biography
Harlem Stomp! A Cultural History of the Harlem Renaissance by Laban Carrick Hill (2004/2005 NBGS)	Informational Book
Jazz: My Music, My People by Morgan Monceaux (1994)	Informational Book
Jazz A B Z: An A to Z Collection of Jazz Portraits by Wynton Marsalis (2005)	Informational Book
Langston Hughes edited by Arnold Rampersad and David Roessel (2006)	Poetry
Shimmy Shimmy Shimmy Like My Sister Kate: Looking at the Harlem Renaissance Through Poems edited by Nikki Giovanni (1996)	Poetry
Stompin' at the Savoy: The Story of Norma Miller by Norma Miller (2006)	Biography
Visiting Langston by Willie Perdomo (2002/2003 NBGS)	Poetry/Picture Book

The Hungry Coat: Explorations of the Reappearing Wise—Yet Foolish—Folk Hero

The Hungry Coat: A Tale From Turkey (Demi, 2004/2005 NBGS) serves as the core title for a web of small text sets centered on a Middle Eastern folk hero who reappears under different names in stories from different countries (see Table 7.6). *The Hungry Coat* is a wisdom tale about judging a man for what he wears in his heart, not by the clothes he wears on his body. This tale is attributed to Nasrettin Hoca, a 13th-century Turkish folk philosopher and humorist. After being ignored when he attends a banquet in an old patched coat, Nasrettin returns in a fancy new coat and is warmly welcomed. He proceeds to stuff the lavish meal into the

Table 7.5. Text Set: "Seeing Beyond Color"

Title	Origin
Help Wanted: Stories by Gary Soto (2005)	Mexican American
An Island Like You: Stories of the Barrio by Judith O. Cofer (1995/1996 NBGS)	Puerto Rican Americans
Moccasin Thunder: American Indian Stories for Today edited by Lori Marie Carlson (2005)	Native American
Out of Bounds: Seven Stories of Conflict and Hope by Beverley Naidoo (2003/2004 NBGS)	South Africa

Table 7.6. Text Set: "The Hungry Coat: Explorations of the Reappearing Wise—Yet Foolish—Folk Hero"

Title	Folk Hero's Name	Culture/Country
Ayat Jamilah: Beautiful Signs: A Treasury of Islamic Wisdom for Children and Parents by Sarah Conover and Freda Crane (2004)	Honorable Joha, Mulla Nasruddin Hodja	Various Islamic cultures
Goha the Wise Fool by Denys Johnson-Davies (2005)	Goha	Egypt
The Hungry Coat: A Tale From Turkey by Demi (2004/2005 NBGS)	Nasrettin Hoca	Turkey
"The Mullah Nasrudin" in *The Barefoot Book of Trickster Tales* by Richard Walker (1998)	Mulla Nasrudin	Iran
"Tales From the Middle East" in *Wisdom Tales From Around the World* by Heather Forest (1996)	Mulla Nasrudin	Sufism

coat ("Eat, coat! Eat!"), reasoning that it was the coat—not he—that had been invited to the banquet.

After reading *The Hungry Coat*, teachers can involve students in the reading of other stories about this wise Muslim teacher who is claimed by several Middle Eastern countries to have originated with them and is identified under several names, including Goha in Egypt and Mulla Nasrudin in Iran. *Goha the Wise Fool* (Johnson-Davies, 2005) is a collection of 15 short tales about sometimes foolish, sometimes wise Goha. "The Mullah Nasrudin" (pp. 50–57) in *The Barefoot Book of Trickster Tales* (Walker, 1998) includes three episodes about this trickster–hero from Iran. Teachers will find *Ayat Jamilah: Beautiful Signs: A Treasury of Islamic Wisdom for Children and Parents* (Conover & Crane, 2004), which includes seven stories of the Honorable Joha, Mulla Nasruddin Hodja, and *Wisdom Tales From Around the World* (Forest, 1996), which has four Sufi stories of Mulla Nasrudin, valuable sources for more short stories attributed to this Middle Eastern wise fool.

Teachers can share information about the origins of the stories they read and help students identify the countries of origin on a map of the Middle East. Students can compare stories, including similarities and differences in the characterization of the wise teacher and the morals or lessons taught by the stories. They can also note how different illustrators portray the wise and foolish folk character. Teachers may also want to have students create their own wise fools, drawing pictures and writing brief descriptions of them, and even writing and illustrating their own stories about them.

Human Tricksters and Fools From Around the World. A related text set involving the wisdom of folklore can include stories about human tricksters and fools from around the world (see Table 7.7), who at times give sage advice and at other times

Table 7.7. Text Set: "Human Tricksters and Fools From Around the World"

Title	Origin
"Anansi's Fishing Expedition" in *A Pride of African Tales* by Donna L. Washington (2004)	Ghana
Horse Hooves and Chicken Feet: Mexican Folktales edited by Neil Philip (2003/2004 NBGS)	Mexico
Just a Minute: A Trickster Tale and Counting Book by Yuyi Morales (2003/2004 NBGS)	Mexico
Porch Lies: Tales of Slicksters, Tricksters, and Other Wily Characters by Patricia C. McKissack (2006)	African American

offer thought-provoking solutions to problems they encounter through their own foolishness. Stories in which seemingly very ordinary people are the tricksters are particularly appealing. The trickster in *Just a Minute: A Trickster Tale and Counting Book* (Morales, 2003/2004 NBGS) is elderly Grandma Beetle, who cleverly cheats the skeleton Señor Calevera when he comes to claim her. In "Pedro the Trickster" in *Horse Hooves and Chicken Feet: Mexican Folktales* (Philip, 2003/2004 NBGS), Pedro de Ordimalas tricks Death. Anansi is a trickster who appears in folklore as either a spider or a man. *A Pride of African Tales* (Washington, 2004) includes "Anansi's Fishing Expedition" (pp. 1–11), a trickster tale from Ghana in which it is Anansi, as a human, who gets tricked. Following the pattern of storytellers she listened to as a child, Patricia McKissack (2006) expands on the legends and historical figures from the African American oral tradition to create nine original stories in *Porch Lies: Tales of Slicksters, Tricksters, and Other Wily Characters*.

Classes can hold their own "Wisdom Tales From Around the World Festival." Students can share wisdom tales through oral telling, writing, drama, and art. *Wisdom Tales From Around the World: Fifty Gems of Story and Wisdom From Such Diverse Traditions as Sufi, Zen, Taoist, Christian, Jewish, Buddhist, African, and Native American* (Forest, 1996) and *Three Minute Tales: Stories From Around the World to Tell or Read When Time Is Short* (MacDonald, 2004/2005 NBGS) are excellent sources of short tales for students to use.

Sharing Food. Demi's *The Hungry Coat*, as well as other tales attributed to the Nasrettin Hoca or his counterpart in other Middle Eastern countries, involves the sharing of food. Teachers can therefore develop a related text set of stories involving the preparation and sharing of food from a particular region or from around the world (see Table 7.8 for a suggested text set). Old Monsieur Gator, in

Table 7.8. Text Set: "Sharing Food"

Title	Origin
Gator Gumbo: A Spicy-Hot Tale by Candace Fleming (2004)	Louisiana, United States
The Hungry Coat: A Tale From Turkey by Demi (2004/2005 NBGS)	Turkey
Mama Panya's Pancakes: A Village Tale From Kenya by Mary Chamberlin and Rich Chamberlin (2005)	Kenya
Yoshi's Feast by Kimiko Kajikawa (2000/2001 NBGS)	Japan

true trickster style, bests the three greedy Louisiana bayou critters who would not help gather the ingredients for gumbo but were eager to eat it in *Gator Gumbo: A Spicy-Hot Tale* (Fleming, 2004). In *Mama Panya's Pancakes: A Village Tale From Kenya* (Chamberlin & Chamberlin, 2005), Mama Panya worries that she won't have enough food to go around as Adika invites everyone they meet on the way to market to join them for dinner. *Yoshi's Feast* (Kajikawa, 2000/2001 NBGS) tells of a dispute between Yoshi and Sabu, an eel broiler, which is eventually settled as Yoshi devises a plan that leaves them enjoying sizzling-hot eels—and each other's company—every evening. The strong storytelling voices of these stories make them good choices for reading aloud, and the illustrations for the books give the tales a strong sense of time and place.

To extend this set of stories involving the sharing of foods, gather variations of "Stone Soup," a story showing that, although giving is hardest when there isn't much to share, when everyone gives a little there is more than enough to go around. Students can read variations of the story and do compare and contrast activities, focusing particularly on how the settings change the stories. Some recommended versions of the "Stone Soup" tale are included in Table 7.9.

Animals as Tricksters and Wise Teachers. Animal tricksters impart wisdom in many folktales from around the world. Table 7.10 includes books that introduce readers to some lesser known animal tricksters. Virginia Hamilton retells 11 trickster tales featuring a host of crafty creatures that made their way from Africa to the West Indies and then to the southern United States in *A Ring of Tricksters* (1997/1998 NBGS). Compère Lapin, a Cajun trickster, is just as pesky as his cousin Brer Rabbit in Sharon Arms Doucet's (2002) trickster tales from the Louisiana bayou, *Lapin Plays Possum*. Monkey King tricks Dragon King, battles

Table 7.9. Recommended Versions of the "Stone Soup" Tale

Title	Hungry Characters	Setting
Cactus Soup by Eric A. Kimmel (2004)	Soldiers from the Mexican Revolution	Mexican village
Kallaloo! A Caribbean Tale by David Gershator and Phillis Gershator (2005)	Granny	Caribbean town
Stone Soup: An Old Tale by Marcia Brown (1947)	Soldiers	French village
Stone Soup by Jon J. Muth (2003)	Three monks	Chinese village

Table 7.10. Text Set: "Animals as Tricksters and Wise Teachers"

Title	Trickster/Wise Teacher	Origin
Lapin Plays Possum: Trickster Tales From the Louisiana Bayou by Sharon Arms Doucet (2002)	Compère Lapin	Southern United States (Cajun)
Love and Roast Chicken: A Trickster Tale From the Andes Mountains by Barbara Knutson (2004)	Cuy the Guinea Pig	Andes
The Magical Monkey King: Mischief in Heaven by Ji-Li Jiang (2002)	Monkey King	China
Raccoon's Last Race: A Traditional Abenaki Story by Joseph Bruchac and James Bruchac (2004)	Azban the Raccoon	Native American (Abenaki)
A Ring of Tricksters: Animal Tales From America, the West Indies, and Africa by Virginia Hamilton (1997/1998 NBGS)	Bruh Rabbit, Bruh Gator, and others (American); Anansí (West Indian); Cunnie Rabbit, Old Mister Turtle, and others (African)	America, the West Indies, and Africa

Jade Emperor, and gets in trouble with Buddha in *Monkey King* (Young, 2001), a picture book introduction to this clever, high-spirited Chinese trickster. Ji-Li Jiang (2002) retells 18 short tales about trickster–hero Monkey King in *The Magical Monkey King: Mischief in Heaven*. Cuy the Guinea Pig repeatedly outfoxes Tio Antonio the Fox, who wants to eat him, in Barbara Knutson's (2004) *Love and Roast Chicken: A Trickster Tale From the Andes Mountains*. The trick is on the trickster in *Raccoon's Last Race* (Bruchac & Bruchac, 2004), a traditional Abenaki story in which Raccoon, the fastest animal on earth, becomes a short, squatty, slow-moving animal as a result of his boasting and failure to keep a promise. Students can compare and contrast these and other tales of animal tricksters, noting particularly the characteristics of the tricksters as well as the origins of the tales and lessons to be learned from the stories.

Perfect Pairs

Reading aloud two related picture books, a picture book and an informational book, poetry and a book, or other books that go together in some way is a good strategy for introducing students to notable books for making global connections. Table 7.11 is a listing of some Perfect Pairs in which one of the books in each pair

Table 7.11. Perfect Pairs, Notable Books for a Global Society (1996–2005)

Title	Genre	Relationship
César: ¡Sí, Se Puede! Yes, We Can! by Carmen T. Bernier-Grand (2004/2005 NBGS)	Poetry	Dramatically illustrated tributes to activist César Chávez
Harvesting Hope: The Story of Cesar Chavez by Kathleen Krull (2003/2004 NBGS)	Biography	
Daniel Half Human and the Good Nazi by David Chotjewitz (2004/2005 NBGS)	Historical Fiction	Stories of youths involved in in the Hitler Youth and the effects of Nazism on young Jews
Hitler Youth: Growing Up in Hitler's Shadow by Susan Campbell Bartoletti (2005)	Informational Book	
The Voice That Challenged a Nation: Marian Anderson and the Struggle for Equal Rights by Russell Freedman (2004/2005 NBGS)	Biography	Introductions to the life of this famous African American vocalist and her role in the U.S. Civil Rights movement
When Marian Sang by Pam Muñoz Ryan (2002)	Biography	
Children of the Great Depression by Russell Freedman (2005)	Informational Book	Two books that give the drought and U.S. Great Depression of the 1930s a "human face"
The Truth About Sparrows by Marian Hale (2004/2005 NBGS)	Historical Fiction	
Henry and the Kite Dragon by Bruce Edward Hall (2004/2005 NBGS)	Picture Book	A story about making and flying kites in New York's Chinatown in the 1920s and a book about the Chinese traditions behind kite flying
Kites: Magic Wishes That Fly Up to the Sky by Demi (1999)	Informational Book	
Facing the Lion: Growing Up Maasai on the African Savanna by Joseph Lemasolai Lekuton (2003)	Biography	Books that deal with coming of age among the Maasai today from the perspectives of a young man and a young woman
Our Secret, Siri Aang by Christina Kessler (2004/2005 NBGS)	Realistic Fiction	
Monsoon Summer by Mitali Perkins (2004)	Realistic Fiction	Stories in which visits to India help girls begin to appreciate their families and heritage
Naming Maya by Uma Krishnaswami (2004/2005 NBGS)	Realistic Fiction	
My Name Is Yoon by Helen Recorvits (2003/2004 NBGS)	Picture Book	Stories about the importance of names to individuals
My Name Was Hussein by Hristo Kyuchukov (2004/2005 NBGS)	Picture Book	
Red Midnight by Ben Mikaelsen (2002/2003 NBGS)	Historical Fiction	Survival stories of children forced to flee Guatemalan villages during military massacres
Tree Girl by Ben Mikaelsen (2004/2005 NBGS)	Historical Fiction	

(continued)

Title	Genre	Relationship
Journey to Ellis Island: How My Father Came to America by Carol Bierman (1998/1999 NBGS)	Biography	Accounts of emigration from Russia by Jews in the late 19th and early 20th centuries
Nothing Here But Stones by Nancy Oswald (2004/2005 NBGS)	Historical Fiction	
Beauty, Her Basket by Sandra Belton (2004)	Picture Book	Grandmothers share family stories and show their granddaughters how to make Gullah coiled-grass baskets
Circle Unbroken: The Story of a Basket and Its People by Margot Theis Raven (2004/2005 NBGS)	Picture Book	
Becoming Naomi León by Pam Muñoz Ryan (2004/2005 NBGS)	Realistic Fiction	Novels set in Mexico and California about spirited young girls facing problems with the support of family and community
Esperanza Rising by Pam Muñoz Ryan (2000/2001 NBGS)	Historical Fiction	
Chanda's Secrets by Allan Stratton (2004/2005 NBGS)	Realistic Fiction	Novels set in Africa in which young women struggle to deal with the devastating effects of AIDS on their families and communities
The Heaven Shop by Deborah Ellis (2004)	Realistic Fiction	
Hachiko: The True Story of a Loyal Dog by Pamela S. Turner (2004/2005 NBGS)	Informational Book	Accounts of the true story of a dog that waited everyday for 10 years at a Tokyo train station for his deceased master to return
Hachiko Waits by Lesléa Newman (2004)	Historical Fiction	
Escape From Saigon: How a Vietnam War Orphan Became an American Boy by Andrea Warren (2004/2005 NBGS)	Informational Book/Biography	Caputo's book provides background for Warren's book about Long, an Amerasian boy who was airlifted to the United States just before the fall of Saigon in 1975.
10,000 Days of Thunder: A History of the Vietnam War by Philip Caputo (2005)	Informational Book	
Rattlesnake Mesa: Stories From a Native American Childhood by Ednah New Rider Weber (2004/2005 NBGS)	Biography	Books about Native American childhoods, including being sent to off-reservation boarding schools
Sweetgrass Basket by Marlene Carvell (2005)	Historical Fiction	
China's Son: Growing Up in the Cultural Revoltuion by Da Chen (2001/2002 NBGS)	Biography	Two accounts of the effects of the Cultural Revolution on young people in China
Chu Ju's House by Gloria Whelan (2004/2005 NBGS)	Realistic Fiction	

(continued)

Table 7.11. Perfect Pairs, Notable Books for a Global Society (1996–2005) (continued)

Title	Genre	Relationship
Coming on Home Soon by Jacqueline Woodson (2004/2005 NBGS)	Picture Book	Stories about children and their concerns about being separated from a parent
Faraway Home by Jane Kurtz (2000/2001 NBGS)	Picture Book	
Oranges on Golden Mountain by Elizabeth Partridge (2001/2002 NBGS)	Picture Book	Stories about Chinese immigrants in America and their family and community ties to China
A Song for Ba by Paul Yee (2004/2005 NBGS)	Picture Book	

is from the 2005 booklist. For example, *César: ¡Sí, Se Puede! Yes, We Can!* (Bernier-Grand, 2004/2005 NBGS), a collection of poems, and *Harvesting Hope: The Story of Cesar Chavez* (Krull, 2003/2004 NBGS), a picture book biography, are dramatically illustrated tributes to activist César Chávez. *Daniel Half Human and the Good Nazi* (Chotjewitz, 2004/2005 NBGS), a novel, and *Hitler Youth: Growing up in Hitler's Shadow* (Bartoletti, 2005), an informational book, both tell stories of youths involved in the Hitler Youth and the effects of Hitler's rise to power in the 1930s on Jewish young people.

Numerous book-related activities can accompany the reading of Perfect Pairs to foster increased global understanding. *Hachiko: The True Story of a Loyal Dog* (Turner, 2004/2005 NBGS) and *Hachiko Waits* (Newman, 2004) are two short books that make great read-alouds for younger students. Both books are based on the true story of a dog that waited every day for nearly 10 years at the Shibuya Station in Tokyo, Japan, for his deceased master to return from work. Using the Internet, students can find photos of the statue of Hachiko and related details on how Hachiko has become a symbol of loyalty and devotion for the people of Japan. Classes can read other stories about real dogs that have been recognized for their loyalty and accomplishments and make a comparison chart, including such items as the dog's name, breed, where it lived, special accomplishments, unique attributes, and hardships or challenges the dog encountered.

Escape From Saigon: How a Vietnam War Orphan Became an American Boy (Warren, 2004/2005 NBGS) tells the story of Long, an Amerasian child orphaned by the Vietnam War who was airlifted to the United States just before the fall of Saigon in 1975. Philip Caputo's *10,000 Days of Thunder: A History of the Vietnam War* (2005) is an accessible introduction to the history of the Vietnam War that provides background for Warren's book and includes a section on the 1975

Operation Baby Lift. Long was one of only a few thousand Vietnamese orphans who made it to adoptive families. Reading this Perfect Pair lends itself to a number of interesting activities for older students, including the following:

- Researching programs of the American government and private agencies that airlifted orphaned children out of Saigon
- Exploring issues related to the discrimination suffered by some Amerasian children after the war
- Learning about the Homecoming Act of 1987, which allowed Amerasian children and their families to emigrate to America
- Reading other books, both fiction and nonfiction, that deal with the effects of the Vietnam War

More teaching suggestions related to Perfect Pairs based on the 2005 Notable Books for a Global Society, as well as lists of related books, can be found in the 2005 Notable Books for a Global Society annotated booklist (Angus et al., 2005).

Reading aloud a Perfect Pair of books is also a good way to assess student interest in a topic. If the interest level is high, teachers may want to develop a text set of related books to continue the topic. For example, *My Name Was Hussein* (Kyuchukov, 2004/2005 NBGS) and *My Name Is Yoon* (Recorvits, 2003/2004 NBGS) are a Perfect Pair of stories exploring the importance of names to individuals and how names are involved in issues of prejudice and discrimination and adjusting to changes, such as immigration and adoption. Other books about the importance of names, such as *The Name Jar* (Choi, 2001/2002 NBGS) and *My Name Is Jorge: On Both Sides of the River* (Medina, 1999) can be displayed to encourage independent reading. Older students might want to read *My Name Is María Isabel* (Ada, 1993) and *When My Name Was Keoko: A Novel of Korea in World War II* (Park, 2002/2003 NBGS). Table 7.12 includes stories about the importance of names to individuals.

Another way of using these Perfect Pairs is to have one student read one of the books and a second student the other book. They can then get together and exchange information about the books. Once teachers have introduced the reading of Perfect Pairs, students will begin to seek out Perfect Pairs of books in their visits to the library.

Conclusion

In this chapter, the use of text sets and Perfect Pairs to connect books for study and discussion has focused on the 2005 Notable Books for a Global Society booklist. Hopefully, educators will want to add to these text sets, develop other

Table 7.12. Stories About the Importance of Names to Individuals

Title	Genre	Origin
My Name Is Jorge: On Both Sides of the River: Poems in English and Spanish by Jane Medina (1999)	Poetry	Mexico and the United States
My Name Is María Isabel by Alma Flor Ada (1993)	Realistic Fiction	United States, Puerto Rican
My Name Is Yoon by Helen Recorvits (2003/2004 NBGS)	Picture Book	United States, Korean
My Name Was Hussein by Hristo Kyuchukov (2004/2005 NBGS)	Picture Book	Bulgaria, Muslim Roma
The Name Jar by Yangsook Choi (2001/2002 NBGS)	Picture Book	United States, Korean
When My Name Was Keoko: A Novel of Korea in World War II by Linda Sue Park (2002/2003 NBGS)	Historical Fiction	Korea

text sets using the Perfect Pairs as starting points, and create other Perfect Pairs using notable books. Nancy L. Hadaway's analysis of different dimensions across 10 years of Notable Books for a Global Society in chapter 1 is a valuable resource to this end. For those who want to plan a genre study, chapter 8 offers excellent examples of books and activities for engaging students with poetry to explore themes of social justice. In addition, educators will want to consider future Notable Books for a Global Society booklists when adding to and creating new text sets that serve as keys to global awareness and understanding.

REFERENCES

Note. Complete bibliographic citations for the Notable Books for a Global Society booklist (1996–2005) can be found at the end of the book.

Angus, C., Corbin, S., Steiner, S.F., Wendelin, K.H., Ernst, S.B., Lamme, L.L., et al. (2005). 2005 Notable Books for a Global Society. *The Dragon Lode, 24*(1), 43–59.

Goss, G. (2003). Helping children think about peace: Children's books that promote peace using a literature cluster. *Bookbird, 41*(4), 33–40.

Hansen-Krening, N. (1992). Authors of color: A multicultural perspective. *Journal of Reading, 36,* 124–129.

Short, K.G., & Harste, J.C. (with Burke, C.). (1996). *Creating classrooms for authors and inquirers* (2nd ed.). Portsmouth, NH: Heinemann.

Sims, R. (1982). *Shadow and substance: Afro-American experience in contemporary children's fiction.* Urbana, IL: National Council of Teachers of English.

Sobol, T. (1990). Understanding diversity. *Educational Leadership, 48*(3), 27–30.

LITERATURE CITED

Ada, A.F. (1993). *My name is María Isabel.* (A.M. Cerro, Trans.). Ill. K.D. Thompson. New York: Atheneum.

Adler, D.A. (2002). *A hero and the Holocaust: The story of Janusz Korczak and his children.* Ill. B. Farnsworth. New York: Holiday House.

Bartoletti, S.C. (2005). *Hitler Youth: Growing up in Hitler's shadow.* New York: Scholastic.

Belton, S. (2004). *Beauty, her basket.* Ill. C.A. Cabrera. New York: Greenwillow.

Brown, M. (1947). *Stone soup: An old tale.* New York: Atheneum.

Bruchac, J., & Bruchac, J. (2004). *Raccoon's last race: A traditional Abenaki story.* Ills. J. Aruego & A. Dewey. New York: Dial.

Caputo, P. (2005). *10,000 days of thunder: A history of the Vietnam War.* New York: Atheneum.

Carlson, L.M. (Ed.). (2005). *Moccasin thunder: American Indian stories for today.* New York: HarperCollins.

Carvell, M. (2005). *Sweetgrass basket.* New York: Dutton.

Chamberlin, M., & Chamberlin, R. (2005). *Mama Panya's pancakes: A village tale from Kenya.* Ill. J. Cairns. New York: Barefoot.

Conover, S., & Crane, F. (2004). *Ayat Jamilah: Beautiful signs: A treasury of Islamic wisdom for children and parents.* Ill. V. Wahl. Spokane: Eastern Washington University Press.

Demi. (1999). *Kites: Magic wishes that fly up to the sky.* New York: Crown.

Doucet, S.A. (2002). *Lapin plays possum: Trickster tales from the Louisiana bayou.* Ill. S. Cook. New York: Farrar, Straus and Giroux.

Ellis, D. (2004). *The heaven shop.* Markham, ON: Fitzhenry & Whiteside.

Fleming, C. (2004). *Gator gumbo: A spicy-hot tale.* Ill. S.A. Lambert. New York: Farrar, Straus and Giroux.

Forest, H. (1996). *Wisdom tales from around the world: Fifty gems from such diverse traditions as Sufi, Zen, Taoist, Christian, Jewish, Buddhist, African, and Native American.* Little Rock, AR: August House.

Freedman, R. (2005). *Children of the Great Depression.* New York: Clarion Books.

Friedman, D.D. (2006). *Escaping into the night.* New York: Simon & Schuster.

Gershator, D., & Gershator, P. (2005). *Kallaloo!: A Caribbean tale.* Ill. D. Greenseid. New York: Marshall Cavendish.

Giovanni, N. (Ed.). (1996). *Shimmy shimmy shimmy like my sister Kate: Looking at the Harlem Renaissance through poems.* New York: Henry Holt.

Graber, J. (2005). *Resistance.* New York: Marshall Cavendish.

Ippisch, H. (1996). *Sky: A true story of resistance during World War II.* New York: Simon & Schuster.

Jiang, J.L. (2002). *The magical Monkey King: Mischief in heaven.* Ill. H. Su-Kennedy. New York: HarperCollins.

Johnson-Davies, D. (2005). *Goha the wise fool.* Ills. H. Ahmed & H. Fattouh. New York: Philomel Books.

Kimmel, E.A. (2004). *Cactus soup.* Ill. P. Huling. New York: Marshall Cavendish.

Knutson, B. (2004). *Love and roast chicken: A trickster tale from the Andes Mountains.* Minneapolis, MN: Carolrhoda.

Kushner, T. (2003). *Brundibar.* Ill. M. Sendak. New York: Michael Di Capua/Hyperion.

Lekuton, J.L. (2003). *Facing the lion: Growing up Maasai on the African savanna.* Washington, DC: National Geographic Society.

Marsalis, W. (2005). *Jazz A B Z: An A to Z collection of jazz portraits.* Ill. P. Rogers. Cambridge, MA: Candlewick.

McKissack, P.C. (2006). *Porch lies: Tales of slicksters, tricksters, and other wily characters.* Ill. A. Carrilho. New York: Schwartz & Wade/Random House.

Medina, J. (1999). *My name is Jorge: On both sides of the river: Poems in English and Spanish*. Ill. F.V. Broeck. Honesdale, PA: Wordsong/Boyds Mills Press.

Miller, N. (2006). *Stompin' at the Savoy: The story of Norma Miller*. (A. Govenar, Ed.). Ill. M. French. Cambridge, MA: Candlewick.

Monceaux, M. (1994). *Jazz: My music, my people*. New York: Knopf.

Muse, D. (Ed.). (2005). *The entrance place of wonders: Poems of the Harlem Renaissance*. Ill. C. Riley-Webb. New York: Harry N. Abrams.

Muth, J.J. (2003). *Stone soup*. New York: Scholastic.

Myers, W.D. (2000). *145th Street: Short stories*. New York: Delacorte Press.

Myers, W.D. (2001). *Bad boy: A memoir*. New York: HarperCollins.

Myers, W.D. (2005). *The autobiography of my dead brother*. Ill. C. Myers. New York: HarperTempest/HarperCollins.

Myers, W.D. (2006). *Street love*. New York: HarperTempest/HarperCollins.

Newman, L. (2004). *Hachiko waits*. Ill. M. Kodaira. New York: Henry Holt.

Perkins, M. (2004). *Monsoon summer*. New York: Delacorte Press.

Rampersad, A., & Roessel, D. (Eds.). (2006). *Langston Hughes*. Ill. B. Andrews. New York: Sterling Press.

Rubin, S.G. (with Weissberger, E.). (2006). *The cat with the yellow star: Coming of age in Terezin*. New York: Holiday House.

Ryan, P.M. (2002). *When Marian sang*. Ill. B. Selznick. New York: Scholastic.

Soto, G. (2005). *Help wanted: Stories*. San Diego, CA: Harcourt.

Walker, R. (1998). *The barefoot book of trickster tales*. Ill. C. Muñoz. New York: Barefoot.

Washington, D.L. (2004). *A pride of African tales*. Ill. J. Ransome. New York: HarperCollins.

CHAPTER 8

Using Poetry to Explore Social Justice and Global Understanding

Mary Napoli

"A literacy education that focuses on social justice educates both the heads and hearts of students and helps them to become thoughtful, committed, and active citizens."

—James Banks (2003, p. 19)

R eading poetry is one way to help foster an emancipatory curriculum. Weaving poetry with a global perspective in our curriculum supports the development of identity, solidarity, critical thinking, and liberatory action (Banks, 1991; Freire, 1970; Nieto, 2002). The power of reading poetry to affect the lives of readers is endless. Poetry appeals to our senses and fosters a love and appreciation for the power of language. In addition, poetry that embraces a global message can introduce children to other languages, cultures, and dialects (Freeman & Lehman, 2001) and has the capacity to transform our lives by shaping new understandings of ourselves and others. In Cahnmann's (2006) recent research, she explores the importance of sharing poetry to explore linguistic and cultural experiences with readers. She states that "reading, living, and writing bilingual poetry can elucidate the goal of bilingual education—to provide an educational environment where students' home languages and cultures are visible and valued as resources in the classroom" (p. 351).

It is critical for classroom and preservice teachers to consider the ways they will engage their students—tomorrow's citizens—to promote global understanding. This critical lens helps educators name and locate their realities within social, cultural, economic, and historical frames of society (Freire, 1970; Giroux, 1988). One way for teachers and preservice teachers to explore a critical

Breaking Boundaries With Global Literature: Celebrating Diversity in K–12 Classrooms, edited by Nancy L. Hadaway and Marian J. McKenna. © 2007 by the International Reading Association.

stance toward literature and to develop the necessary skills to help their students embrace diversity is to share global poetry. Certainly, poetry can guide today's youth to challenge the injustices and navigate the contradictions of their world. Reading poetry serves as an excellent catalyst for class discussion about thematic strands such as culture, identity, and gender, and it provides rich learning experiences for students at all grade levels (Damico, 2005; Hadaway, Vardell, & Young, 2001, 2002; McCall, 2004; Perfect, 1999). Sharing poems from the Notable Books for a Global Society booklists is a particularly effective way to encourage conversations about these themes and to help students see that they are not powerless to bring about social change.

This chapter first describes ways that educators at all levels can utilize poetry to foster "participatory spaces" (hooks, 1994) within the classroom and enhance students' understanding of global issues through these experiences with poetry. Then, information is shared about a project where preservice teachers examined issues of global understanding and social justice and then implemented various strategies using global poetry with elementary students. These interactions between elementary students and preservice teachers during their experiences with reading global poetry can be highly useful for educators of all grade levels, as educators can use this information to apply similar approaches in their own classrooms.

Strategies for Exploring Social Justice and Global Understanding Through Poetry

There are many benefits of incorporating global poetry into the classroom. In this chapter, readers will learn about several strategies to implement with their students. When reading global poetry with students, conversations about social justice and social change will become a natural part of individual, small-group, and whole-group instruction. It is important to keep in mind that the strategies presented in this chapter are not exhaustive. There are many ways to integrate poetry with global messages within the curriculum, and as we share these poems with students, the possibilities become endless.

Surveying Students' Experiences With Poetry

Many students have had very little exposure to global poetry and view reading poetry as an unpleasant task. Surveying students' perceptions of poetry can guide educators to design meaningful experiences (Apol & Harris, 1999; Mathis, 2002; Sloan, 2003). It is critical to understand students' familiarity and prior experiences with poetry for several reasons. First, as educators, we need to assess our students' prior knowledge with poetry in order to facilitate meaningful instruction. The surveys also serve as a self-reflection tool for the students and can encourage their independent exploration of the genre. Another benefit of using the survey is to acquire information about students' familiarity with popular and classical poetry writers. In addition, the results of the surveys can assist teachers to select the appropriate titles for poetry browsing. To create a written survey, teachers can include general prompts such as these:

- Poetry makes me feel....
- I like or do not like reading poetry because....
- What sort of poetry do you like?
- What types of poetry do you know about (e.g., ballad, acrostic, limerick)?
- Name your favorite poet.

Surveys can also include a simple Likert-type scale with various prompts to gauge students' interest and familiarity with poetry.

Poetry Browsing and Personal Responses to Poetry

Before class, teachers need to arrange multiple copies of multicultural poetry anthologies that pertain to gender, social class, poverty, identity, and race issues. For example, the poems in *19 Varieties of Gazelle: Poems of the Middle East*, an anthology of poems about the Middle East (Nye, 2002/2003 NBGS), and *Bronx Masquerade*, a novel in verse intertwining prose and fiction (Grimes, 2002/2003 NBGS), provide opportunities for readers to consider their perspectives on discrimination, identity, stereotyping, culture, and identity. Teachers can post a visually appealing poster labeled "Poetry Browsing Session in Progress" when beginning a classroom poetry exploration. The directions for this activity are simple: Students walk around the room, read the poetry selections, and find one that "speaks" to them.

When working with students, it's important to keep in mind that their background, discourse, gender, and culture influence their responses toward global poetry and issues of social justice (Edelsky, 1999). As students browse the collections, teachers need to encourage them to consider their personal, emotional, and social responses to various poems. During follow-up discussion, educators can encourage students to explore their own values and attitudes about global issues.

For example, the poem "When I Was a Child" by Yehunda Amichai, which appears in *The Space Between Our Footsteps: Poems and Paintings From the Middle East* (Nye, 1998/1999 NBGS), describes an adult reminiscing about his childhood, which was filled with words of hope from his mother and uncertainty about his father's return. This poem was embraced by a male preservice educator during my undergraduate children's literature course. During our whole-group discussion, he shared a deeply emotional story that touched the hearts and minds of his classmates. He indicated that, for him, the poem paid homage to his best friend, a young father of twin boys who was killed by a roadside bomb in the Middle East. Like Rosaen (2003), I found that providing the space for preservice teachers to read and discuss poetry can facilitate connections between their own lives and issues of social justice. Although this took place in an undergraduate children's literature course, it is important to keep in mind that all readers of poetry have the capacity to personally respond to poems on the basis of their individual experiences. Reading poetry with global themes can bring readers of any age closer to their own cultural experiences as well as those of others. The more we share poetry with our students, the more they will feel compelled to share personal responses and feelings. Reading poetry aloud on a daily basis will undoubtedly shape students' written and oral expressions to the genre.

Reading Aloud and Performing Poetry

To help students make connections between global poetry and their everyday lives, opportunities to dramatize, read aloud, collect, and present poetry are an integral part of any classroom. For example, many of the selections in *Confetti: Poems for Children* (Mora, 1996/1997 NBGS) are excellent for reading aloud or for choral reading. The lively language and rhythmic verses make this a perfect book for elementary grades. Told from a Mexican American girl's point of view, the poems help readers to better understand the experiences of bilingual youth. This collection captures a cultural richness for enjoyment and discussion. When reading aloud *I hear, I hear*, students can read the first line of the poem in a natural voice and then read the phrase *pom pom* in a louder voice accompanied by sound effects.

Dramatizing poetry also invites readers into the language of the text. When students dramatize a poem, they are not only reading the poem but interpreting the situations and feelings with motions and expression. In Medina's (2004) research about drama and multicultural literature, she discovered that weaving drama throughout the curriculum serves as a catalyst for promoting critical discourse among students. To simulate the dramatic experience, students can act out several poems in *The Distant Talking Drum: Poems From Nigeria* (Olaleye, 1995/1996 NBGS). Some of the poems are appropriate to recite as "poems for two voices" (Fleischman, 1988). Following the example in *Three Voices: An Invitation to Poetry Across the Curriculum* (Cullinan, Scale, & Schroeder, 1995), educators can turn the poem "Village Market" into a play where different groups of students portray the mothers, children, dogs, and other animals that surround the market. Teachers can encourage students to apply simple movements to a few keywords of the poem "Market Square Dance" while other students read aloud (pp. 110–111).

Moreover, teachers can work with their students to create and dramatize interpretations of poetry that explore issues of relationships, identity, culture, and social justice. For example, after reading *Bronx Masquerade* (Grimes, 2002/2003 NBGS), teachers can invite students to engage in a discussion exploring character dialogues and their similarities and differences. In small groups, students can collaborate on dramatic interpretations to capture the essence of the voices. To provide the context for dramatization, teachers and students can discuss issues of gender, race, and identity and explore the tensions and possibilities presented in this novel in verse. As Medina stated, "words and actions [can become] the center of powerful explorations through drama" (p. 275).

AUTHOR REFLECTIONS

Unmasked

NIKKI GRIMES

Rich or poor, young or old, black or white—when the subject is people, the most important common denominator is the human heart. I write with that in mind every time I set pen to paper. Why? Because we live in a global society, in a multihued, multicultural world, and we need to understand one another, learn of one another. There is no safer place to do that than between the pages of a book.

Love is love, pain is pain, and we all bleed when cut. Literature can remind us of this sameness, even as it celebrates our differences. It is particularly critical to promote that understanding in children's literature.

A literary environment in which our fear of "the other" is allowed to flourish and fester is an environment in which the seeds of racism can, all too easily, take root and spread. But it need not be so. We can change that environment, and children's literature is the perfect place to begin. That's what a book like *Bronx Masquerade* is all about. That's what, I hope, every one of my books is all about.

Book by Nikki Grimes selected for the Notable Books for a Global Society:

Bronx Masquerade (2002/2003 NBGS)

When modeling dramatization of poetry, it is imperative to move students beyond a literal interpretation of the poem. One way to encourage critical dialogue about the poem is to provide chart paper for students to illustrate the most powerful mental image that was evoked and to explain their reasons for the illustration. Another approach is to maintain a poetry response journal where students can freely express their insights and interpretations about the poem as well as record their wonderings.

Integrating Poetry and Social Studies

Integrating poetry in the content areas can enhance connections between social studies and reading. As previously discussed, poetry provides insights on global issues to increase our understanding and awareness of the world. Moreover, poetry can influence teachers to embrace a social-reconstructionist approach (McCall, 2004; Vardell, 2003) in which classroom teachers can incorporate poetry to address social issues within the curriculum. For example, in small groups, invite students to read the poem "Unveiled" in *The Space Between Our Footsteps: Poems and Paintings From the Middle East* (Nye, 1998/1999 NBGS). This particular poem addresses the issue of gender inequality based on the cultural and social standards of one family. The young girl hungers for activities and opportunities that will nourish her intellectual curiosities, but instead of receiving approval or encouragement for setting goals for her future she is reminded of her place and the expectations of her family. Using other poems from this anthology may also challenge students' ideas about cultural and gender inequality. After reading several of the poems aloud, direct students to work with a partner to explain, draw, or write what they learned from the poems.

As educators, it is imperative to serve as coparticipants in the process of critically reading poetry connecting to social themes with our students. For instance, adapting a critical questioning strategy utilized by Ava McCall (2004), classroom teachers can develop possible prompts to facilitate small-group discussion among students, such as the following:

- Problematize the issue that this young girl is facing. Discuss the rights and privileges that she was arguing for.
- In what ways was she silenced and for what purpose(s)?
- Have you been or known someone who has been in a similar situation? If so, describe your initial reaction to the way in which this individual was treated.

Poetry Circles

Another way to include global poetry in the classroom is to form poetry circles. Similar to literature circles (Daniels, 2002; Harste, Short, & Burke, 1988; Schlick-Noe & Johnson, 1999), poetry circles offer opportunities for readers to read and respond to poems. Literature circles, as defined by Daniels (2002), are small, peer-led discussion groups whose members have chosen to read and respond to the same text. Group members read portions of the text, take notes as they read, and come to the group with ideas to share. Daniels recommends that establishing roles at the beginning of literature circles provides some guidance and direction. In order to simulate this experience within the classroom, teachers might want to use the suggested roles provided in Table 8.1 as one way to organize poetry circles. However, it is important to emphasize that there is no one way to organize poetry circles. The most important component of the poetry circle experience is to provide students with ample opportunities to discuss and explore poetry within the classroom setting.

Throughout the poetry circle exploration, teachers will want to encourage their students to form a written response to the overall collection and, in some cases, to respond to one poem that particularly evoked personal connections and be prepared to share these responses during the discussion (Daniels, 2002; Rosenblatt, 1978). For example, teachers can invite their students to read and respond to the following Notable Books for a Global Society poetry selections during the poetry circle engagement. Middle school and high school students would enjoy reading poems from the collection entitled *Skin Deep and Other Teenage Reflections* (Medearis, 1995/1996 NBGS). The poems pertain to issues such as dating, puberty, and identity, which directly affect young adolescents. After reading these poems, students can share their own adolescent experiences

Table 8.1. Suggested Poetry Circle Roles

Poetry Circle Role	Responsibility
Image creator	Offers visual representation of how the poem affected their senses
Poet researcher	Conducts background research about the poet or anthologist
Critical dialogue leader	Encourages critical conversations with students and poses questions to initiate group discussion
Reader	Practices reading the poem aloud several times before doing so in the group
Idea generator	Facilitates the process of dramatizing the poem for the rest of the class and encourages everyone to participate

in small-group discussions or in a poetry response journal. Teachers can model reading aloud poetry by sharing selected poems before reading realistic fiction books containing similar issues.

The poems in the anthology entitled *The Tree Is Older Than You Are: A Bilingual Gathering of Poems and Stories From Mexico* (Nye, 1995/1996 NBGS) ignite images and stories about Mexican life and culture. Upper elementary and middle school students can interview one another about their backgrounds, cultural heritage, and memories. They can also write individual poems to celebrate their own heritage, family background, and interests. One possibility is to direct students to use the bio-poem template as a framework to record their ideas. In the elementary classroom, teachers can share *Visiting Langston* (Perdomo, 2002/2003 NBGS), a story in verse that introduces readers to a young African American girl who accompanies her father on his visit to Langston Hughes's house in Harlem, New York, USA. Classroom teachers and their students can conduct a poet study about Langston Hughes to research his other poems, such as "I, Too, Sing America." Teachers can then invite their students to clap to the rhythm during a shared reading experience.

During poetry circles, teachers can encourage their students to critically evaluate and discuss the poems. As students begin to grapple with text and go beyond the surface meaning to unpack themes and issues, they challenge their prior discourses and experiences in learning about literature, in this case, poetry. For instance, one component of critical literacy is to consider the background research conducted by the poet, the poet's purpose for writing about the theme, and the point of view and biases expressed in the poem (Creighton, 1997). When reading poems about the culture and memories of people in the Middle East from *19 Varieties of Gazelle: Poems of the Middle East* (Nye, 2002/2003 NGBS), for example, teachers can share the opening pages of this collection. During a poet study about Naomi Shihab Nye, the class can read the foreword from Nye's collection and discuss the importance of learning about the poet's background in addition to reading about the culture. In this case, students will learn more about the poet's Palestinian father and how he shared both fond and sad memories of growing up in the Middle East. Nye grew up with rich cultural influences of music, food, and language. She has traveled extensively and has returned to the Middle East numerous times.

Educators can also explore the problems that are associated with stereotyping people on the basis of race, gender, or family background. In addition, they can discuss the negative and harmful effects of bullying or teasing individuals on the basis of race, gender, or culture. By actively engaging in critical dialogues about poetry and social justice, students will begin to shape new understandings about themselves and their world.

Poetry Exploration Strategies in Action: A Teacher Research Project

In one of the children's literature courses I taught, I modeled the various activities for using poetry to explore global understanding and issues of social justice appropriate for K–12 classrooms, as discussed in the previous section. I provided preservice teachers with an opportunity to practice reading aloud poetry to small groups of elementary students, and the following section highlights some of the significant results of this experience. Educators of students in all grades from preschool to high school can apply a similar approach within their own classrooms, as these experiences can be adapted to any grade level as needed.

In the Classroom: Preservice Teachers Sharing Poetry With Elementary Students

Over numerous class sessions, preservice teachers engaged in coteaching experiences to model and simulate the instructional process. Before visiting the students, preservice teachers worked with a partner to develop a series of poetry experiences using a recommended list of poems addressing social and global issues. During the planning process, preservice teachers discussed the age appropriateness of the poems and the types of questions and response activities that would match content standards and enhance literacy. Here, the focus will be on the interactions between the elementary students and two preservice teachers, Amy and Paul (all names are pseudonyms).

Amy and Paul decided to plan response activities for *César: ¡Sí, Se Puede! Yes, We Can!* (Bernier-Grand, 2004/2005 NBGS), a set of biographical poems that chronicle the life and struggles of activist César Chávez. Neither Amy nor Paul knew about the significant accomplishments of César Chávez and decided to locate additional information. They also decided that it would be helpful to find additional picture books and nonfiction books to read, summarize, and share with the elementary students. Amy and Paul agreed that they would dramatize several poems in addition to posing critical questions.

During our visits, preservice teachers brought bags of props, materials, and their poetry collections. As they launched their beginning activities, elementary students shared personal connections to the poems while exploring real-world issues. As I observed Amy and Paul work with their small group of fourth graders, I noticed how they were able to simulate an engaging experience using poetry with global themes. As they worked with their group, they guided students to consider the meaning of the poems and solicited their thoughts about how to dramatize the words. Amy and Paul modeled the process and enthusiastically shared the poems about César Chávez. The critical dialogue and questions that were being shared within their poetry circle was notably effective at engaging students with the poetry and social justice issues related to the poem, and this type of dialogue can be adapted in any classroom to generate students' critical thinking. In the following vignette, Amy and Paul lead students through a discussion during their first visit.

Student 1: Did you know that we talked about César Chávez in Social Studies?

Amy: Really? Why don't you tell us what you already know about him?

Student 1: He spent his entire life fighting for equal rights for farmers.

Student 2: Yeah, they were not treating them right.

Amy: That's really interesting. I didn't know much about César Chávez's ideas or about his love for his people. I read this poetry book (holds up *César: ¡Sí, Se Puede! Yes, We Can!*) and learned that one of his dreams was to make sure that the farm workers got better pay.

Paul: You know, Amy, I am wondering how we could learn from his example?

Amy: Yeah, that's a good idea.

Student 1: What do you mean?

Paul: Well, I wonder how kids and adults today could learn from all of the things that César Chávez did for his people.

Student 2: Um...let me think. I'm not sure.

Paul: That's OK. Take your time and think about what you learned so far.

Student 2: OK, I have something. Maybe, we could learn to speak up if something is not fair.

Amy: That's good. Does anyone else have something to add?

Student 3: Yeah...to work together to make a difference.

Student 1: OK, I see what you mean.

Amy: OK, would you like to add something?

Student 1: Um...yeah, I would say...um...that we can try to change things if they are not fair.

Paul: Great ideas. Can you think of anything that is unfair or that you want to change?

On our last visit, Paul and a fourth-grade student with whom he worked shared a poem written by the fourth grader with the entire group of preservice teachers and fourth-grade students (see Figure 8.1). In addition, the elementary students and preservice teachers exchanged poems as "gifts" of appreciation

Figure 8.1. Poem for Two Voices Written by Fourth-Grade Student

Birds fly across the sky	
	They fly in the clouds
They fly over water	
Flying	*flying*
All around the world	
	They are free
I wish I could fly	*I wish I could fly*
Just one day	
To teach people	
	Something important
	To be happy
To be kind	
	To be fair
To work together	*To make a difference*

(Heard, 1999). Some of the students wrote their own words while others found poems in anthologies.

The preservice teachers' experience with these students illustrates the power of sharing global poetry with students. Quality poetry is meant to be read aloud and can also serve as a model for student writing. In this case, the student wrote his poem using the format found in "poems for two voices" to create an original verse based on his exposure to global poetry and conversations that were held in his classroom. Teachers can encourage their students to "borrow" the format from their favorite poets in order to create meaningful texts.

Preservice Teachers' Reflections

When I asked Amy and Paul to reflect upon their experience, they were surprised that fourth graders were beginning to consider issues of justice. Paul mentioned that it was clear that the classroom teachers were committed to adding these discussions to their curriculum. Throughout the discussion, the fourth graders not only shared their insights, but also stretched their understanding of the issues by listening to others. As a group, they demonstrated new awareness of the world around them while also providing meaningful connections with global literature. During our subsequent visits, the elementary students surprised us by writing and acting out their own poems that connected to their lives.

After each classroom visit, preservice teachers reflected upon how their instruction influenced student learning, what they discovered about reading global poetry, and how their initial reactions about poetry had remained the same or had changed based on the experience. Amy and Paul expressed different reactions based on their background experience with poetry. Amy indicated that she would never have thought that children would be able to discuss difficult and challenging subject matter about their world. She was not prepared for the conversation that took place in the classroom. At the end of the experience, she wrote,

> Now I am more aware of the importance of integrating global poetry in the classroom. I did not understand how important it really is for teachers to expose students to literature from different cultures. I never had this experience growing up. I went to school in a fairly upper class community and I cannot remember having been exposed to poetry or to books that shared the rich cultural experiences that Paul and I used with the fourth graders. I am beginning to realize that a teacher's role is more than just following the text, but to open your students' world to make connections, and to think about social justice. I have a better appreciation for using literature in this way. I am still a bit unsure how to do all of this when I go into the classroom, but I think that using poetry is a good way to start. I was never a fan of poetry, so after reading so many poems this semester and sharing them at the elementary school, I am now more excited to use poetry in my classroom.

On the other hand, Paul had different experiences with poetry especially in middle and high school. His original perceptions of poetry were very positive. At his high school, his English class held weekly poetry readings and students wrote and read their own works or the works of others. Paul recalled that he created a poetry anthology in 11th grade, which consisted of many self-authored poems that touched on social issues. He also explained that both of his parents had extensive libraries and that he was a voracious reader throughout his life. In fact, he remembers that in 11th grade his class had a poetry celebration where everyone shared poems and acted them out or set them to music. As a result of the experience, he explained,

> I have always loved poetry. I think that some of my classmates find it unusual to know that a "guy" can like poetry, but I hope that my example will raise their awareness that poetry can be enjoyed by everyone regardless of race, sex, class, etc. It was interesting to work with a classmate who was not as enthusiastic about reading poetry. This made me realize that I will encounter reluctant students in my own classroom and I would need to find creative ways to encourage them to read poems. This happened in our group a bit. One of the boys did not seem very interested in poetry. He called it "a girl thing." But then when he found out that I had written poetry and created songs and special rhythms to voice my views and ideas, he started to rethink his position. I told him that I listen to songs a lot to get ideas for poems. Even though we only had a chance to work with the kids a few times, I made it a point to really try to make a difference for that student. I am glad that we selected to use the poems from César Chávez because his actions and accomplishments changed the lives of many people. I could tell that this student was drawn to Chávez's story. On the last day of our visit, Jay (one of the boys in the group)

presented me with a poem in two voices that he asked me to read with him. The message in the poem made me realize the power that poetry has on our lives. I know that poetry will be a part of my classroom regardless of the grade level I teach.

Conclusion

Overall, reading selections from the Notable Books for a Global Society booklist presents multiple benefits for students at all levels. Global literature has the capacity to foster personal and social change, enrich our curriculum, and have an impact on our hearts. As educators, we need to guide students to embrace global poetry to build hopeful futures and to make the world a better place. The final chapter of this section, "Transformative Literature: A Teaching/Learning Model for Using Global Literature to Positively Influence Our World" by Marian J. McKenna, continues the exploration of literature for social justice by proposing a three-level model designed to help readers discover the transformative process that results from reading global literature.

REFERENCES

Note. Complete bibliographic citations for the Notable Books for a Global Society booklist (1996–2005) can be found at the end of the book.

Apol, L., & Harris, J. (1999). Joyful noises: Creating poems for voices and ears. *Language Arts, 76,* 314–322.

Banks, J.A. (1991). Teaching multicultural literacy to teachers. *Teaching Education, 4*(1), 135–144.

Banks, J.A. (2003). Teaching literacy for social justice and global citizenship. *Language Arts, 81,* 18–19.

Cahnmann, M. (2006). Reading, living, and writing bilingual poetry as scholARTistry in the language arts classroom. *Language Arts, 83,* 342–352.

Creighton, D.C. (1997). Critical literacy in the elementary classroom. *Language Arts, 74,* 438–445.

Cullinan, B., Scale, M., & Schroeder, V. (1995). *Three voices: An invitation to poetry across the curriculum.* York, ME: Stenhouse.

Damico, J. (2005). Evoking hearts and heads: Exploring issues of social justice through poetry. *Language Arts, 83,* 137–146.

Daniels, H. (2002). *Literature circles: Voice and choice in book clubs and reading groups.* Portland, ME: Stenhouse.

Edelsky, C. (Ed.). (1999). *Making justice our project: Teachers working toward critical whole language.* Urbana, IL: National Council of Teachers of English.

Freeman, E., & Lehman, B. (2001). *Global perspectives in children's literature.* Boston: Allyn & Bacon.

Freire, P. (1970). *Pedagogy of the oppressed.* New York: Continuum.

Giroux, H. (1988). *Teachers as intellectuals: Toward a critical pedagogy of learning.* Granby, MA: Bergin & Garvey.

Hadaway, N., Vardell, S., & Young, T. (2001). Scaffolding oral language development through poetry for students learning English. *The Reading Teacher, 54,* 796–806.

Hadaway, N., Vardell, S., & Young, T. (2002). Poetry for language development of English language learners. *The Dragon Lode, 20*(2), 68–76.

Harste, J., Short, K., Burke, C. (1988). *Creating classrooms for authors: The reading-writing connection*. Portsmouth, NH: Heinemann.

Heard, G. (1999). *Awakening the heart: Exploring poetry in elementary and middle school*. Portsmouth, NH: Heinemann.

hooks, b. (1994). *Teaching to transgress: Education as the practice of freedom*. New York: Routledge.

Mathis, J. (2002). Poetry and preservice teachers: Perceptions and possibilities. *The Dragon Lode, 20*(2), 12–19.

McCall, A. (2004). Using poetry in social studies classes to teach about cultural diversity and social justice. *The Social Studies, 95*(4), 172–176.

McClure, A. (1999). 1999 Notable books for a global society. *The Dragon Lode, 18*(1), 18.

Medina, C. (2004). Drama wor(l)ds: Explorations of Latina/o realistic fiction: Drama encourages critical dialogue through exploration of multiple voices and perspectives. *Language Arts, 81*, 272–282.

Nieto, S. (2002). *Language, culture, and teaching: Critical perspectives for a new century*. Mahwah, NJ: Erlbaum.

Perfect, K. (1999). Rhyme and reason: Poetry for the heart and head. *The Reading Teacher, 52*, 728–737.

Rosaen, C. (2003). Preparing teachers for diverse classrooms: Creating public and private spaces to explore culture through poetry writing. *Teachers College Record, 105*(8), 1437–1485.

Rosenblatt, L. (1978). *The reader, the text, the poem: The transactional theory of the literary work*. Carbondale: Southern Illinois University Press.

Schlick-Noe, K., & Johnson, N. (1999). *Getting started with literature circles*. Norwood, MA: Christopher-Gordon.

Sloan, G. (2003). *Give them poetry! A guide for sharing poetry with children K–8*. New York: Teachers College Press.

Vardell, S.M. (2003). Poetry for social studies: Poems, standards, and strategies. *Social Education, 67*(4), 206–211.

LITERATURE CITED

Fleischman, P. (1988). *Joyful noise*. New York: HarperCollins.

CHAPTER 9

Transformative Literature: A Teaching/Learning Model for Using Global Literature to Positively Influence Our World

Marian J. McKenna

"The second 'island' is the separation between what is near in time and space from what is far away, the illusion that our individual well-being can be disconnected from the well-being of the biological and social systems that sustain us...and the local and global communities we live in. If we understand instead that our lives are seamlessly connected to the biocultural whole, then we might find our own integrity, acknowledging that the special care we take of our own interests and homes, we owe also to the future and to the larger world."

—Kathleen Dean Moore (2004, pp. 6–7).

I have always been amazed that the oceans of the world can be distinguished from one another. It is a mystery to me. The waters move throughout the planet, and it is all the same water, rising, falling, changing temperature, and being pulled about by the tug of the moon. It is all the same water, and we are a part of it all. Perhaps an oceanographer could tell me the exact point where the North Atlantic becomes the South Atlantic, but by the time his or her explanation was complete, the waters would have moved on to another place.

As the waters flow across the face of the globe, so do people move from place to place for a variety of reasons. Cultural and religious freedom, financial opportunities, displacement, and refuge from war and natural disasters are among the many reasons that our restless species moves. But unlike the waters that sustain us, people create artificial barriers between and among us where no physical barriers exist. We create barriers and differences that separate us along racial, cultural, religious, gender, and other classification schemes.

This chapter makes the case that, as the waters of the sea are the same waters, no matter where they roam over the planet, so is the human condition the same, no matter where we live. Our stories have a resounding commonality at their heart. The following discourse provides a rationale and model for using global literature not only to teach students about the world in which they live but also to transform them into engaged, active citizens, willing and able to live fully chosen, authentic lives.

In the use of global literature, we can ask our children and students to consider the notion that what happens in one place can happen anywhere. As the Berlin wall has come down, so can we bring down barriers and boundaries in the minds of our students, no matter the origin of those boundaries. We have an obligation as educators to heighten the awareness of our students that social injustice—no matter where it is found—is untenable, unthinkable. As we expose our students to the universal potential of the human spirit, to love, to work, to protect our young, to choose our way of worship, we can ask them to consider the truth behind a popular window sign: "War is Obsolete." There are other ways to resolve differences and other ways to celebrate one another. Indeed, there are challenges that we must face together as a species trying to live in a global society on a finite planet.

This chapter proposes a three-stage Transformative Teaching/Learning Model (see Figure 9.1) that combines the best we have in global literature, what we know about best practices in the classroom, and what research tells us about the efficacy of academic service learning to provide opportunities for our students to become dynamic readers who connect the text with their own lives and the lives of those near and far. "Transformative learning occurs when learners engage in a thorough process of critical reflection and rational discourse. Experiential learning is central to this process" (Mezirow, 1991, 1995). Teaching also transforms those of us who teach, making this Transformative Teaching/Learning Model one that acknowledges teaching and learning as part of the same cycle of events. Then, our students, our next generation of leaders, must go outward with these connections into constructive activism.

A fitting analogy for these three levels of engagement can be found in a deeper analogy from Ralph Waldo Emerson when he said, "Thought is the blossom, language is the bud, action is the fruit behind it." In the teaching model described in this chapter, the blossom is the Information Stage, the bud is the

Figure 9.1. The Three-Stage Transformative Teaching/Learning Model

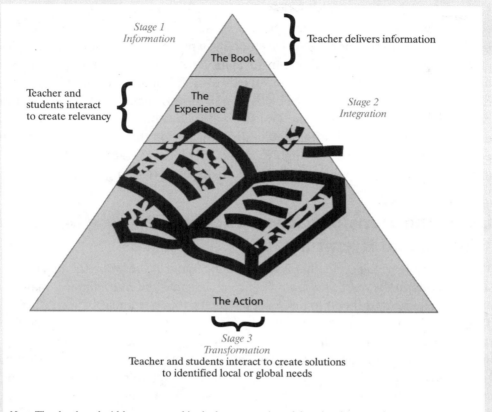

Stage 1
Information

The Book

} Teacher delivers information

Teacher and
students interact
to create relevancy
}

The
Experience

Stage 2
Integration

The Action

Stage 3
Transformation
Teacher and students interact to create solutions
to identified local or global needs

Note. The depth and width represented in the bottom section of the triangle comes from
the connections and richness that are added as a result of family, community, and cultural interchanges.

Integration Stage, and the fruit (or in this case, the action) is the Transformation Stage, where we are transformed by the action we take and the action we take transforms us and our world. The model builds upon pedagogical theories and practices for supporting our students' development through three stages of engagement so that students may learn from global literature, grow, and take action for a better and more just world.

The press to use quality literature as teaching and learning tools in our classrooms is a well-researched and supported practice. However, to be called literature, to win prestigious awards, books and the authors who write them have the responsibility to change the lives of their readers. In what way does global literature succeed? Do students move beyond the world of their neighborhoods, their schools, and their immediate concerns to realize that they live in a global village? Can we ask students to develop compassion, insight, and perhaps even constructive activism as a result of being exposed to such books, such stories? Certainly some of my more sensitive students, whether in elementary grades or graduate classes, may make this transformation without any input or guidance, but it is seldom an automatic response. However, it is imperative to elicit such responses from our students as our planet grows ever smaller and our classrooms richer with cultural diversity. The Transformative Teaching/Learning Model, as illustrated in Figure 9.1, is grounded in the anticipation that teachers and teacher educators are themselves thoroughly engaged in global literature as well as understanding the unapologetically political nature of teaching.

Using the Transformative Teaching/Learning Model With Global Literature

The teaching/learning cycle, that is the dynamic interplay between the teacher, student, community, and classroom, is such an organic and multidimensional entity that it is very difficult to discuss a model for it in our linear language. Therefore, let me thoroughly emphasize that there is not meant to be a step-by-step "procedure" in following or adapting this model. A teacher can use this model from any beginning point depending on his or her students and educational goals. For example, those teachers who are lucky enough to be teaching from an inquiry-based curriculum may want to start with what I am calling Stage 3, Transformation, the identification of a community-based need and taking action to address that need. A class can then work outward from there to Integration (Stage 2) and Information (Stage 1) as needed to take positive action and be able to reflect deeply concerning the impact and relevance of such action. In a constructivist classroom, the teacher may want to start with a piece of quality literature such as those recommended in this book, allowing the students the aesthetic experience of the transaction with a text before framing that experience with data or instruction around the time, place, and events leading up to the story. Therefore, the following model will necessarily be an oversimplification of a very complex process. As teachers who strive to translate this model into our own classrooms, we will all move through it in different ways and create our own adaptations according to our teaching styles, our tolerance for not knowing all of the answers, and our ability to let go of our students' learning and move outward into the larger community as learners and teachers with our students. Much will also depend on the courage and the amount of support or lack thereof of those in administrative positions in our schools and universities.

Stage 1: Information

Perhaps the best way to visualize this model is as a pyramid with the Information Stage being at the top and most narrow part of the model. This stage can be aligned with the knowledge and comprehension stages of Bloom's taxonomy. Students get information from their teachers and textbooks. This is what Rosenblatt (1978) refers to as the efferent reading experience or reading for information. This is the beginning scaffolding from which students can and will build a deeper understanding of people and the events happening in places around the globe as well as in our own backyards. The Information Stage of engagement is characterized by the teacher providing background knowledge such as introducing the book, the author, setting, history, and rationale for choosing the particular text. At this stage we see traditional interactions between teacher and students, such as direct instruction, assignments, and discussion over the various literary elements. The focus at this stage is primarily on the efferent experience or information about the text under study. Again, please note that although the Information Stage of engagement is being discussed first, this does not mean that it necessarily has to come first in the chronology of the classroom. For the sake of presentation, I am discussing the model from the simplest level of engagement to the deepest and most personal level of engagement, which is Transformation.

The Information Stage can be described as the level where knowledge is acquired, comprehension is developed, and interest on the part of the students is heightened concerning the topic being introduced. In this stage of engagement, the classroom is teacher-centered where the teacher is providing information and sources for investigation. The classroom looks much like a traditional classroom where one might observe students asking questions for clarification and the teacher is engaged in lecture, read-alouds, and some interrogative and guided discussion.

Stage 2: Integration

The second stage of engagement, Integration, is what Rosenblatt (1976) referred to as the transactions between the reader and the text, such that the personal or aesthetic meaning of the text is created for and by the reader. Students are given the opportunity to read the literature that is central to the Transformative Teaching/Learning Model. They learn about conditions for people in Afghanistan (*Parvana's Journey*, Ellis, 2002/2003 NBGS) or Guatemala (*Tree Girl*, Mikaelsen, 2004/2005 NBGS). They learn about processes people may have to go through as they emigrate to the United States from their home countries (*Tangled Threads: A Hmong Girl's Story*, Shea, 2003/2004 NBGS). However, it is evident in working with students at any grade level that simply being provided with quality literature, no matter how stirring the actual story may be, does not directly translate into integrated or transformative learning.

This is where a sensitive and highly qualified teacher comes into the equation. Almost anyone can deliver information. It takes a skilled, educated, and compassionate teacher to move students inward and onward for the learning to become truly meaningful and relevant and to provide opportunities for students to develop a social empathy and take action that addresses specific community needs. This is the process described by Emerson as moving us from thought to action via the use of language. We can apply this quote (see p. 166) directly to the proposed model.

The Integration Stage of engagement is characterized by a more constructivist classroom where the teacher serves as the facilitator of discussion and discovery among the students as they go deeper into the text and find the relevancy of it to their own lives and time. The focus at this stage is on the experience of reading the book and the creation of individual, personal meaning. At the second stage the understanding and experience gained becomes wider and deeper by applying it to our own lives and situations. The Integration Stage brings in the depth of personal culture and the ability to see the lives of others through our own lives. After reading *Any Small Goodness: A Novel of the Barrio* (Johnston, 2001/2002 NBGS), a sixth grader reported, "I think global books are important because it can tell you how to solve problems or how not to be a bully or something like that." This statement indicates that the student is moving into the Integration Stage of understanding the literature and is engaged in a transaction with the story. She has been able to personalize and make relevant the stories and events in this book. Beyond information, this book is becoming integrated into the child's experiences of the world.

At the Integration Stage of engagement, an observer may see a classroom full of students reading the same or different books about a topic or event. This is the stage of Rosenblatt's transaction with the text where the students are reading high-quality literature for aesthetic purposes. It is here that the students are free to consider the connections of the literature under study to their own situations, inner lives, or imaginations. Students are able to create personal meaning around a text. In this scenario, the teacher serves as a guide and participant in guided and reflective discussions in order to deepen students' understanding of the context, history, and reality of the story. Students may be participating in book clubs, pairing activities, or writing unsent letters and journal entries. Up to this stage of engagement, we are not seeing anything out of the normal range of activities in a classroom conducted by a highly qualified teacher—with the exception that global literature is at the heart of the curriculum.

Stage 3: Transformation

The final stage proposed for this model is that of Transformation, the notion supported by John Dewey's theories of experiential learning and Rosenblatt's transactional theory. Theirs was a call for literary critics and teachers to be political activists, and they promoted the very powerful movement toward academic service learning at all levels of educational institutions. Neither Rosenblatt's theories nor this Transformative Teaching/Learning Model end with the aesthetic event for the reader. As educators at any level, it is imperative that we move our students further and more comprehensively than ever before. The world is changing and schools and educational practices are changing with it. It is action that defines this level of engagement, or the fruit of all of our labors, where we are both transformed by our actions and our actions may transform our world and how we move through it.

Students move from a level of knowing about something, someplace, or someone to understanding and being able to relate to that situation or person, to being willing and able to take positive action addressing a situation or an injustice. In other words, they begin to push the envelope of Morton's (1995) service-learning continuum from volunteerism to service learning for social justice and begin to ask important questions about why things are the way they are: Why do people not take care of each other as we should, and what can be done about the myriad of social and political injustices in our neighborhoods and in our world? The model proposed in this chapter has as its goal the development of educated citizens as defined by Sumida and Meyer (2006): "At the heart of teaching and learning, an educated citizen is viewed as one who can 'read the world,' think critically, question relationships of power, and become an agent of social change" (p. 444).

It is at the Transformation Stage of engagement that students and their teachers go beyond personal and academic learning to the development of a social empathy and awareness of social injustices being perpetrated in our neighborhoods as well as around the world. It is at this stage of engagement that the classroom begins to look and sound different as teachers and students become coinvestigators asking questions such as, What can we do in our classroom? What can we do in our communities? What skills do we have and what skills can we develop to address some of the injustices of which we are now aware? How can we take our learning and our skills out into the community so that we may learn more deeply while addressing needs expressed by our community members? In this classroom, teacher and students are working together to identify a problem and possible solutions *with* their community partners and resources. Teachers, students, and interested community partners work as a group, individually, or in teams to develop a plan of action to address mutually identified needs.

At this stage of engagement, the walls between classroom and community become more transparent. It is here that action becomes the fruit of the study and consequent transformation as students, teachers, and community partners work together toward a common goal, using the skills of all participants. Action, as embodied in a service-learning project, transforms the partners by creating links from the learning to the community and the world. Learning is deepened through relevant action, and the human spirit is expanded through connections and mutual support with all types of people and situations. The understanding that students gain as a result of having something to offer to their community or world affects their learning and the rest of their lives. These are the deeper understandings and behaviors that students (and their teachers) will take with them into their futures, long after "lessons" have been forgotten.

Extending the Model Through Service Learning

Academic service learning is the culminating piece of the pyramid. It is broad and deep as it takes us outside of the realm of the classroom and demands that we interact with our neighborhoods, our own preconceived biases, and the learning in which we are engaged. It is a dynamic pedagogy that has been on the rise in the United States particularly in the last 20 years. To say that it has been on the rise connotes that it is a new theory or pedagogy, but that is not the case. Academic service learning has been embedded in the goals of public and higher education since the inception of these noble institutions. Therefore, the vehicle for personal as well as social transformation in the Transformative Teaching/Learning Model is the pedagogy of academic service learning, particularly as it extends from high-quality global literature.

Service learning is primarily and foremost connected to the curriculum and curricular goals so that what is being learned in the classroom is taken out into the community to address local or global needs. This pedagogy can work for almost any age group or class size. A kindergarten or first-grade classroom might define its community as the playground connected to the school. A graduate class of students may want to provide service learning to an entire school district, or a team of teachers may want to adopt a school in a beleaguered community or in some other part of the country or world. The learning can be any area of literacy studies or other curricular connections, such as history, science, music, art, diet and exercise, or economics, to name just a few. The "service" aspect of the service learning will be dictated by the size of the community, the expressed

Learning From History

CHRIS CROWE

AUTHOR REFLECTIONS

At 14, I was a certifiable knucklehead.

Sports were the only things I took seriously, and I didn't know—or care much—about anything else going on in 1968. Of course, I wasn't a total idiot, so I'd heard about the Vietnam War and the U.S. Civil Rights movement, but for me those events existed only in newspaper headlines and two-minute TV news bites. Sports pages and the coolest magazine ever, *Sports Illustrated*, provided me with the *real* news of 1968, including the Packers' victory in Super Bowl II, Denny McClain's 30-win season, and another NBA title for the Boston Celtics.

Fortunately, thanks to the combined effects of high school, college, and maturity, I outgrew my knuckleheadedness and became more knowledgeable about the world around me.

Somehow, though, the years and the education never taught me about Emmett Till. It wasn't until 1998 when researching Mildred D. Taylor that I stumbled onto the story of this 14-year-old boy from Chicago who was kidnapped, tortured, and murdered by white men. I eventually dug up the original issue of *Jet* magazine that featured a story about the crime and the trial of Till's killers and a grotesque photo of the boy's mutilated corpse. Fascinated by the story, I read everything I could find about Till, and I learned that the Emmett Till case was a significant catalyst for the U.S. Civil Rights movement: He was killed in August 1955; a jury pronounced his killers innocent in September 1955; and on December 1, 1955, Rosa Parks helped trigger the Montgomery Bus Boycott.

Why hadn't I known that?

The historical importance of the Till case and my ignorance of it inspired me to try to write a young adult novel built around the murder of the boy from Chicago, a novel that would introduce teen readers to the Emmett Till case.

But in addition to learning the awful truth about the murder of Emmett Till, I wanted readers of *Mississippi Trial, 1955* to learn how slippery and subtle racism can be. Like many teenagers (and like me as a teenager), my narrator, Hiram Hillburn, thinks that all Americans enjoy the same freedoms he does. He assumes that because racism isn't a problem for him, it's not a problem for anyone. He also assumes that bad people are always bad and that good people are always good. Well, the summer of 1955 turns Hiram's worldview upside down.

I hoped that my novel would have a similar effect on young adult readers, that my fictional account of Hiram Hillburn and his encounter with Emmett Till would help them understand the very real complexities and consequences of racism.

Book by Chris Crowe selected for the Notable Books for a Global Society:
Mississippi Trial, 1955 (2002/2003 NBGS)

needs of the community, and the expertise the students bring to that need. It is often the most productive to work with existing community organizations.

One such outstanding example is one of my undergraduate students who, after reading and discussing *Zulu Dog* by Anton Ferreira (2002/2003 NBGS) in our class, signed up with a humanitarian science organization and is currently in Tanzania working on developing and teaching sustainable agriculture. Of course, the particular text under question was not the only influence on this outstanding young man, but the experience of this powerful book certainly helped to focus his plans for continued service learning activities and critical reflection for his growth as a teacher.

However the service-learning projects are designed, the hallmarks of successful and meaningful service-learning projects are the integration of the classroom curriculum and community, critical reflection where students bring their learning and experience back into the classroom discussion, involvement of student voice in the design of the service-learning project, and an ever-growing awareness of the importance of civic responsibility.

Using the Transformative Teaching/Learning Model With Notable Books for a Global Society Booklists in Grades K–12

In this section, three books selected to the Notable Books for a Global Society booklists, each at a different age level, have been selected to serve as specific examples of how student engagement may evolve from information consumption to integration to transformation. Even very young children can be encouraged in their ability to make decisions, negotiate with their peers, and select courses of action that have the most or least positive impacts on their community. Keep in mind that the notion of community is determined by the age and skill levels of the students so that the community for a kindergarten class could be some feature of the school itself or the immediate neighborhood.

The goal for students at any grade level is to naturally move through a world that recognizes, celebrates, and respects people and cultures from all over the world. Make sure that each one of your students can find themselves in the pages of a book in your classroom library. Eventually the goal is one of not talking about global literature, or inserting it into the curriculum. The goal is to fully live in a global society. Using quality global literature as a starting point for both learning and living is powerfully expressed by the writer Anne Lamott:

> What a miracle it is that out of these small, flat, rigid squares of paper unfolds world after world after world, worlds that sing to you, comfort and quiet or excite you. Books

help us understand who we are and how we are to behave. They show us what community and friendship mean; they show us how to live and die. (Lamott, 1994, p.15)

Using the Transformative Teaching/Learning Model in the Primary Grades

When examining Demi's *One Grain of Rice: A Mathematical Folktale* (1997/1998 NBGS) at the Information Stage, we see a thoughtful young girl outwit a greedy and heartless raja with a little bit of cleverness and an understanding of mathematics. This book, though written in a folklore style, offers a wonderful insight on a culture and the theme of good versus evil. Although the mathematical concept of fractals may be too advanced for early primary students, they can certainly discuss the characters, the theme, the plot, and events of the story.

At the Integration Stage of engagement, students may be asking why the people in this story were hungry. They may want to discuss what it feels like to be hungry, times when they themselves felt hungry, and even express the understanding that there are people who are hungry in our own community. In addition to any mathematical demonstrations that this book lends itself to, there are rich opportunities for oral and written communication skills to be enhanced and many reading or language arts standards to be addressed.

Even students at the primary level can progress to the Transformation Stage and begin to question why there is hunger in their community and think about what they might be able to do about it. Can they be as clever and thoughtful as the young girl in the story? Consider some ways that these students can address and more deeply understand the notion of hunger in their communities. For example, the class could save their snack allowance for a week and donate that money to the local food bank. This falls more on the volunteerism end of Morton's (1995) continuum, but it does get young students thinking about the larger world. An even richer experience would be for the students to go to the local food bank or homeless shelter and help measure and weigh portions of food into storage bags to be used for cooking or donations. In this scenario, students move out of their classrooms, address cross-curricular standards, and reach out to the community to become aware of and transformed by engagement with the lives of their friends and neighbors.

Other suggested booklist selections for primary classrooms are *Just a Minute: A Trickster Tale and Counting Book* by Yuyi Morales (2003/2004 NBGS), *The Barking Mouse* by Antonio Sacre (2003/2004 NBGS), *The Color of Home* by Mary Hoffman (2002/2003 NBGS), *The Day Gogo Went to Vote: South Africa, April 1994* by Elinor Batezat Sisulu (1996/1997 NBGS), and *Gleam and Glow* by Eve Bunting (2001/2002 NBGS).

Using the Transformative Teaching/Learning Model in the Upper Elementary Grades

Black Angels (Murphy, 2001/2002 NBGS) is a wonderful upper elementary novel about an adolescent girl who becomes embroiled with the Jim Crow laws and the Freedom Fighters of the United States, even though she vows to stay away from "all of that fuss." At the Information Stage, the book is rich with information about U.S. history, segregation in the South, and the U.S. Civil Rights movement in the 1960s, so students' knowledge and awareness of U.S. history and geography can be enhanced through this book. They may want to discuss and conduct research activities to discover more of the stories and history of this period, asking such questions as, Who were the heroes and heroines of the times?

At the Integration Stage of engagement, students' understanding and sympathy with people of this era is deepened and becomes a personal experience with the novel and the activities guided by the classroom teacher. Students may want to write unsent letters to some of the people they have researched. Engage in a book pair activity, comparing the experience of *Through My Eyes* (Bridges, 1999/2000 NBGS) or other related titles. It is important for students to understand what racism, bigotry, and segregation are and how they have been manifested in the United States. This can lead to a discussion of whether we have biases about things we don't understand or to which we have no exposure.

Discussions such as these lead the way for transformative experiences and questions. Questions such as the following can be used: What groups in our school or neighborhood are subject to the cruelties of prejudice or segregation? Why? What can be done about some of these injustices? Students, teachers, principals, and community members who want to make changes in the social framework of their schools and neighborhoods can be very powerful partners in changing the way we treat one another on a daily basis. Together, service-learning partners such as those just mentioned may want to instigate new games for the playground that include everyone. The team may decide to do an educational campaign in the community or school about the damage of prejudice and racism and how to stop it. Students may want to take a presentation to another grade level or the school board or to a town meeting. Remember, we all must be able to understand that our lives and our efforts can and do make a difference in how we work and live—we all have something to offer and we can make the world a better place, no matter how large or small our efforts.

Using the Transformative Teaching/Learning Model in Middle School and High School

Parvana's Journey (Ellis, 2002/2003 NBGS) is a recommended book for mature middle school students or young adult readers. When using this book, it is recommended that a teacher begin with the aesthetic experience and simply allow the students to read the book for enjoyment and comprehension before couching it in any background or efferent information—allow the discussion and questions to come from the students and then from the teacher. Using this book with young adults, a teacher can very readily see how the three levels of engagement presented in this model can merge and appear to be seamless.

Once students have read and had the opportunity to discuss the book in small groups, provide opportunities to study the history and geography of Afghanistan (Information Stage). Give direct instruction with reference books, videos, and news reports. The "What would you do if...?" kind of questions, which indicate the Integration Stage of the model, can be posed for students to deliberate in their journals or discussion groups, but there is still more to be done to both strengthen the learning and provide support for people in disastrous situations. There are numerous activities to use to lead students to the Transformation Stage. For instance, some students may have loved ones in the armed forces. Letters can be sent to the troops from your hometown. Have students research some of the nongovernmental relief organizations that are working in Afghanistan to see where they can have an opportunity to help. The royalties for the sale of the book *Parvana's Journey* are all going to Women for Women, an organization that helps women in Afghanistan—students may want to see how and what they can contribute to this organization. Find out the real stories of some of the people who live in Afghanistan, particularly in refugee camps, and find out how relief may be sent to them. Adopt a refugee camp and send clothing and school supplies to them. Research the mileage the children in *Parvana's Journey* walked as they traversed their country in search of their families. Raise money by doing a walk or relay of this length and send it to a struggling school either abroad or at home. Research the horrific reality of minefields throughout the world and find out what is being done and what can be done to protect innocent people. See also *Secrets in the Fire* (2003/2004 NBGS) by Henning Mankell. This is a very poignant companion text to *Parvana's Journey* and contains further information about minefields at the end of the text.

As students become involved in these projects, their learning is deepened and made more immediate and relevant. Their ability to be critically reflective of their own actions and those of others is greatly enhanced and, again, students realize that they can make a difference even through small efforts. We should never underestimate the power of these feelings for our students. The world around them and their role in it begins to be transformed as they become more active and engaged participants.

Reconsidering Our Responsibilities

In my undergraduate literacy courses my students and I have been steadily moving toward reading more and more global literature. Specifically, we have read *Iqbal: A Novel* (D'Adamo, 2003/2004 NBGS), the true story of a boy chained to a life of servitude in weaving rugs; *Keeper of the Night* (Holt, 2003/2004 NBGS), where a young woman in Guam must keep her family together after her mother's suicide; *Becoming Naomi León* (Ryan, 2004/2005 NBGS), a beautiful coming-of-age story set in Avocado Acres Trailer Rancho in California, USA; *Parvana's Journey* (Ellis, 2002/2003 NBGS), set in Afghanistan; *Tree Girl* (Mikaelsen, 2004/2005 NBGS), an achingly poignant story based on the events in the life of a young woman who must travel across Guatemala in search of safety from guerilla warfare; *Secrets in the Fire* (Mankell, 2003/2004 NBGS), which is set in Mozambique and tells of the outrageous heartbreak of land mines; *Zulu Dog* (Ferreira, 2002/2003 NBGS), a story of post-apartheid and an unlikely but beautiful friendship; and *The Winter People* (Bruchac, 2002/2003 NBGS), a historical novel of the French and Indian War told from the Abenaki perspective.

We discuss these books in a structured book club format, focusing on literary elements and activities that ask for creative thoughtfulness and that demonstrate the students' ability to support their elementary and secondary students in finding relevance and integrating the stories into their own lives. In this way, beginning teachers have the opportunity to experience what they are going to be asking their students to do in their future classes. Once we have conducted our book clubs in the fashion of a pre-K–12 classroom setting, we then do a critical review of both the books and their usefulness in the literacy or content area classrooms.

Most of the students are thrilled with these selections and are eager to know more about the people and culture at the heart of these books. These students have engaged in a transaction with the book under discussion and have integrated it on some level to their own lives. However, I have been alarmed at some student responses, such as "I have never been to Guam, so I don't really care about what goes on there" and "I can't relate to historical events." These and other expressions give evidence to an appalling lack of empathy or even interest in the larger world on the part of some students.

Concerns for my students and the efficacy of my teaching led to the realization that many of our students need and deserve a very articulated model to support them in moving from where they may be numbed by or overwhelmed with media, text messages, and bad news to an understanding of the connections and responsibilities inherent in a global society. They must be given the tools, the dialogue, and the experiences to "read the world" and in so doing develop a respect, an understanding, and perhaps even an ethic of care for people and places all over the globe: "Much cries out for reform, but an indiscriminately negative attitude may alienate youth from the very democratic means necessary for constructive, humane change" (Louise Rosenblatt, quoted in Probst, 2005, p. 12).

Therefore, our task as teachers and citizens is to use everything at our disposal to bring some of the realities of life to our students, not to depress them or reveal global horrors to them but to allow them to discover that these depredations are not tolerable or acceptable and that there are things we all can do about them. The wonderful literature that is the subject of this book, the Notable Books for a Global Society, are not just good books that have passed through rigorous review, nor are they simply the tools for our educational tasks. We are going beyond what Pat Mora refers to as the four "Fs" of Food, Fashion, Festivals, and Folklore (although some of the folk literature selections on these lists are wonderful). These books provide our students and ourselves with experiences that become a part of us. We do not just read these books as words on the page. We feel these stories in our hearts and are transformed by them.

Conclusion

We could not continue to have the stamina to be teachers of any age or grade level if we did not somehow believe that we could change and are changing the world. As our world becomes more globally interactive and delicately sustained, we are increasingly aware of our connections and responsibilities to one another. As teachers it is imperative for us to support our students in moving from feelings of paralysis and hopelessness to a place where they can take actions, no matter how small, to make the world a better place. "What we need next is a new ethic—call it an 'ecological ethic of care,'.... It's an ethic built...on the intricate and beautiful ways that love for places and love for people nurture each other and sustain us all" (Moore, 2004, p. 65). Once students realize that they do have a very real ability to take action and contribute to our global society, it will reverberate throughout all of their learning and living efforts.

Rosenblatt, in her work of finding the meaning of literature through a transaction between the reader and the text, encourages us to take that transaction out to the transformation of our society:

I am not under the illusion that the schools alone can change society. However, I can affirm the belief uttered so many years ago: we teachers of language and literature have a crucial role to play as educators and citizens. We phrase our goals as fostering the growth of the capacity for personally meaningful, self-critical literary experience. The educational process that achieves this aim most effectively will serve a broader purpose, the nurturing of men and women capable of building a fully democratic society. (quoted in Probst, 2005, p. 12)

As teachers, we cannot rest with the notion that our students are capable of building a fully democratic society; we must provide examples and models for them to learn from and build upon. Great global literature such as those books presented here and the hundreds of titles that are published every year provide the portals through which we and our students can pass to develop deeper and deeper engagement with ourselves, our communities, and our world. The Transformative Teaching/Learning Model uses quality global literature and the pedagogy of academic service learning to achieve our larger goal as educators. Above and beyond the teaching of the curriculum, it is our goal and responsibility to support the development of fully engaged citizens, capable and interested in choosing the life they lead.

REFERENCES

Note. Complete bibliographic citations for the Notable Books for a Global Society booklist (1996–2005) can be found at the end of the book.

Dewey, J. (1938). *Experience and education*. New York: Macmillan.
Lamott, A. (1994). *Bird by bird: Some instructions on writing and life*. New York: Random House.
Mezirow, J. (1991). *Transformative dimensions of transformative learning*. San Francisco: Jossey-Bass.
Mezirow, J. (1995). Transformation theory of adult learning. In M.R. Welton (Ed.), *In defense of the lifeworld: Critical perspectives on adult learning* (pp. 39–70). New York: SUNY Press.
Moore, K.D. (2004). *The Pine Island paradox*. Minneapolis, MN: Milkweed Editions.
Morton, K. (1995). The irony of service: Charity, project and social change in service-learning. *Michigan Journal of Community Service-Learning, 2*, 19–32.
Probst, R.E. (2005). In memory of Louise Rosenblatt. *Voices From the Middle, 12*(3), 9–12.
Rosenblatt, L.M. (1976). *Literature as exploration*. New York: Noble and Noble Publishers.
Rosenblatt, L.M. (1978). *The reader, the text, the poem: The transactional theory of the literary work*. Carbondale: Southern Illinois University Press.
Sumida, A.Y., & Meyer, M.A. (2006). T4=Teaching to the fourth power: Transformative inquiry and the stirring of cultural waters. *Language Arts, 83*, 437–449.

CONCLUSION

Crossing the Bridge

Marian J. McKenna

"Can there be any doubt, then, that we need our graduates—this new American generation of such great privilege and promise—to become active participants in the world, potent advocates for human rights, confident leaders willing to take risks in the pursuit of intellectual honesty, of freedom to disagree, of justice and fairness, global citizenship, and mutual responsibility? And so the question arises then: How can we support our students in becoming passionate and powerful moral leaders?"

—Diana Chapman Walsh (2006, p. 4)

The world we are leaving to our children and students is one that demands that they be creators of knowledge. Despite what the minimalist mandates of No Child Left Behind may suggest, our students cannot survive in this world simply by being receptacles of knowledge; they also must be creative problem solvers. Therefore, in the preceding chapters of this text, we have not only tried to cover some of the most germane topics in the use of high-quality global literature, but we have also addressed some of the fundamental social issues facing a global society. We have discussed why it is important to use global literature and have provided theories, strategies, and models for using it in our classrooms. However, beyond these instructional goals exists an even greater one: to nurture the imaginations and generosity of spirit of our students and ourselves.

Changing the World With Education and Understanding

We need to support our students in maintaining hope and vigor in the face of wrenching problems and seemingly insurmountable obstacles to human justice throughout the world. We need to allow our students the experiences and opportunities to believe that our lives and our efforts matter in determining how we live together in the natural and human world. We need to face the challenges before us, not with despair but with vigor in the delight of a challenge that can be met not only with resources but also with intentions for justice and equality, with a willingness to open our hearts to the tough questions within and outside of us. As we listen to the news about the cruelty and brutality in the world today, we cannot just turn off the radio or television and go about our business. Our business is the evolution of our species beyond the caves and into the light of the 21st century and the building of a world where we can conquer poverty and starvation, a world where war is obsolete, a world where our hearts are open to find in the world's suffering our own bonds of humanity. Some may say that it is easy to talk about building a better world and to make such optimistic statements, but it is these very statements—the energy of our thoughts and attention—that must be directed toward positive solutions to some of the world's most pressing problems.

Teaching and Learning as Political Acts

Education is a profession that is based on hope for the future—in fact, hope for *a* future—and within this profession teaching and learning are profoundly political acts, and they are acts that should be continually engaged. The political and personal are forged in our professions of teaching and learning—it has always been so. When we walk into our classrooms, no matter the level at which we teach, we carry with us not only our lesson plans but our personas, our attitudes, biases, political leanings, and intentions. These underpinnings of who we are cannot be hidden within the notion of objective teaching. For example, in one of my graduate literacy classes, I asked my students for rigorous self-examination and gave them some textual tools for doing so. After reading *Reclaiming Democracy: Multicultural Educators' Journeys Toward Transformative Teaching* (Romo, Bradfield, & Serrano, 2004), one of my students reported in front of our whole class, "I think that I might be a racist. I don't mean to be a racist, and I don't really want to be one, but after reading this book, I think that I just might be a racist." This comment reflects how we as teachers must subject ourselves to rigorous self-examination before we ask our public K–12 students to do so. Imagine the courage of this graduate student to make that announcement in front of her peers and fellow teachers. Of course, in making this statement she is on her way to examining and eliminating her racism. This is the kind of courage and true self-examination that is called for in us as teachers before we ask our students to examine their own prejudices and ignorance of other cultures. In becoming and being teachers, we must peel back the layers of ourselves and be clear about what we are presenting to our students. Perhaps it can be said that becoming a teacher is becoming our most honest self.

Learning Through Literature

It is our responsibility as educators to take charge of the selection and choices of texts to be used in our classrooms. Chapter 1 gave us a road map for the books selected to the Notable Books for a Global Society booklists from 1996–2005. We must take it upon ourselves to read these titles and the ones to follow and be investigative in regard to trends and changes in global literature. In chapter 2, the authors alert us to the many places where books can fall through the cracks and not get to our shelves. We have to be participants and activists in our classrooms and professional societies. We must move beyond representing underrepresented groups, beyond using quality global literature as instructional tools. Our students cannot know the world in which they live without the perspectives of the people who populate it. None of us can know the various perspectives of an event without the stories of the people who were involved. All voices must be heard. The authors of this volume and the celebrated global literature they highlight have given us the voices of many times, places, and characters. We have heard the voices of women coming out of oppression, the voices of immigrants finding their way in a new culture, and the voices of children caught up in the horrors of war and displacement. In this complex, difficult, and often frightening world, students need and deserve more than platitudes and timed vocabulary tests. They need knowledge construction around real issues instead of knowledge reproduction, authentic dialogue instead of repetition, and the chance to articulate problems confronting them instead of following instructions. They need collaboration with people like and unlike themselves instead of competition, deep and critical reflection instead of prescription, and avenues for action versus hopelessness and retreat. We can do this for our students and our communities through our stories, old and new.

In addition to hearing the messages of other people's stories and how they view the world, we must respect these stories and the views reflected in them. We should embrace what these stories tell us about ourselves, as was the case with the graduate student illustrated in the previously mentioned example, and how they can help us better understand how we might live together on this planet. Our stories tell us who we are and what we believe to be true. Stories from other cultures allow us to get behind the eyes of other people and learn to respect how they see the world and how it is different from our own view. This is a great gift and it enlarges us and the way we can think about our lives.

This is a lesson I learned not long ago during a trip to Kenya with my husband, Ralph. As we were hiking through desert scrublands near the area of Lake Barrunga, we crossed the paths of several isolated families with their goats, carving out their place in this barren landscape in an attempt to live in peace. At some point, a little girl with dusty, bare feet and a pretty pink dress began to follow us through the scrub. At first we couldn't even get a good look at her as she would hide behind rocks or bushes when we turned. My husband eventually welcomed the girl to come closer to us, inviting her to examine the binoculars he was wearing. I already knew that her people feared cameras and considered it a great insult, if not a danger, to be photographed. But the image of Ralph bending down to communicate with this little girl, in what to me was "the middle of nowhere," was so piercingly sweet and momentous that I forgot the "stories" of the people in whose culture I was a visitor and raised the camera to capture the moment. And, in that moment, the little girl was gone. She scooted behind Ralph and took off across the scrublands, leaving dust puffs with every step.

I had been so captivated by the beauty and trust in the image of this beautiful little girl in the middle of the brush that I forgot to respect her "story," her culture's fear of the lens. I forgot to respect her beliefs, and in an instant miles of slowly built trust vanished. The lesson here was personal and immediate. But all of us can learn these types of cultural sensitivity lessons through the global literature both within and outside of our own countries and experiences. These lessons can be both windows and mirrors—reflections on our experiences and windows into the experiences of others like and different from us.

Creating Relevant Classrooms With Global Literature

No matter our highest intentions as teachers, these higher goals and engaged classrooms are not easy to achieve or create, and we must support one another on a daily and personal basis. Currently, we find ourselves in a time where we as people across the globe are dangerously dividing ourselves along religious and political lines. We have become denizens of the Tower of Babel once again, unable to realize how so often we are saying the same thing in different ways. Unfortunately, this global climate of conflict and confusion is having an effect on the climate of classrooms today as classrooms increasingly become political battlegrounds. In my own classroom experience, I see that many of my students are not engaged and instead are "leaving" class. By saying they are "leaving," I don't mean that they are getting up and walking out of the classroom; they are sitting there in front of me. Yet they are leaving in the sense that their minds and attention are no longer engaged or present in the classroom—the students are simply "checking out." I struggle to reach them and engage them in the larger issues at stake in literacy education, but this seems so much harder than it used to be. Many of the students just seem to want the class to get the job and get out of school.

As I think about how to restructure my classes to bring students back to not only attention but an authentic interaction with the course dialogue, material, and beyond, I think that it is not just that our current students are not as bright as students once were. Instead it seems that students today choose to be anesthetized, rather than face a world that is out of control and about which they feel helpless. The "leaving" is perhaps a way to escape the undercurrent of anxiety that pervades their world and their lives, and in this case it is certainly understandable. Perhaps a pervasive anxiety can be found in all of us regardless of where we live. There is a powerful urge for our students and many others to bury their heads in the sands of our social climate. Students are pulling their lives in to a place where it is manageable for them, focusing on roommates, grades, jobs, and relationships.

So what do we teach our students in times like these? How can we help them understand the world of which they are such a vital part? We tell our stories. We listen to the stories others tell to us. We seek out and use the best of global literature through such agencies the Notable Books for a Global Society booklists, which selects 25 titles with global themes each year. Through extended experiences with literature and learning, we remember respect, compassion, dialogue, and community. We remember hope and how much we all have to offer one another. We take our stories and move outside of our homes, classrooms, and businesses to become an interdependent community once again. In chapter 2, authors Freeman, Lehman, and Scharer invoke the memory of Jella Lepman who in 1953 founded the International Board on Books for Young People (www.ibby.org), based on the belief that literature could serve as a bridge to understanding among children around the globe. With the increased recognition of the necessity of global literature by publishers and teachers alike, we can think that perhaps the bridge Lepman believed in has been built. In this book, the authors hope that you have been given the tools and inspirations to cross that bridge with your students.

REFERENCES

Romo, J.J., Bradfield, P., & Serrano, R. (Eds.). (2004). *Reclaiming democracy: Multicultural educators' journeys toward transformative teaching*. Upper Saddle River, NJ: Pearson Prentice Hall.

Walsh, D.C. (2006). *Trustworthy leadership: Can we be the leaders we need our students to become?* Kalamazoo, MI: The Fetzer Institute.

NOTABLE BOOKS FOR A GLOBAL SOCIETY
(1996–2005) BOOKLISTS BY YEAR

1996 Notable Books for a Global Society: A K–12 List

Adler, D. (1995). *One yellow daffodil: A Hanukkah story*. Ill. L. Bloom. San Diego, CA: Gulliver Books/Harcourt Brace.

Ayer, E.H. (1995). *Parallel journeys*. New York: Atheneum.

Begay, S. (1995). *Navajo visions and voices across the mesa*. New York: Scholastic.

Bradby, M. (1995). *More than anything else*. Ill. C. Soentpiet. New York: Orchard Books.

Chinn, K. (1995). *Sam and the lucky money*. Ill. C. Van Wright & Y-H. Hu. New York: Lee & Low.

Cofer, J.O. (1995). *An island like you: Stories of the barrio*. New York: Orchard.

Curtis, C.P. (1995). *The Watsons go to Birmingham—1963*. New York: Delacorte Press.

Grifalconi, A. (1995). *Not home*. Boston: Little, Brown.

Hamilton, V. (1995). *Her stories: African American folktales, fairy tales, and true tales*. Ill. L. Dillon & D. Dillon. New York: Blue Sky/Scholastic.

Hoffman, M. (1995). *Earth, fire, water, air*. Ill. J. Ray. New York: Dutton.

Kindersley, B., & Kindersley, A. (1995). *Children just like me*. New York: Dorling Kindersley.

Medearis, A.S. (1995). *Skin deep and other teenage reflections*. Ill. M. Bryant. New York: Macmillan.

Nye, N.S. (1995). *The tree is older than you are: A bilingual gathering of poems & stories from Mexico*. New York: Simon & Schuster.

Olaleye, I. (1995). *The distant talking drum: Poems from Nigeria*. Ill. F. Lessac. Honesdale, PA: Boyds Mills Press.

Rappaport, D. (1995). *The new king*. Ill. E.B. Lewis. New York: Dial.

Ritter, L.S. (1995). *Leagues apart: The men and times of the Negro baseball leagues*. Ill. R. Merkin. New York: Morrow.

Sandler, M.W. (1995). *Immigrants*. New York: HarperCollins.

Shea, P.D. (1995). *The whispering cloth: A refugee story*. Ills. A. Riggio & Y. Yang. Honesdale, PA: Boyds Mills Press.

Smith, R. (1995). *Thunder cave*. New York: Hyperion.

Taylor, M.D. (1995). *The well: David's story*. New York: Dial.

Taylor, T. (1995). *The bomb*. New York: HarperTrophy.

Temple, F. (1995). *Tonight by sea*. New York: Orchard.

Williams-Garcia, R. (1995). *Like sisters on the homefront*. New York: Lodestar/Dutton.

Woodson, J. (1995). *From the notebooks of Melanin Sun*. New York: Scholastic.

1997 Notable Books for a Global Society: A K–12 List

Balgassi, H. (1996). *Peacebound trains*. Ill. C. Soentpiet. New York: Clarion Books.

Bash, B. (1996). *In the heart of the village: The world of the Indian banyan tree*. San Francisco: Sierra Club.

Breckler, R. (1996). *Sweet dried apples: A Vietnamese wartime childhood*. Ill. D.K. Ray. Boston: Houghton Mifflin.

Bruchac, J. (1996). *Between earth & sky: Legends of Native American sacred places*. Ill. T. Locker. San Diego, CA: Harcourt Brace.

Freedman, R. (1996). *The life and death of Crazy Horse*. Ill. A.B.H. Bull. New York: Holiday House.

Breaking Boundaries With Global Literature: Celebrating Diversity in K–12 Classrooms, edited by Nancy L. Hadaway and Marian J. McKenna. © 2007 by the International Reading Association.

Garza, C.L. (1996). *In my family/En mi familia*. San Francisco: Children's Book Press.

Ho, M. (Compiler). (1996). *Maples in the mist: Children's poems from the Tang Dynasty*. (M. Ho, Trans.). Ills. J. Tseng & M. Tseng. New York: Lothrop, Lee & Shepard.

Lewin, T. (1996). *Market!* New York: Lothrop, Lee & Shepard.

Martin, R. (Reteller). (1996). *Mysterious tales of Japan*. Ill. T. Kiuchi. New York: G.P. Putnam's Sons.

Mora, P. (1996). *Confetti: Poems for children*. Ill. E. Sanchez. New York: Lee & Low.

Onyefulu, I. (1996). *Ogbo: Sharing life in an African village*. New York: Gulliver.

Osofsky, A. (1996). *Free to dream—The making of a poet: Langston Hughes*. New York: Lothrop, Lee & Shepard.

Pausewang, G. (1996). *The final journey*. (P. Crampton, Trans.). New York: Viking/Penguin.

Rinaldi, A. (1996). *Hang a thousand trees with ribbons: The story of Phyllis Wheatley*. San Diego, CA: Harcourt Trade.

Schroeder, A. (1996). *Minty: A story of young Harriet Tubman*. Ill. J. Pinkney. New York: Dial.

Schur, M.R. (1996). *When I left my village*. Ill. B. Pinkney. New York: Dial.

Sisulu, E.B. (1996). *The day Gogo went to vote: South Africa, April 1994*. Ill. S. Wilson. Boston: Little, Brown.

Smalls-Hector, I. (1996). *Irene Jennie and the Christmas masquerade: The Johnkankus*. Ill. M. Rosales. Boston: Little, Brown.

Staples, S.F. (1996). *Dangerous skies*. New York: Farrar, Straus and Giroux.

Tamar, E. (1996). *The garden of happiness*. Ill. B. Lambase. San Diego, CA: Harcourt Brace.

Tunnell, M.O., & Chilcoat, G.W. (1996). *The children of Topaz: The story of a Japanese-American internment camp*. New York: Holiday House.

White, R. (1996). *Belle Prater's boy*. New York: Farrar, Straus and Giroux.

Wisniewski, D. (1996). *Golem*. Photographs by L. Salsbery. New York: Clarion Books.

Wood, M., & Igus, T. (1996). *Going back home: An artist returns to the South*. Ill. M. Wood. San Francisco: Children's Book Press.

Yep, L. (1996). *Ribbons*. New York: G.P. Putnam's Sons.

1998 Notable Books for a Global Society: A K–12 List

Bentley, J. (1997). *"Dear friend": Thomas Garrett & William Still, collaborators on the Underground Railroad*. New York: Cobblehill/Dutton.

Bial, R. (1997). *Mist over the mountains: Appalachia and its people*. New York: Houghton Mifflin.

Bruchac, J. (1997). *Lasting echoes: An oral history of Native American people*. Ill. P. Morin. San Diego, CA: Harcourt Brace.

Buettner, D. (1997). *Africatrek: A journey by bicycle through Africa*. New York: Lerner.

Davol, M.W. (1997). *The paper dragon*. Ill. R. Sabuda. New York: Atheneum.

Demi. (1997). *One grain of rice: A mathematical folktale*. New York: Scholastic.

Dolphin, L. (1997). *Our journey from Tibet: Based on a true story*. Photographs by N.J. Johnson. New York: Dutton.

Dorris, M. (1997). *The window*. New York: Hyperion.

Hamilton, V. (1997). *A ring of tricksters: Animal tales from America, The West Indies, and Africa*. Ill. B. Moser. New York: Blue Sky/Scholastic.

Hest, A. (1997). *When Jessie came across the sea*. New York: Candlewick.

Hurmence, B. (1997). *Slavery time: When I was chillun*. New York: Putnam.

King, M.L., Jr. (1997). *I have a dream*. Ills. 15 Coretta Scott King Award and Honor Book artists. New York: Scholastic.

Lee, M. (1997). *Nim and the war effort*. Ill. Y. Choi. New York: Farrar, Straus and Giroux.

Mastoon, A. (1997). *The shared heart: Portraits and stories celebrating lesbian, gay, and bisexual young people*. New York: Morrow.

McKissack, P. (1997). *Ma Dear's aprons*. New York: Atheneum.

Meyer, C. (1997). *Jubilee journey*. New York: Gulliver.

Mochizuki, K. (1997). *Passage to freedom: The Sugihara story*. Ill. D. Lee. New York: Lee & Low.

Myers, W.D. (1997). *Harlem*. Ill. C. Myers. New York: Scholastic.

Normandin, C. (Ed.). (1997). *Echoes of the elders: The stories and paintings of Chief Lelooska*. New York: Dorling Kindersley.

Nye, N.S. (1997). *Habibi*. New York: Simon & Schuster.

Rappaport, D. (1997). *The flight of red bird: The life of Zitkala-Sa*. New York: Dial.

Schur, M.R. (1997). *Sacred shadows*. New York: Dial.

Spivak, D. (1997). *Grass sandals: The travels of Basho*. Ill. Demi. New York: Atheneum.

Wood, N. (Ed.). (1997). *The serpent's tongue: Prose, poetry, and art of the New Mexico pueblos*. New York: Dutton.

Young, E. (1997). *Voices of the heart*. New York: Scholastic.

1999 Notable Books for a Global Society: A K–12 List

Aliki. (1998). *Marianthe's story: Painted words/Spoken memories*. New York: Greenwillow.

Ayers, K. (1998). *North by night: The story of the Underground Railroad*. New York: Delacorte Press.

Bennett, J.W. (1998). *Blue star rapture*. New York: Simon & Schuster.

Bierman, C. (1998). *Journey to Ellis Island: How my father came to America*. New York: Hyperion.

Bunting, E. (1998). *So far from the sea*. Ill. C. Soentpiet. New York: Clarion Books.

Flake, S.G. (1998). *The skin I'm in*. New York: Jump at the Sun/Hyperion.

Fletcher, S. (1998). *Shadow spinner*. New York: Atheneum.

Gollub, M. (1998). *Cool melons—turn to frogs! The life and poems of Issa*. Ill. K. Stone. New York: Lee & Low.

Hoyt-Goldsmith, D. (1998). *Lacrosse: The national game of the Iroquois*. Photographs by L. Migdale. New York: Holiday House.

Khan, R. (1998). *The roses in my carpets*. Ill. R. Himler. New York: Stoddart Kids.

Kurtz, J. (1998). *The storyteller's beads*. San Diego, CA: Harcourt Brace.

Lewin, T. (1998). *The storytellers*. New York: Lothrop, Lee & Shepard.

Lobel, A. (1998) *No pretty pictures: A child of war*. New York: Greenwillow.

Luenn, N. (1998). *A gift for Abuelita: Celebrating the Day of the Dead/Un regalo para Abuelita: En celebración del Día de los Muertos*. Ill. R. Chapman. Flagstaff, AZ: Rising Moon/Northland.

Morin, P. (1998). *Animal dreaming: An Aboriginal dreamtime story*. San Diego, CA: Silver Whistle/Harcourt Brace.

Myers, W.D. (1998). *Amistad: A long road to freedom*. Ill. P. Lee. New York: Dutton.

Nye, N.S. (Selector). (1998). *The space between our footsteps: Poems and paintings from the Middle East*. New York: Simon & Schuster.

Park, F., & Park, G. (1998). *My freedom trip: A child's escape from North Korea*. Ill. D.R. Jenkins. Honesdale, PA: Boyds Mills Press.

Rinaldi, A. (1998). *Cast two shadows*. San Diego, CA: Gulliver/Harcourt Brace.

San Souci, R.D. (1998). *Fa Mulan: The story of a woman warrior*. Ills. J. Tseng & M. Tseng. New York: Hyperion.

Swann, B. (1998). *Touching the distance: Native American riddle-poems*. Ill. M. Rendon. San Diego, CA: Harcourt.

Waldman, N. (1998). *Masada*. New York: Morrow.

Woodson, J. (1998). *If you come softly*. New York: G.P. Putnam's Sons.

Wyeth, S.D. (1998). *Something beautiful*. Ill. C. Soentpiet. New York: Doubleday.

Zemser, A.B. (1998). *Beyond the mango tree*. New York: Greenwillow.

2000 Notable Books for a Global Society: A K–12 List

Bell, W. (1999). *Zack*. New York: Simon & Schuster.

Bridges, R. (1999). *Through my eyes*. New York: Scholastic.

Cooney, C.B. (1999). *Burning up*. New·York: Delacorte Press.

Coy, J. (1999). *Strong to the hoop*. Ill. L. Jean-Bart. New York: Lee & Low.

Curtis, C.P. (1999). *Bud, not Buddy*. New York: Delacorte Press.

Diakité, B.W. (1999). *The hatseller and the monkeys*. New York: Scholastic.

Echewa, T.O. (1999). *The magic tree: A folktale from Nigeria*. New York: Morrow.

English, K. (1999). *Francie*. New York: Farrar, Straus and Giroux.

Erdrich, L. (1999). *The birchbark house*. New York: Hyperion.

Hamanaka, S., & Ohmi, A. (1999). *In search of the spirit: The living national treasures of Japan*. Ill. S. Hamanaka. Calligraphy by A. Ohmi. New York: Morrow Junior Books.

Harrell, B.O. (1999). *Longwalker's journey: A novel of the Choctaw Trail of Tears*. New York: Dial.

Holtwijk, I. (1999). *Asphalt angels*. (W. Boeke, Trans.). Asheville, ND: Front Street.

Hopkinson, D. (1999). *A band of angels: A story inspired by the Jubilee Singers*. Ill. R. Colón. New York: Atheneum.

Left Hand Bull, J., & Haldane, S. (1999). *Lakota hoop dancer*. Photographs by S. Haldane. New York: Dutton.

Look, L. (1999). *Love as strong as ginger*. Ill. S.T. Johnson. New York: Atheneum.

McGill, A. (1999). *Molly Bannaky*. Ill. C. Soentpiet. Boston: Houghton Mifflin.

McLaren, C. (1999). *Dance for the land*. New York: Atheneum.

McMahon, P. (1999). *One Belfast boy*. Photographs by A. O'Connor. Boston: Houghton Mifflin.

Myers, W.D. (1999). *At her majesty's request: An African princess in Victorian England*. New York: Scholastic.

Naylor, P.R. (1999). *Walker's crossing*. New York: Atheneum.

Ray, M.L. (1999). *Basket moon*. Ill. B. Cooney. Boston: Little, Brown.

Say, A. (1999). *Tea with milk*. Boston: Houghton Mifflin.

Silverman, E. (1999). *Raisel's riddle*. Ill. S. Gaber. New York: Farrar, Straus and Giroux.

Wells, R. (1999). *Streets of gold*. Ill. D. Andreasen. New York: Dial.

Woodruff, E. (1999). *The memory coat*. Ill. M. Dooling. New York: Scholastic.

2001 Notable Books for a Global Society: A K–12 List

Bagdasarian, A. (2000). *Forgotten fire*. New York: Dorling Kindersley.

Carmi, D. (2000). *Samir and Yonatan*. (Y. Lotan, Trans.). New York: Scholastic.

Collier, B. (2000). *Uptown*. New York: Henry Holt.

Deedy, C.A. (2000). *The yellow star: The legend of King Christian X of Denmark*. Ill. H. Sørensen. Atlanta, GA: Peachtree.

Delacre, L. (2000). *Salsa stories*. New York: Scholastic.

Gold, A.L. (2000). *A special fate: Chiune Sugihara, hero of the Holocaust*. New York: Scholastic.

Govenar, A. (Ed.). (2000). *Osceola: Memories of a sharecropper's daughter*. Ill. S. Evans. New York: Hyperion.

Herrera, J.F. (2000). *The upside down boy/El niño de cabeza*. Ill. E. Gomez. San Francisco: Children's Book Press.

Herschler, M.B. (2000). *The darkest corner*. Asheville, NC: Front Street.

Hill, K. (2000). *The year of Miss Agnes*. New York: Simon & Schuster.

Isaacs, A. (2000). *Torn thread*. New York: Scholastic.

Joseph, L. (2000). *The color of my words*. New York: HarperCollins.

Kajikawa, K. (2000). *Yoshi's feast*. Ill. Y. Heo. New York: Dorling Kindersley.

Kurtz, J. (2000). *Faraway home*. Ill. E.B. Lewis. New York: Gulliver Books.

Levitin, S. (2000). *Dream freedom*. San Diego, CA: Harcourt.

Madrigal, A.H. (2000). *Blanca's feather/La pluma de Blanca*. Ill. G. Suzán. Flagstaff, AZ: Rising Moon.

Marrin, A. (2000). *Sitting Bull and his world*. New York: Dutton.

Osborne, M.P. (2000). *Adaline Falling Star*. New York: Scholastic.

Polacco, P. (2000). *The butterfly*. New York: Philomel Books.

Pressler, M. (2000). *Anne Frank: A hidden life*. (A. Bell, Trans.). New York: Dutton.

Rubin, S.G. (2000). *Fireflies in the dark: The story of Friedl Dicker-Brandeis and the children of Terezin*. New York: Holiday House.

Ryan, P.M. (2000). *Esperanza rising*. New York: Scholastic.

Staples, S.F. (2000). *Shiva's fire*. New York: Farrar, Straus and Giroux.

Whelan, G. (2000). *Homeless bird*. New York: HarperCollins.

Wong, J.S. (2000). *The trip back home*. Ill. B. Jia. San Diego, CA: Harcourt.

2002 Notable Books for a Global Society: A K–12 List

Bunting, E. (2001). *Gleam and glow*. Ill. P. Sylvada. San Diego, CA: Harcourt.

Chen, D. (2001). *China's son: Growing up in the Cultural Revolution*. New York: Delacorte Press.

Choi, Y. (2001). *The name jar*. New York: Alfred A. Knopf.

Cooney, C. (2001). *The ransom of Mercy Carter*. New York: Delacorte Press.

Cooper, M.L. (2001). *Slave spirituals and the Jubilee Singers*. New York: Clarion Books.

Garland, S. (2001). *Children of the dragon: Selected tales from Vietnam*. Ill. T. S. Hyman. San Diego, CA: Harcourt.

Hesse, K. (2001). *Witness*. New York: Scholastic.

Hoyt-Goldsmith, D. (2001). *Celebrating Ramadan*. Photographs by L. Migdale. New York: Holiday House.

Johnston, T. (2001). *Any small goodness: A novel of the barrio*. Ill. R. Colón. New York: Blue Sky/Scholastic.

Johnston, T. (2001). *Uncle Rain Cloud*. Ill. F. VandenBroeck. Watertown, MA: Charlesbridge.

Lipp, F. (2001). *The caged birds of Phnom Penh*. Ill. R. Himler. New York: Holiday House.

Littlesugar, A. (2001). *Freedom school, yes!* Ill. F. Cooper. New York: Philomel Books.

McKissack, P.C. (2001). *Goin' someplace special*. Ill. J. Pinkney. New York: Atheneum.

Mead, A. (2001). *Girl of Kosovo*. New York: Farrar, Straus and Giroux.

Mosher, R. (2001). *Zazoo*. New York: Clarion Books.

Murphy, R. (2001). *Black angels*. New York: Delacorte Press.

Na, A. (2001). *A step from heaven*. Asheville, NC: Front Street.

Nelson, M. (2001). *Carver: A life in poems*. Asheville, NC: Front Street.

Park, L.S. (2001). *A single shard*. New York: Clarion Books.

Partridge, E. (2001). *Oranges on Golden Mountain*. Ill. A. Sogabe. New York: Dutton.

Rice, D. (2001). *Crazy loco*. New York: Dial.

Stock, C. (2001). *Gugu's house*. New York: Clarion Books.

Taylor, M.D. (2001). *The land*. New York: Dial.

Tunnell, M.O. (2001). *Brothers in valor: A story of resistance*. New York: Holiday House.

Woodson, J. (2001). *The other side*. Ill. E.B. Lewis. New York: Putnam.

2003 Notable Books for a Global Society: A K–12 List

Ada, A.F. (2002). *I love Saturdays y Domingos*. New York: Atheneum.

Andrews-Goebel, N. (2002). *The pot that Juan built*. Ill. D. Diaz. New York: Lee & Low.

Bial, R. (2002). *Tenement: Immigrant life on the Lower East Side*. Boston: Houghton Mifflin.

Bruchac, J. (2002). *The winter people*. New York: Dial.

Clinton, C. (2002). *A stone in my hand*. Cambridge, MA: Candlewick.

Crowe, C. (2002). *Mississippi trial, 1955*. New York: Phyllis Fogelman/Penguin Putnam.

Ellis, D. (2002). *Parvana's journey*. Toronto, ON: Groundwood.

Ferreira, A. (2002). *Zulu dog*. New York: Farrar, Straus and Giroux.

Freedman, R. (2002). *Confucius: The golden rule*. Ill. F. Clement. New York: Arthur A. Levine/Scholastic.

Grifalconi, A. (2002). *The village that vanished*. Ill. K. Nelson. New York: Dial.

Grimes, N. (2002). *Bronx masquerade*. New York: Dial.

Hoffman, M. (2002). *The color of home*. Ill. K. Littlewood. New York: Phyllis Fogelman/ Penguin Putnam.

McCaughrean, G. (2002). *The kite rider*. New York: HarperCollins.

Mikaelsen, B. (2002). *Red midnight*. New York: HarperCollins.

Nye, N.S. (2002). *19 varieties of gazelle: Poems of the Middle East*. New York: Greenwillow.

Orozco, J.L. (2002). *Fiestas: A year of Latin American songs of celebration*. Ill. E. Kleven. New York: Dutton.

Park, F., & Park, G. (2002). *Good-bye, 382 Shin Dang Dong*. Ill. Y. Choi. Washington, DC: National Geographic Society.

Park, L.S. (2002). *When my name was Keoko: A novel of Korea in World War II*. New York: Clarion Books.

Perdomo, W. (2002). *Visiting Langston*. Ill. B. Collier. New York: HarperCollins.

Sierra, J. (2002). *Can you guess my name? Traditional tales around the world*. Ill. S. Vitale. New York: Clarion Books.

Stanley, D. (2002). *Saladin: Noble prince of Islam*. New York: HarperCollins.

UNICEF. (2002). *A life like mine: How children live around the world*. New York: Dorling Kindersley.

Wong, J.S. (2002). *Apple pie 4th of July*. Ill. M. Chodos-Irvine. San Diego, CA: Harcourt.

Woods, B. (2002). *The red rose box*. New York: Putnam.

Yee, P. (2002). *Dead man's gold and other stories*. Ill. H. Chan. Toronto, ON: Groundwood.

2004 Notable Books for a Global Society: A K–12 List

Cameron, A. (2003). *Colibri*. New York: Frances Foster Books.

Cave, K. (2003). *One child, one seed: A South African counting book*. Ill. G. Wulfsohn. New York: Henry Holt.

D'Adamo, F. (2003). *Iqbal: A novel*. (A. Leonori, Trans.). New York: Atheneum.

Dennis, Y.W., & Hirschfelder, A. (2003). *Children of Native America today*. Watertown, MA: Charlesbridge.

Edwardson, D.D. (2003). *Whale snow*. Ill. A. Patterson. Watertown, MA: Talewinds/Charlesbridge.

Fleming, C. (2003). *Boxes for Katje*. Ill. S. Dressen-McQueen. New York: Farrar, Straus and Giroux.

Holt, K.W. (2003). *Keeper of the night*. New York: Henry Holt.

Jung, R. (2003). *Dreaming in black & white*. (A. Bell, Trans.). New York: Phyllis Fogelman/Penguin Putnam. (1996 published in German)

Krull, K. (2003). *Harvesting hope: The story of Cesar Chavez*. Ill. Y. Morales. San Diego, CA: Harcourt.

Levine, K. (2003). *Hana's suitcase*. Downer's Grove, IL: Albert A. Whitman.

Mankell, H. (2003). *Secrets in the fire*. (A.C. Stuksrud, Trans.). Willowdale, ON: Annick Press.

Morales, Y. (2003). *Just a minute: A trickster tale and counting book*. San Francisco: Chronicle.

Morpurgo, M. (2003). *Kensuke's kingdom*. New York: Scholastic. (1999 published in Great Britain)

Myers, W.D. (2003). *The beast*. New York: Scholastic.

Myers, W.D. (2003). *Blues journey*. Ill. C. Myers. New York: Holiday House.

Naidoo, B. (2003). *Out of bounds: Seven stories of conflict and hope*. New York: HarperCollins.

Philip, N. (2003). *Horse hooves and chicken feet: Mexican folktales*. Ill. J. Mair. New York: Clarion Books.

Pressler, M. (2003). *Malka*. New York: Philomel Books.

Recorvits, H. (2003). *My name is Yoon*. New York: Farrar, Straus and Giroux.

Sacre, A. (2003). *The barking mouse*. Ill. A. Aguirre. Morton Grove, IL: Albert Whitman & Company.

Shea, P.D. (2003). *Tangled threads: A Hmong girl's story*. New York: Clarion Books.

Shea, P.D., & Weill, C. (2003). *Ten mice for Tet*. Ill. T.N. Trang. Embroidery by P.V. Dinh. San Francisco: Chronicle.

Smothers, E.F. (2003). *The hard-times jar*. Ill. J. Holyfield. New York: Frances Foster Books/ Farrar, Straus and Giroux.

Tingle, T. (2003). *Walking the Choctaw road: Stories from red people memory*. El Paso, TX: Cinco Puntos Press.

Tryszynska-Frederick, L. (2003). *Luba: The angel of Bergen-Belsen*. Ill. A. Marshall. Berkeley, CA: Tricycle Press.

2005 Notable Books for a Global Society: A K–12 List

Bernier-Grand, C.T. (2004). *César: ¡Sí, se puede! Yes, we can!* Ill. D. Diaz. New York: Marshall Cavendish.

Chotjewitz, D. (2004). *Daniel half human and the good Nazi*. (D. Orgel, Trans.). New York: Richard Jackson/Atheneum/Simon & Schuster.

Demi. (2004). *The hungry coat: A tale from Turkey*. New York: Margaret K. McElderry/Simon & Schuster.

Freedman, R. (2004). *The voice that challenged a nation: Marian Anderson and the struggle for equal rights*. New York: Clarion Books.

Hale, M. (2004). *The truth about sparrows*. New York: Henry Holt.

Hall, B.E. (2004). *Henry and the kite dragon*. Ill. W. Low. New York: Philomel Books.

Hesse, K. (2004). *The cats in Krasinski Square*. Ill. W. Watson. New York: Scholastic.

Hill, L.C. (2004). *Harlem stomp! A cultural history of the Harlem Renaissance*. New York: Megan Tingley/Little, Brown.

Kessler, C. (2004). *Our secret, Siri Aang*. New York: Philomel Books.

Krishnaswami, U. (2004). *Naming Maya*. New York: Farrar, Straus and Giroux.

Kyuchukov, H. (2004). *My name was Hussein*. Ill. A. Eitzen. Honesdale, PA: Boyds Mills Press.

MacDonald, M.R. (2004). *Three minute tales: Stories from around the world to tell or read when time is short*. Little Rock, AR: August House.

Mikaelsen, B. (2004). *Tree girl*. New York: Rayo/HarperTempest/HarperCollins.

Myers, W.D. (2004). *Here in Harlem: Poems in many voices*. New York: Holiday House.

Oswald, N. (2004). *Nothing here but stones*. New York: Henry Holt.

Raven, M.T. (2004). *Circle unbroken: The story of a basket and its people*. Ill. E.B. Lewis. New York: Farrar, Straus and Giroux.

Ryan, P.M. (2004). *Becoming Naomi León*. New York: Scholastic.

Singer, M. (Ed.). (2004). *Face relations: 11 stories about seeing beyond color*. New York: Simon & Schuster.

Stratton, A. (2004). *Chanda's secrets*. Willowdale, ON: Annick Press.

Turner, P.S. (2004). *Hachiko: The true story of a loyal dog*. Ill. Y. Nascimbene. Boston: Houghton Mifflin.

Warren, A. (2004). *Escape from Saigon: How a Vietnam War orphan became an American boy*. New York: Farrar, Straus and Giroux.

Weber, E.N.R. (2004). *Rattlesnake Mesa: Stories from a Native American childhood*. Photographs by R. Renkun. New York: Lee & Low.

Whelan, G. (2004). *Chu Ju's house*. New York: HarperCollins.

Woodson, J. (2004). *Coming on home soon*. Ill. E.B. Lewis. New York: Putnam.

Yee, P. (2004). *A song for Ba*. Ill. J.P. Wang. Toronto, ON: Groundwood.

AUTHOR INDEX

Note. Page numbers followed by *f* or *t* indicate figures or tables, respectively.

HO, M., 27, 188
HOFFMAN, M., 28, 75*t*, 102, 105, 175, 187, 192
HOLM, A., 49*t*
HOLT, K.W., 178, 192
HOLTWIJK, I., 46, 190
HOLUB, J., 49*t*
HOOKS, B., 152, 164
HOPKINSON, D., 190
HOYT-GOLDSMITH, D., 189, 191
HUNT, I., xv, xviii
HUNT, P., 42
HURMENCE, B., 188

I

IGOA, C., 100, 111
IGUS, T., 188
IPPISCH, H., 133*t*, 134, 149
ISAACS, A., 190
ISAACS, K., 3, 4, 6, 22

J

JIANG, J.-L., 143, 143*t*, 149
JIMÉNEZ, F., 101, 102, 112
JOHNSON, N., 157, 164
JOHNSON-DAVIES, D., 139*t*, 140, 149
JOHNSTON, T., 73, 74, 75*t*, 80, 86–88, 106, 107, 170, 191
JOSEPH, L., 190
JUNG, R., 21, 192
JURMAIN, S., 65, 72
JUSTICE FOR IMMIGRANTS, 75, 91

K

KADOHATA, C., 95, 112
KAJIKAWA, K., 141*t*, 142, 190
KESSLER, C., 144*t*, 193
KHAN, R., 20, 189
KIMMEL, E.A., 142*t*, 149
KINDERSLEY, A., 23, 187
KINDERSLEY, B., 23, 24, 187
KINDLER, A., 93, 98, 111
KING, M.L., JR., 188
KNUTSON, B., 143, 143*t*, 149
KODAMA, T., 49*t*
KRISHNASWAMI, U., 144*t*, 193
KRULL, K., 95, 144*t*, 146, 192
KURTZ, J., 22, 38–39, 59, 75*t*, 146*t*, 189, 190
KUSHNER, T., 134, 149
KYUCHUKOV, H., 20, 144*t*, 147, 148*t*, 193

L

LAMME, L.L., xxii, 21, 148
LAMOTT, A., 174–175, 180
LARSEN, L.J., 75, 76, 91
LAZARUS, E., 73, 91
LEE, M., 113, 114*t*, 115, 121, 124, 126, 188
LEFT HAND BULL, J., 190

LEHMAN, B.A., xxi, 5, 6, 34, 35, 44, 50, 151, 163
LEHR, S., 56, 72
LEKUTON, J.L., 144*t*, 149
LEPMAN, J., 34, 50
LEVINE, E., 101, 104, 105, 112
LEVINE, K., 192
LEVITIN, S., 21, 190
LEWIN, T., 23, 188
LINDGREN, A., 43, 51
LIPP, F., 191
LITTLESUGAR, A., 67, 191
LOBEL, A., 24, 98, 189
LOOK, L., 190
LOUIE, B., 31
LUENN, N., 189
LYON, G.E., 69

M

MACDONALD, M.R., 136, 137*t*, 141, 193
MACHADO, A.M., 49*t*
MADRIGAL, A.H., 20, 190
MAGGIO, R., 127
MAHY, M., 49*t*
MANKELL, H., 21, 46, 177, 178, 192
MARRIN, A., 190
MARSALIS, W., 138*t*, 149
MARTIN, B. Jr, xv, 16, 31
MARTIN, R., 137*t*, 188
MARTINEZ-ROLDAN, C.M., 55, 72
MASTOON, A., 23, 25, 188
MATHIS, J.B., xxii, 50, 152, 164
MCCALL, A., 152, 156, 164
MCCANN, M.R., 133*t*
MCCARTHY, S.J., 56, 72
MCCAUGHREAN, G., 192
MCCLURE, A., 164
MCCORMICK, P., 21, 31
MCGILL, A., 190
MCGLINN, J.M., 71
MCKENNA, M.J., ix–x, xxiii, 163,
MCKISSACK, P.C., 20, 140*t*, 141, 149, 188, 191
MCLAREN, C., 190
MCMAHON, P., 25, 190
MEAD, A., 114, 114*t*, 115, 116, 121, 191
MEDEARIS, A., 27, 157, 187
MEDINA, C., 154, 164
MEDINA, J., 103–104, 112, 147, 148*t*, 150
MENDOZA, J., 15–16, 31
MERRIAM, E., 113
MEYER, C., 188
MEYER, M.A., 171, 180
MEZIROW, J., 166, 180
MICHENER, J.A., xiv, xviii
MIKAELSEN, B., 21, 65, 114*t*, 115, 117–118, 120, 121, 144*t*, 169, 178, 192, 193
MILLER, N., 138*t*, 150

SUBJECT INDEX

Note. Page numbers followed by *f* or *t* indicate figures or tables, respectively.

A

ACCESS, 43–44

ACTIVITIES: literature response activities, 68–71, 88–90, 108–110, 121–126; for Perfect Pairs, 146, 147

ADOPTION: Perfect Pairs, 146–147, 147

ADULTS, 107–108

AFGHANISTAN, 64

AFRICA: books about, 29; in fiction picture books, 20; growing up in, 38–39; in nonfiction, 25; Perfect Pairs, 145*t*; in poetry, 28; in realistic fiction, 21

AFRICAN AMERICANS, 2, 4; books about, 28–29; books published by, 40; in fiction picture books, 20; in folklore, 27; in historical fiction, 22; in nonfiction, 25; in poetry, 28

AIDS EPIDEMIC: Perfect Pairs, 145*t*; in realistic fiction, 21

ALBERT WHITMAN, 17*f*

ALFRED A. KNOPF, 17*f*

ALIKI, 100

AMERICAN COUNCIL ON THE TEACHING OF FOREIGN LANGUAGES, 95

AMERICAN LIBRARY ASSOCIATION: Mildred L. Batchelder Award, 46

AMERICAS AWARD, 11

ANDERSON, MARIAN, 63, 144*t*

"ANIMALS AS TRICKSTERS AND WISE TEACHERS" TEXT SET, 142–143, 143*t*

ANNICK PRESS, 17*f*

ANTIN, MARY, 78

APPRECIATING DIVERSE LANGUAGES RESPONSE STRATEGY, 69–70, 70*t*

ART, 125–126

ARTHUR A. LEVINE, 17*f*

ASIA, 40, 43–44; books about, 29; in fiction picture books, 20; in folklore, 26–27; in nonfiction, 25; in poetry, 28; in realistic fiction, 21; U.S. immigration from, 75, 76

ASIAN AMERICANS, 2, 4, 29, 34

ATHENEUM, 17*f*

AUGUST HOUSE, 17*f*

AUSTRALIAN FOLKLORE, 26

AUTHENTICITY, 14, 39–40; cultural, 15, 44–45

AUTHOR REFLECTIONS, xxiii–xxiv; on children becoming authors of their lives, 117–118; on fostering a global outlook, 135; on humanity unmasked, 155; on the importance of global literature, 13; on

language diversity, 97; on learning from history, 173; on the magic of story, 66; on race, 83–84; on third cultures, 38–39; on words, 97

AUTHOR STUDIES, 136

AUTHORS, 14–15; children becoming authors of their lives, 117–118; international, 48, 49*t*; notable contemporary international, 48, 49*t*

AWARD-WINNING BOOKS, 46

AWARDS FOR TRANSLATED BOOKS, 46

B

BIAL, RAYMOND, 23

BILINGUAL BOOKS, 59, 96–99, 122; picture books, 104

BILINGUAL BOOKS FOR CHILDREN BOOKLIST, 96–97

BILINGUAL EDUCATION ACT, 95

BIOGRAPHIES, 24

BLUE SKY, 17*f*

BOOK AWARDS, 11

BOOK ILLUSTRATION, 125–126

BOOKS: award-winning, 46; bilingual, 59, 96–99, 104, 122; Christian, 25, 30; about immigration, 74, 75*t*; interlingual, 96–99; international, 47, 48, 49*t*; Muslim, 25; picture, 19*t*, 19–21, 77–80, 101, 104; Quaker, 25; sharing with students, 46–47; translated, 46

BOOKSTORES, 41

BOSTON HERALD, 78

BOYDS MILL PRESS, 17*f*

BRUCHAC, JOSEPH, xxiv, 13

BULGARIA, 148*t*

BUNTING, EVE, 19

C

CALIFORNIA: Perfect Pairs, 145*t*; Proposition 227, 95

CANDLEWICK PRESS, 17*f*

CANON, 42

CARLISLE INDIAN INDUSTRIAL SCHOOL, 95

CARTER G. WOODSON AWARD, 11

CELEBRATING LANGUAGE DIVERSITY, 108

CENTER FOR HOLOCAUST STUDIES, 134

CHARLESBRIDGE, 17*f*

CHÁVEZ, CÉSAR, 95; Perfect Pairs, 144*t*, 146; poetry exploration strategies, 159–160

CHENG, ANDREA, 60

CHILDREN: as authors of their lives, 117–118; as interpreters for adults who speak their first language, 104; language acquisition of, 103–106;

lost innocence of, 116–119; refugees, 119, 120; resilient, 113–127; war experiences as reflected in literature, 116–121

J

JAPANESE AMERICANS, 95

JENKINS, DEBRA REID, 125

JEWS: books about, 19, 25, 29; "Heroes of the Holocaust" text set, 132–134; in historical fiction, 22; Perfect Pairs, 145*t*, 146

JOHN STEPTOE AWARD, 11

JUMP AT THE SUN, 16, 17*f*

JUSTICE: poetry to explore, 151–164; social, 151–164, 152–158

JUSTICE FOR IMMIGRANTS (WEBSITE), 89

K

KELLOGG, STEVEN, 41

KITE-FLYING: Perfect Pair, 144*t*

KORCZAK, JANUSZ, 134

KOREA, 121; emigration from, 82–86; stories about the importance of names, 148*t*

KOREAN WAR STORIES, 122–123

KURTZ, JANE, xxiv, 39, 60

L

LANGUAGE: adjustment to, 100–102; home, 105–106; influence in U.S. geography, 108–109, 109*t*; learning about, 99; losing touch with, 105–106; loss of, 99–100; sharing roots of, 106

LANGUAGE ACQUISITION: adults and, 107–108; children's, 103–106; discomfort with, 103–104; process of, 104

LANGUAGE DIVERSITY, 69–70, 70*t*; author reflection on, 97; historical overview of, 94–96; mapping, 109–110; promoting awareness of, 96–100; in United States, 93–112; visual displays celebrating, 108

LATIN AMERICA: books about, 29; in fiction picture books, 20; in nonfiction, 25; in poetry, 28; in realistic fiction, 21; U.S. emigration from, 75, 76

LATINO/HISPANIC CULTURE, 43–44

LATINOS, 34

LEARNING: from history, 173; as political, 182–183; through literature, 183–184

LEE, DOM, 134

LEE & LOW, 15, 16, 17*f*

LEP STUDENTS. *See* Limited English proficient students

LEPMAN, JELLA, 34

LERNER PUBLISHING GROUP, 17*f*

LIMITED ENGLISH PROFICIENT (LEP) STUDENTS, 93

LINGUISTIC IDENTITY, 93–112; themes in literature, 100–108

LINGUISTIC ROOTS, 106

LITERACY: critical, 3

LITERARY CANON, 41–43

LITERATURE, 1, 3–4; as bridge to understanding, 1–6; children's experiences with war as reflected in, 116–121; connecting to science and nutrition studies, 122–123; diverse perspectives in, 7–51; diversity through, xix–xxv; global, 4–5, 5*f*, 30, 36–41, 53–127, 165–180, 184–185; with global perspective, 10–12; international, 4–5, 30, 33–51; learning through, 183–184; linguistic identity themes in, 100–108; multicultural, 2, 4, 18; multiethnic, 4; to positively influence our world, 165–180; to promote global awareness, 129–180; promoting awareness of language diversity through, 96–100; publishing trends in, 36–41; themes of diversity in, 53–127; transformative, 165–180

LITERATURE CIRCLES, 157

LITERATURE RESPONSE ACTIVITIES, 68–71, 88–90, 108–110, 121–126; appreciating diverse languages strategy, 69–70, 70*t*; "Where I'm From" poem response strategy, 69

LITTLE, BROWN, 17*f*

LODESTAR, 17*f*

LOST INNOCENCE, 116–119

LOTHROP, LEE & SHEPARD, 17*f*

M

MACMILLAN, 17*f*

MAHY, MARGARET, 43

MANDARIN CHINESE, 96, 106

MAPPING LANGUAGE DIVERSITY, 109–110

MAPPING LANGUAGE INFLUENCE, 108–109, 109*t*

MARGARET K. MCELDERRY, 17*f*

MARSHALL CAVENDISH, 17*f*

MASAI, 144*t*

MCCANN, MICHELLE, 67

MCKISSACK, PATRICIA, 19

MEXICAN AMERICANS: bilingual books about, 101; books about, 28, 29, 101; realistic portrayals of, 86–88

MEXICO, 120; in fiction picture books, 20; Perfect Pairs, 145*t*; stories about the importance of names, 148*t*

MIDDLE EAST: books about, 29; in historical fiction, 22; "The Hungry Coat: Explorations of the Reappearing Wise—Yet Foolish—Folk Hero" text set, 139*t*, 139–143; in nonfiction, 25; in poetry, 27, 28

MIDDLE SCHOOL: Transformative Teaching/Learning Model in, 177–178

MIKAELSEN, BEN, xxiv, 21, 117–118

MILDRED L. BATCHELDER AWARD, 46

MILITARY STUDIES, 123–124

MISSISSIPPI SUMMER PROJECT, 67

MIXED GENRES, 19*t*, 28

MONTGOMERY, L.M., 43

MORA, PAT, xxiv, 97

MORAL ECOLOGY, 179

MORMON CHURCH, 134

MOTIF-INDEXES, 136

TRANSLATED BOOKS, 46

TRICKSTERS: "Animals as Tricksters and Wise Teachers" text set, 142–143, 143*t*; "Human Tricksters and Fools From Around the World" text set, 140*t*, 140–141; "The Hungry Coat: Explorations of the Reappearing Wise—Yet Foolish—Folk Hero" text set, 139*t*, 139–143

TRICYCLE PRESS, 17*f*

TUNNELL, MICHAEL O., xxiv, 135

U

UNITED STATES: immigrant experience, 73–91; immigration in, 75–77, 77–80, 88–89; language diversity in, 93–112; mapping language influence in, 108–109, 109*t*; as promised land, 78–79

UNITED STATES BOARD ON BOOKS FOR YOUNG PEOPLE (USBBY), 48

UNITED STATES HOLOCAUST MEMORIAL MUSEUM, 134

UPPER ELEMENTARY GRADES: Transformative Teaching/Learning Model in, 176

U.S. BOARD ON BOOKS FOR YOUNG PEOPLE, 3

U.S. DEPARTMENT OF HOMELAND SECURITY, 76

U.S. IMMIGRANT EXPERIENCE, 73–91

USBBY. *See* United States Board on Books for Young People

V

VAN ALLSBURG, CHRIS, 41

VIETNAM WAR, 119, 120; Perfect Pairs, 145*t*, 146–147

VIKING, 17*f*

VIOLENCE, POLITICAL, 21

VISUAL DISPLAYS, 108

W

WAR STORIES, 64, 115–116, 122–123; for bilingual education and cultural appreciation, 122; children's experiences as reflected in literature, 116–121; resilient children in, 113–127; Social Studies unit on war and the military, 123–124

WARCHILD WEBSITE, 123

WEISSBERGER, ELA, 134

"WHERE I'M FROM" POEM RESPONSE STRATEGY, 69

WHITES, 2

WILLIAM MORROW, 17*f*

"WISDOM TALES FROM AROUND THE WORLD FESTIVAL", 141

WOMEN FOR WOMEN, 177–178

WONG, JANET S., xxiv, 19, 60, 83–84

WOODSON, JACQUELINE, 19, 21

WORLD WAR II, 62, 64, 67–68, 95; books about, 29, 120–121; family upheaval and separation during, 119–120; "Heroes of the Holocaust" text set, 132–134, 133*t*; Perfect Pairs, 144*t*, 146; stories about the importance of names, 148*t*

WRITING WORKSHOP, 124–125

Z

ZIPATONE, 37